A History of Modern Linguistics

For M.P.

A History of Modern Linguistics
From the Beginnings to World War II

James McElvenny

EDINBURGH
University Press

Edinburgh University Press is one of the leading university presses in the UK. We publish academic books and journals in our selected subject areas across the humanities and social sciences, combining cutting-edge scholarship with high editorial and production values to produce academic works of lasting importance. For more information visit our website: edinburghuniversitypress.com

© James McElvenny, 2024

Edinburgh University Press Ltd
The Tun – Holyrood Road
12(2f) Jackson's Entry
Edinburgh EH8 8PJ

Typeset in 9.75/12 Janson by
Cheshire Typesetting Ltd, Cuddington, Cheshire

A CIP record for this book is available from the British Library

ISBN 978 1 4744 7001 8 (hardback)
ISBN 978 1 4744 7002 5 (paperback)
ISBN 978 1 4744 7003 2 (webready PDF)
ISBN 978 1 4744 7004 9 (epub)

The right of James McElvenny to be identified as the author of this work has been asserted in accordance with the Copyright, Designs and Patents Act 1988, and the Copyright and Related Rights Regulations 2003 (SI No. 2498).

Contents

List of figures	viii
Acknowledgements	ix

1 Introduction — 1
  1.1 What is modern linguistics? — 2
  1.2 How to read this book — 3
  1.3 Further reading — 4

2 Comparative-historical grammar — 6
  2.1 Sir William Jones and Sanskrit — 7
  2.2 Friedrich Schlegel and comparative grammar — 8
  2.3 Franz Bopp and the elaboration of comparative grammar — 11
  2.4 Jacob Grimm and sound laws — 14
  2.5 Further reading — 18

3 Language classification — 19
  3.1 The Schlegel brothers and the 'inner structure' of languages — 19
  3.2 Wilhelm von Humboldt's 'anti-semiotics' — 22
  3.3 Humboldt's linguistics of structure and linguistics of character — 25
  3.4 Heymann Steinthal and *Völkerpsychologie* — 27
  3.5 Steinthal's characterisation of languages — 29
  3.6 Further reading — 32

4 The consolidation of comparative-historical linguistics — 34
  4.1 August Schleicher and realism — 35
  4.2 Darwinism and scientific materialism — 37
  4.3 Morphology of languages — 41
  4.4 Inner and outer form — 43
  4.5 Further reading — 46

5 The pragmatic turn of the mid-nineteenth century — 47
  5.1 William Dwight Whitney and his enemies — 47
  5.2 Language as an 'institution' — 50
  5.3 Common Sense philosophy — 53
  5.4 Uniformitarianism — 54
  5.5 Further reading — 57

6	Neogrammarian doctrine	58
	6.1 Young Turks	58
	6.2 Sound laws and analogy	60
	6.3 Hermann Paul's science of principles	63
	6.4 Further reading	66
7	Critiques of Neogrammarian doctrine	67
	7.1 Schuchardt, Gabelentz and Whitney on the limits of sound laws	69
	7.2 Schmidt, Schuchardt and the wave theory	72
	7.3 Karl Vossler and idealism in linguistics	75
	7.4 Further reading	78
8	Language as a system	80
	8.1 Ferdinand de Saussure, Neogrammarian extraordinaire	80
	8.2 The Course in General Linguistics	83
	8.3 Saussure's sources	87
	8.4 Further reading	90
9	The phoneme	91
	9.1 The first steps towards theorisation	92
	9.2 Phonetic alphabets	95
	9.3 Further reading	98
10	Prague Circle structuralism	100
	10.1 Structuralism and phonology	101
	10.2 The sources of structuralism	103
	10.3 The spread of structuralism	106
	10.4 Further reading	108
11	The beginnings of functionalism	109
	11.1 Philipp Wegener and language as action	109
	11.2 Wegener's sources	112
	11.3 Wegener and syntax	115
	11.4 Further reading	117
12	Meaning and British linguistics	118
	12.1 John Rupert Firth and the 'study of meaning in its own terms'	118
	12.2 Bronislaw Malinowski and the context of situation	123
	12.3 The background to Malinowski's functional model of language	124
	12.4 Further reading	128
13	Functionalism in Central Europe and North America	130
	13.1 Karl Bühler's *Sprachtheorie*	131
	13.2 Bühler and the Prague Circle	135
	13.3 Roman Jakobson and cybernetics	136
	13.4 Further reading	140

14	The beginnings of American structuralism	142
	14.1 Franz Boas and the Boasians	143
	14.2 Boasian anthropology	144
	14.3 Alternating sounds	147
	14.4 Further reading	150
15	Linguistic relativity	151
	15.1 The Sapir–Whorf hypothesis	152
	15.2 Boasian linguistics and relativity	155
	15.3 Analytic philosophy and mysticism	157
	15.4 Further reading	162
16	The culmination of American structuralism	163
	16.1 Edward Sapir, Leonard Bloomfield and formalism	164
	16.2 Bloomfield and behaviourism	167
	16.3 Bloomfield and logical positivism	171
	16.4 Distributionalism	173
	16.5 Further reading	175
17	Conclusion	177
Bibliography		181
Index		199

Figures

3.1	Steinthal's (1860a: 327) classification of languages	31
4.1	Schleicher's (1861–2, vol. 1: 7) family tree showing the main branches of Indo-European	38
5.1	Whitney's (1874: 274) table of the frequency of English sounds	52
7.1	Insert map of dialects in the Rhineland from Wenker (1877)	74
7.2	Schmidt's (1871–5, vol. 2: 199) diagram of the wave model	76
8.1	The sign according to Saussure (1922 [1916]: 158)	85
8.2	Saussure's (1922 [1916]: 159) illustration of 'value', the mutually delimiting character of signs	85
9.1	The letters of Alexander Melville Bell's (1867: 37) Visible Speech	96
12.1	Malinowski's (1956 [1923]: 324) stages of language development	126
12.2	Ogden and Richards's (1956 [1923]: 11) 'Triangle of Reference' or 'Semiotic Triangle'	127
13.1	Karl Bühler's (1934: 28) Organon model	132

Acknowledgements

It would not have been possible to write this book without the assistance of a number of superb colleagues. First among these are Chloé Laplantine, Martin Konvička and Luca Dinu, who with me run the History and Philosophy of the Language Sciences media empire, which includes the podcast where much of the material contained in this book had its first airing. John Joseph and Clemens Knobloch were the first readers of the book manuscript. Their comments have led to many revisions that have improved the final book.

Clemens Knobloch and Erhard Schüttpelz have given me employment over the past few years, ensuring that I had a roof over my head while producing this book. My position during this time has been as a researcher at the Collaborative Research Centre 'Media of Co-operation', based at the University Siegen and funded by the Deutsche Forschungsgemeinschaft (DFG, German Research Foundation) – Project-ID 262513311 – SFB 1187 [Gefördert durch die Deutsche Forschungsgemeinschaft (DFG) – Projektnummer 262513311 – SFB 1187].

My thanks to all these colleagues and institutions for providing the support needed to compose this compendium of misplaced erudition.

1 Introduction

The following pages offer a concise history of the main currents in linguistic theory from the beginnings of the modern field around the turn of the eighteenth to the nineteenth century up to the end of World War II. We focus on academic linguistics, and look at how scholars – working in their specific social, cultural and political contexts – came to their ideas and methods. The emphasis of our account lies on the debates, controversies and unresolved problems that have shaped the outlook of linguistics as a discipline.

The scope of this book is therefore much narrower than that of many classic histories of linguistics, such as R. H. Robins's (1997 [1967]) *A Short History of Linguistics*, which can still claim to be the standard one-volume overview of the subject in English, or Vivien Law's (2003) *The History of Linguistics in Europe*. These works take linguistics to be any systematic reflection or technical treatment of language, and project the beginnings of the field back to the dawn of Western civilisation in Ancient Greece. Both Robins and Law begin their story with assorted pronouncements on language from Greek philosophers and the first grammarians, and then proceed through the centuries to trace the transmission of ideas and methods through the Roman world, the Middle Ages, the Renaissance, and into our own modern period.

There is an undeniable continuity in thought and practice between those ancient philosophers holding forth in their academies and us in our own academic setting today, and there is great value in this panoramic perspective that strains to see all of history at once. Everyone who takes an interest in the history of linguistics should be aware of this context in the *longue durée*. But at the same time there is a danger of misunderstanding and misrepresentation in seeking to subsume such diverse and even divergent material under our modern notion of linguistics. These forebears of ours were no doubt talking about language and languages, and their ideas and techniques have no doubt contributed to our thinking and methods, but were they really doing linguistics?

In the world today, 'linguistics' refers to a specific academic discipline. Of course, even among contemporary linguists there is a diverse range of views on the nature of language and how to approach its study. There is also a diverse range of specialisations that concentrate on very different aspects of language. What brings these disparate lines of research together is not so much any single cluster of ideas or methods, but rather a sociological context. What unites linguists as linguists is the institutionalised discipline in which they were raised, and which they perpetuate and strive to develop in new directions. This is the fundamental premise that determines the approach taken in this book.

1.1 What is modern linguistics?

The modern field of linguistics first became established in Germany in the early nineteenth century, in the new research universities that appeared around this time (see Turner 2014: chap. 5; Morpurgo Davies 1998: chap. 1). Whereas the primary purpose of universities had traditionally been the cultivation and transmission of an age-old learned canon, the research university was designed to support novel investigations leading to new knowledge and insights (see Rüegg 2004). These principles were first explicitly articulated in the mission of the University of Berlin, founded in 1809, where professors were expected to pursue original research in their respective fields and to induct their students into the research mindset. The research university was a German invention, but by the second half of the century, the German model was being emulated in France, the United States and other countries around the world.

Our story begins with the emergence of the modern discipline of linguistics in the nineteenth century through these facts of institutionalisation. This is the immediate historical context of linguistics as we know it today – and it also provides us with a network of direct personal connections we can trace. The narrative we construct will be like a collective biography of the field and its figures, or perhaps a kind of family history. In fact, in the German tradition – which, as we have seen, is the starting point for our story – the relationship of teacher to student is, at least at the level of conventional metaphor, considered to be so much like a family relationship that it is normal to refer to someone's doctoral supervisor as their *Doktorvater* (literally 'doctor-father'). In the twentieth century, with the gradual opening up of universities to a wider clientele than just the sons of well-to-do households, the term *Doktormutter* (literally 'doctor-mother') also came into use.

But our story does not start with an Adam and Eve of linguistics. The linguist has evolved from preceding scholarly life forms; what came before the institutionalisation of the discipline is therefore at many points relevant to the account here, and we will make reference to it. In similar fashion, we will not seek to erect an absolute boundary around disciplinary linguistics and isolate it from the world outside. Disciplinary linguistics merely serves as the centre of gravity of this book, the point at which its weight lies, but which draws into its orbit many other ideas, events, methods and figures.

Our account in this volume ends just after World War II, an event that marked a clear break in academic and intellectual life in Germany, in Europe and around the world. As is well known, World War II was precipitated by the aggression of Nazi Germany and its fascist allies against neighbouring countries. Already before the war, there was a climate of intolerance and deadly persecution in those countries where fascist dictatorships, in their various forms, had come to power. This political situation, and the unprecedented destruction wrought by the war it brought about, drove the best European scholars into exile, most usually in the United States. The exodus of talent from the Continent, and the political, economic and military hegemony of the United States after the war, shifted the centre of the academic world to America. Before the war, Americans typically looked to Europe as the source of scholarly and scientific innovation; after the war, the poles were reversed. This is especially true in linguistics: although linguistics continued to be practised in European universities after World War II – and indeed continues to be practised today – the field became increasingly oriented towards American models.

Even though disciplinary linguistics from the beginning of the nineteenth century to the end of World War II may seem like a rather brief and tightly circumscribed episode in the grand scheme of human history, we still have had to be selective in order to fit the whole story into the 200-odd pages of this book. This book is intended above all to be short and easily digestible – without, however, being dumbed down. The aim is to present a coherent narrative, with an arc that follows the dominant theoretical approaches of each era, the work that set the tone for the field. In each chapter, we examine the tenets and techniques of the leading scholars in linguistics and their adherents, and look at the developments they inspired and reactions they provoked. There remain, however, numerous scholars and schools of linguistics in our period who have missed out on the dubious honour of gracing these pages.

1.2 How to read this book

There is no single correct way to read this book. Every reader should feel free to find their own way through the text, whether that means poring over each page consecutively, skipping randomly from paragraph to paragraph, or taking a more moderate path somewhere between those two extremes. Each of the following chapters narrates a more or less self-contained episode and is infused with cross-references, both forwards and backwards, linking the various plot lines. The chapters can therefore be treated as a Choose Your Own Adventure and read non-sequentially, although those seeking a chronological account may prefer a sequential reading.

To assist with entry into the web of scholarship surrounding the topics discussed in this book, each chapter closes with recommendations for further reading, along with commentary designed to provide orientation in the literature. Most of the sources cited in the text and recommended at the end of each chapter should be available in university libraries and large public libraries, often in digital editions. For many older works that are no longer in copyright, it is usually possible to find public domain digital versions online. A commendable resource in this regard is the non-profit Internet Archive (https://archive.org/), or even the very much for-profit but still freely accessible Google Books (https://books.google.com/).

In choosing which versions of primary sources to cite, this book tries to steer a course between authoritativeness and accessibility: some sources are cited from the first published version, and others from volumes of collected works or later critical editions. Primary sources in German and French are cited from editions in the original language, but direct quotations are always given in English translation. The translations into English are my own, although they are generally informed by existing published translations where available. In such cases, a reference to the published translation is also provided. Cross-references within the Bibliography link the different editions of texts cited, including translations and originals.

Much of the material contained in this book has already been broadcast to the world in the *History and Philosophy of the Language Sciences Podcast* (https://hiphilangsci.net/category/podcast/). Although the topics are arranged somewhat differently and dealt with in greater depth in this book, those who would like to hear this content delivered in my dulcet tones would do well to listen to the podcast. The podcast also includes numerous interviews with experts on specific topics. Edited versions of interview transcripts have been published in the open access volume *Interviews in the History of Linguistics: Volume I* (McElvenny 2022). The podcast is ongoing and covers many topics beyond the scope of this book.

1.3 Further reading

There is no shortage of secondary material sketching the history of linguistics. As mentioned at the beginning of this chapter, the classic single-volume panoramic account of Western study of language is R. H. Robins's (1997 [1967]) *A Short History of Linguistics*. A more recent classic is Vivien Law's (2003) *The History of Linguistics in Europe: From Plato to 1600*, the focus of which lies on the pre-modern period. Lia Formigari's (2004 [2001]) *A History of Language Philosophies*, originally published in Italian, provides a superb overview of the interaction between language study and philosophy of language on the same timescale of Antiquity to the present. John Goldsmith and Bernard Laks's (2019) *Battle in the Mind Fields* offers a comprehensive survey of the emergence of modern linguistic ideas amid developments in philosophy, psychology and related fields. A concise who's who of linguistic thought with pointers to further reading is Margaret Thomas's (2011) *Fifty Key Thinkers on Language and Linguistics*.

Among the best sources for highly detailed accounts of specific periods and individual approaches in linguistic scholarship are the two-volume *Historiography of Linguistics*, edited by Thomas A. Sebeok (1975); the monograph series *History of Linguistics*, edited by Giulio Lepschy (1994–8), the volumes of which were originally published in Italian but later translated into English; and the trilingual, three-volume encyclopaedia *History of the Language Sciences*, edited by Sylvain Auroux, E. F. Konrad Koerner, Hans-Josef Niederehe and Kees Versteegh (2000–6).

In recent years, there has been great interest in the historical development of disciplines that study the human world, among which linguistics occupies a prominent place. James Turner's (2014) *Philology: The Forgotten Origins of the Modern Humanities* is a masterly examination of the emergence of several modern humanities disciplines, including linguistics, from earlier philological scholarship, with a focus on nineteenth-century Europe and North America. Rens Bod's (2013 [2010]) *A New History of the Humanities: The Search for Principles and Patterns from Antiquity to the Present*, originally published in Dutch, undertakes a grand survey of the humanities from all corners of the globe. One caveat on Bod's book is that its sweeping scope results in the assimilation of very different traditions to a single overarching narrative, robbing these traditions of their uniqueness and individuality. Despite this problem, the book offers a good preliminary introduction to the recent historiography of the humanities.

2 Comparative-historical grammar

The first kind of linguistics to be institutionalised as an academic discipline – with professors, textbooks, classes and students – was comparative-historical grammar. This is the branch of linguistics that tells us that languages are related to one another in a genealogical sense; for example, that French, Italian, Spanish and many other languages are siblings descended from the common ancestor Latin. Such close-knit family relationships are fairly obvious and have long been acknowledged, but the great insight that made comparative-historical grammar possible was to recognise much more distant relationships of this kind. Specifically, the similarities between classical languages of the East – such as Sanskrit and Persian – and classical languages of the West – such as Latin and Ancient Greek – led European scholars to imagine a great Indo-European language family and to undertake the task of sketching its family tree.

For almost as long as linguistics has existed as a discipline, it has had a standard history. In this standard history, the genealogical approach is generally considered the first truly 'scientific' study of language. One of the earliest claims of this nature comes from the German scholar Theodor Benfey (1809–1899) in his 1869 *Geschichte der Sprachwissenschaft und orientalischen Philologie in Deutschland* (History of linguistics and Oriental philology in Germany). Describing the new impulses in language study in the first half of the nineteenth century, he wrote: '[T]he turn that now occurred was so tremendous that hardly a stone was left standing from what came before, that previous work [. . .] sank to being of purely historical value, that linguistics now began to become a science' (Benfey 1869: 332). As we will see in the following chapters, such claims to a new scientific status that sweeps away all preceding scholarship are a recurrent motif in the history of linguistics and allied fields, an attitude that C. F. 'Carl' and Florence Voegelin (1963), in discussing the later history of linguistics in North America, have called the 'eclipsing stance'.

Benfey's book is one of the earliest works to start canonising the history of linguistics. The first classics in this canon are the writings of the British Orientalist Sir William Jones (1746–1794) and the German philologist and philosopher Friedrich Schlegel (1772–1829). Together their texts are credited with giving the initial impetus to comparative-historical grammar. These are followed closely by the works of Franz Bopp (1791–1867) and Jacob Grimm (1785–1863), in which the methods underlying the new field were elaborated. It is to these pillars of the emerging discipline that we turn in the following sections.

2.1 Sir William Jones and Sanskrit

In introducing Sir William Jones, Benfey quoted a passage that has achieved the status of a ritual incantation, recited at the opening of every history of modern linguistics. Let us participate in this ritual and quote the passage here in full. In 1786, in Calcutta, Jones made the following observation:

> The *Sanscrit* language, whatever be its antiquity, is of a wonderful structure; more perfect than the *Greek*, more copious than the *Latin*, and more exquisitely refined than either, yet bearing to both of them a stronger affinity, both in the roots of verbs and in the forms of grammar, than could possibly have been produced by accident; so strong indeed, that no philologer could examine all three, without believing them to have sprung from some common source which, perhaps, no longer exists: there is a similar reason, though not quite so forcible, for supposing that both the *Gothick* and the *Celtick*, though blended with a very different idiom, had the same origin with the *Sanscrit*; and the old *Persian* might be added to the same family, if this were the place for discussing any question concerning the antiquities of *Persia*. (Jones 1807 [1786]: 34–5)

This passage – commonly referred to as the 'philologer passage' because of the occurrence of this rather archaic term, 'philologer' – can be read as prefiguring the fundamental principles of later comparative-historical grammar. Jones identifies similarities in verb roots and grammatical forms across the great classical languages – Sanskrit, Greek, Latin, Gothic, Celtic and Persian – and attributes these similarities to common ancestry, where the common ancestor has been lost to time.

The passage appeared in Jones's third 'Anniversary Discourse' to the Royal Asiatic Society in Calcutta (Jones 1807 [1786]), a scholarly club for learned British gentlemen stationed in India. Jones had long been a student of 'Oriental' languages, and his primary motivation in going to India was to master Sanskrit. In Calcutta, he was central to European scholarship on India and the East and instrumental in the founding of the Asiatic Society.

Jones is in many ways the archetypal representative of the eighteenth-century scholar-cum-colonial administrator, the kind of figure that serves as grist to the mill of the young field of postcolonial studies. As Edward Said (2003 [1978]: 77–9) pointed out in his *Orientalism*, the book that more or less launched postcolonial studies, Jones was undeniably a member of the colonial caste appropriating the cultural knowledge of India and repackaging it for a European audience. Jones's scholarly engagement with India was made possible by the political and military power of the British East India Company on the subcontinent at the time. Indeed, Jones's day job was judge at the British Supreme Court of Calcutta, where he quite literally sat in judgment on the Company's Bengali subjects.

Jones's image of European and Indian kinship is most certainly a colonial projection. However, as historian Thomas Trautmann argues in his 1997 book

Aryans and British India, Jones's scholarly generation emphasised the commonalities between East and West. At least in the domain of Sanskrit studies, orientalising scholarship that highlighted what from a European perspective might seem exotic and strange and used this as a justification and instrument of colonial control was something that became more prevalent in subsequent generations.

We may pause here for a moment to ask why Jones's preferred explanation for the similarities he noticed was common descent. This mode of explanation is so deeply ingrained in our ideas about how the history of languages should be conceived that we may even take it for granted. The answer is that the point of departure for Jones – and for many of his contemporaries – was the account of human origins and history contained in the Bible. Jones assumed what Trautmann (1997: 8–9, 42–52) calls a 'Mosaic ethnology'. That is, Jones's picture of the origin and descent of humanity was shaped by the account sketched in Genesis, the Book of Moses. He took the observed similarities between languages as evidence for the spreading of Noah's descendants across the world after the great flood. According to Jones (1807 [1792]), in another of his 'Anniversary Discourses', each of the three sons of Noah – Shem, Ham and Japheth – begat distinct lineages that populated different regions of the world. Japheth's descendants moved to the north of Asia and Europe and became the nomadic herders to be encountered there today, Shem's people settled in the Near East, and Ham's children established themselves in Africa and India, and then later moved on to Greece, Italy and Europe.

Suddenly Jones's flash of insight igniting a new scientific linguistics looks like a medieval hangover. Within a generation of Jones, no one would adopt such a literal interpretation of biblical genealogy – even if some biblical terminology survived, such as the label for the 'Semitic' family (which includes such languages as Hebrew and Arabic), derived from the name of Noah's son Shem. Nevertheless, the principles underlying Jones's approach still colour comparative-historical grammar up to the present day. Linguists still speak of language families and draw family trees that preserve the principle of patrilineal descent: each tree branches out as a parent language begets its child languages. Other kinds of linguistic relationship, such as developments attributable to contact between languages, are frequently treated as aberrations that disturb this scheme (see McElvenny 2021).

Even though the family tree model was challenged at many points – as we see in particular in Section 7.2 – the history of comparative-historical grammar in the nineteenth century is largely a story of working out the finer details of the supposed genealogical relations between languages and of attempts to find a modern, scientific footing for this enterprise.

2.2 Friedrich Schlegel and comparative grammar

Although the standard narrative of comparative-historical grammar starts with a quotable quote from a Briton in Calcutta, its focus quickly shifts to the country in which this new paradigm would find an institutional home: Germany. The text credited with introducing Sanskrit studies to an eager audience in Germany is the 1808 bestseller *Ueber die Sprache und Weisheit der Indier* (On the language and wisdom of the Indians) by Friedrich Schlegel (1772–1829). This book is perhaps also the first text to establish the tradition of citing the philologer passage.

Friedrich Schlegel is best known as one of the chief initiators of Romanticism, a cultural movement emphasising nature, emotions and individual creativity as a reaction against the cool and condescending rationalism of the Enlightenment. Romanticism swept through the artistic and intellectual world of Europe around the turn of the eighteenth to the nineteenth century, and gained significant traction in the German-speaking lands. Schlegel's *Ueber die Sprache und Weisheit der Indier* is a book born of Romantic sentiment: it offers the European reader an exploration, infused with mysticism, of ancient Indian language, philosophy, history and literature.

Schlegel's book opens with the observation that Sanskrit 'has the greatest affinity with the Greek and Latin, as well as the Persian and German languages' (Schlegel 1808: 3; English translation in Schlegel 1900 [1808]: 428–9). The affinity he postulated is, however, not precisely the same as that earlier put forward by Jones. Schlegel saw Sanskrit as the most ancient of the languages he named, from which the others were derived, whereas Jones imagined an ancestor common to all of them lost to time.

But Schlegel looked to the same kind of linguistic evidence in constructing his genealogical relationships, namely the thoroughgoing similarities in words and grammatical forms across the languages. The first part of Schlegel's book is largely dedicated to the detailed exemplification of these similarities. Most important for demonstrating genealogical relationships, according to Schlegel, are the correspondences in the 'inner' grammatical structure of languages, to be determined by 'comparative grammar':

> But the decisive point that will illuminate everything is the inner structure of the languages or comparative grammar, which will inform us about the genealogy of languages in a similar way to which comparative anatomy has cast light on the higher levels of natural history. (Schlegel 1808: 28; English translation in Schlegel 1900 [1808]: 439)

Here we see the sense in which the 'comparative' in 'comparative-historical grammar' is meant. The analogy is with comparative anatomy, a science that had made great advances in these years and had accrued significant prestige. Through the work of such scholars as Johannes Friedrich Blumenbach (1752–1840) in Göttingen and Georges Cuvier (1769–1832) in Paris, the fledgling field of comparative anatomy began painting a vivid picture of the antediluvian world. Working with nothing but fragments of fossilised skeletons and the similarities of these to those of living creatures, the comparative anatomists were able to reconstruct prehistoric animals and put forward hypotheses about their lifestyles and habits (see Rudwick 2005: chaps 6 and 7).

The inspiration was not unidirectional but reciprocal. Just as the grammarians sought to model themselves on the anatomists, the anatomists looked to the example of the antiquarians. The antiquarians of the outgoing eighteenth century, in their efforts to understand and reconstruct the ancient world, moved beyond their traditional sources in literary documents to examine archaeological remains: inscriptions, coins, ruins and the remnants of daily life (see Turner 2014). Both Blumenbach and Cuvier commented that, following the same principles as the antiquarians, their own work aimed to reconstruct the past from fragments.

The common practice of the antiquarians, comparative anatomists and grammarians reflects a philosophy which sees history as the stories of unique individuals – whether individual civilisations, creatures or languages – living in contingent circumstances. The only way to understand these individuals is to examine the empirical evidence they have left behind. This approach is in contrast to the ambition of such natural sciences as physics or chemistry, which seek to discover overarching principles to explain and predict individual observed phenomena. The philosophical and methodological tension between these two approaches played out also in linguistics and resurfaces repeatedly in the coming chapters.

At this point, we must note that empirically oriented efforts to uncover language origins and relationships were pursued prior to Jones, Schlegel and those who lined up as their successors. Indeed, alternative approaches to empirical language comparison continued even after academic comparative-historical grammar had become established. The end of the seventeenth century – a hundred years before Jones and Schlegel – saw increasing interest in the philosophy of language. The rampant empiricism of this era, in which experimental sciences rose to prominence, led to increasing debate about the nature of language, the medium in which we formulate our thoughts and communicate our observations. How do words have meaning, and can this meaning ever be reliable, given the inherent subjectivity of language?

The English philosopher John Locke (1632–1704) argued that the signification of words is arbitrary and therefore there is no in-built guarantee of their reliability. Responding to Locke, the German philosopher and polymath Gottfried Wilhelm Leibniz (1646–1716) insisted to the contrary that there is at base a natural connection between words and their meanings, although this connection has become obscured through the historical development of languages (we explore these positions in greater detail in Section 3.2). To find the original correspondences between words and meaning, suggested Leibniz, we should explore words' etymologies. In addition, comparing etymologies across languages would reveal the 'cognations and migrations' (Aarsleff 1982: 66) of peoples across the world in cases where we have no other evidence (see Aarsleff 1982: chaps 2 and 3; Vermeulen 2018).

Although Leibniz acknowledged that etymology in his day was a largely speculative pastime, he held out the hope that it would one day become a rigorous science. To this end, he proposed collecting large samples of empirical data from the languages of the world. By Leibniz's time, there was already a tradition of using a translation of the Lord's Prayer as a standard sample for comparing languages. In his correspondence, Leibniz repeatedly expressed the hope that such a project could be undertaken on a large scale, in particular in the multilingual Russian Empire. The project Leibniz envisaged later found a patron in Tsarina Catherine the Great (1729–1796), who commissioned the German naturalist and explorer Peter Simon Pallas (1741–1811) to compile a comparative vocabulary of the world's languages, with a focus on those spoken in Russian territories (see Archaimbault 2010).

This brand of linguistic comparativism reached its culmination in the work *Mithridates*, compiled by Johann Christoph Adelung (1732–1806) and continued after his death in three further volumes by Johann Severin Vater (1771–1826). Adelung and Vater's compendium is named after the ancient king Mithridates of Asia Minor, who was reputed to command all twenty-two of the languages spoken in his empire. The name Mithridates had already famously been used as the allegorical title of a 1555 book by the Swiss polymath Conrad Gessner (1516–1565), a book which similarly sought to survey the world's languages.

The four volumes of Adelung and Vater's *Mithridates* contain a comprehensive selection of the world's languages and offer a translation of the Lord's Prayer with interlinear glosses for each language, accompanied by ethnographic information about the speakers and bibliographic references. The first volume of *Mithridates* appeared in the year of Adelung's death, 1806, and the final volume in 1817, well into the period in which the parallel tradition of comparative-historical grammar had become established.

2.3 Franz Bopp and the elaboration of comparative grammar

Although figures like Sir William Jones and Friedrich Schlegel pointed out the similarities between Indian and European languages and suggested the direction research should take, the actual task of systematically comparing forms in detail fell to others. This laborious undertaking was first attempted by the German scholar Franz Bopp (1791–1867). As a pupil in the Gymnasium – that is, an academically oriented German secondary school – Bopp was carried away by the contemporary enthusiasm for Sanskrit and Oriental learning. Particularly piquing his interest was Schlegel's (1808) *Ueber die Sprache und Weisheit der Indier*. According to the legend, after reading this book, Bopp made it his mission to uncover the relationships between the languages of East and West.

Bopp's apprenticeship in Oriental languages took him as a young man to Paris, the centre of Sanskrit studies in Europe at the time, where he studied alongside August Wilhelm Schlegel (1767–1845), the brother of Friedrich. August Wilhelm was perhaps the more accomplished Sanskritist of the two brothers, and would go on to become the first professor of Sanskrit and Oriental languages in Germany with his appointment to the University of Bonn in 1818. The contact between Bopp and A. W. Schlegel continued throughout their careers and turned into rivalry. Bopp moved in an increasingly technical direction, trying to tease out the commonalities in the grammatical forms of languages, without regard for how the languages were actually used. A. W. Schlegel, on the other hand, maintained stronger ties to the older philological tradition, in which grammar was treated merely as an auxiliary for understanding and appreciating the literature written in a language.

The product of Bopp's Paris sojourn was his first book, the 1816 *Über das Conjugationssystem der Sanskritsprache in Vergleichung mit jenem der griechischen, lateinischen, persischen und germanischen Sprache* (On the conjugational system of the Sanskrit language in comparison with those of the Greek, Latin, Persian and German language). In this book, Bopp analysed and compared the conjugational systems of the languages named in the title. That is, he examined the inflectional forms of verbs in these languages and used these to chart their historical relationships. In the following years, Bopp continued his research in London, where he published in 1820, among many other texts, a revised English version of the *Conjugationssystem* under the title 'Analytical comparison of the Sanskrit, Greek, Latin, and Teutonic languages' (Bopp 1820).

The great innovation in Bopp's work was to unite the 'philosophical and historical' sides of linguistic scholarship; this is how Bopp described his contribution himself (see Lefmann 1891–7, vol. 1: chap. 3). The 'historical' element was the empirical language data that many scholars were collecting and curating in this period. In the previous section we saw not only the example of Friedrich Schlegel but also the parallel tradition of Adelung and Vater. The 'philosophical' component was the analytic step. Although many of Bopp's predecessors highlighted the desirability of analysis, in practice they did not go much further than offering an impressionistic discussion of surface similarities. By contrast, Bopp, for each language, dissected words and factored out changes in form caused by laws of 'euphony'. For Bopp, 'euphony' was a cover term for all the sound changes he observed, a term that he did not theorise any further. Through his analytic procedure, Bopp arrived at putative underlying forms of words and grammatical inflections that he could then compare like for like across languages.

Bopp's decomposition of words follows along the lines of what are often described as 'rationalist' approaches to the study of language, of which there were several different traditions that were active in his day. One of the most prominent of these traditions, to which Bopp was exposed during his time in Paris, is that of *grammaire générale* or 'general grammar'. The general grammarians subjected grammatical forms across a number of languages – mainly French, Latin, Greek and Hebrew – to a highly abstract analysis in order to uncover the universal cognitive processes that the forms were assumed to reflect.

The work that initiated the general grammar tradition is the 1660 *Grammaire générale et raisonnée* (*General and Rational Grammar*) by Antoine Arnauld (1612–1694) and Claude Lancelot (1615–1695), also known as the 'Port-Royal grammar', after the Port-Royal monastery in which Arnauld and Lancelot lived and worked (see Harris and Taylor 1997 [1989]: chap. 8). The tradition of general grammar continued to exercise an influence well into the nineteenth century – whether that influence was to serve as a source of inspiration or to trigger a negative reaction.

Like the general grammarians, Bopp believed that verbs at base reflect the structure of logical propositions, even if this logical structure may have become obscured in the course of historical language change. On this understanding, each verb must be analysed as containing a subject term, an attribute that is assigned to the subject, and a copula linking the subject and attribute. In his analyses of verb conjugations, Bopp broke down verbs into the root, corresponding to the idea attributed to the subject, and inflectional endings which he believed were ultimately derived from the copula verb 'to be'. This original structure, he thought, has become obscured over time because of changes effected by the rules of euphony in each language. This analysis formed the basis of 'agglutination theory', which we discuss in Section 4.3.

There was also an Indian tradition of linguistic scholarship that may have provided some inspiration to Bopp, and certainly influenced many European linguists later in the nineteenth century. This tradition centred on the work of the ancient Indian grammarian Pāṇini, who most likely lived some time around the sixth to the fourth century BC. Pāṇini is credited as the author of the *Aṣṭādhyāyī* (Eight chapters), a treatise offering a highly abstract description of the grammar and sound system of Classical Sanskrit (on Pāṇini, see Thomas 2011: 3–8). From the earliest days of Sanskrit scholarship in Europe, the *Aṣṭādhyāyī* was a key source used in studying the language and as a basis for Sanskrit grammars written by Europeans. Bopp actually disparaged the Indian grammatical tradition – a point on which he was criticised by A. W. Schlegel (see McGetchin 2009: 150–1) – but there is a case to be made that the abstract base forms and rules of derivation found in the *Aṣṭādhyāyī* partly inspired or at least reinforced Bopp's own analyses, which similarly involved positing underlying forms. The debt European linguistics owed to Pāṇini and the Indian grammatical tradition was acknowledged by later scholars, including Ferdinand de Saussure (1857–1913; Section 8.3), John Rupert Firth (1890–1960; Section 12.1) and Leonard Bloomfield (1887–1949; Section 16.1).

In recognition of his pioneering research, Bopp was awarded an honorary doctorate from the University of Göttingen in 1820, which opened up the possibility of a university career. In the following year, he was called to an extraordinary professorship for Sanskrit and general linguistics at the young University of Berlin, and was promoted within five years to ordinary professor, the highest and most secure rank. Bopp's appointment in Berlin was pushed forward by his acquaintance Wilhelm von Humboldt (1767–1835), a key figure in the founding of the University of Berlin and in the wider educational reforms that were implemented in Prussia at this time. Humboldt was himself an influential language scholar, who is introduced properly in the next chapter.

The institutional foothold Bopp secured in Berlin allowed him to train up a group of students to populate the new field of comparative-historical grammar that was taking shape. It also granted him the time and resources to continue his comparative project and expand its scope. The chief product of these efforts was his *Vergleichende Grammatik des Sanskrit, Zend, Griechischen, Lateinischen, Litthauischen, Gotischen und Deutschen* (Comparative Grammar of Sanskrit, Zend [i.e. Ancient Persian], Greek, Latin, Lithuanian, Gothic and German), which appeared in six hefty volumes from 1833 to 1852, expanding along the way to include most of the major groups of Indo-European languages.

The increasing technical focus – or perhaps narrowness – of the approach coalescing around Bopp received some somewhat sarcastic commentary from A. W. Schlegel. As we saw at the beginning of this section, Schlegel maintained a more traditional, philological approach. For Schlegel, studying grammar was just a way to gain access to a language and its literature, not an end in itself. For this reason, Schlegel could not muster much enthusiasm for the minute technical details of Bopp's comparative grammar, which were taking the academic world by storm. In 1831, Schlegel quipped about Bopp's work:

> Der Boppart [Boppard] ist ein Ort am Rhein;
> die Bopp-Art sind Pedanterei'n
> [Boppard is a place on the Rhine;
> Bopp-style is pedantry]
> (Schlegel 1831: 321; see Lefmann 1891–7, vol. 1: 173–4)

2.4 Jacob Grimm and sound laws

Bopp's comparative method provided a means for identifying the putative genealogical relationships between languages, but it had very little to say about how the languages have actually changed historically. In the standard narrative, another scholar is credited with putting the historical into comparative-historical linguistics: Jacob Grimm (1785–1863).

Jacob Grimm and his brother Wilhelm Grimm (1786–1859) made foundational contributions to the study of law, literature and language in Germany. Today the Brothers Grimm are best known for two of their collaborative works: the *Kinder- und Hausmärchen* (Grimm and Grimm 1812–15), their collection of German fairy tales; and the *Deutsches Wörterbuch* (Grimm and Grimm 1854–1960), the first comprehensive dictionary of German that illustrates the histories of individual words with quotations from texts.

Linguists remember Jacob Grimm most fondly for a book he wrote alone, his *Deutsche Grammatik* (Grimm 1822–37 [1819]), a comparative grammar of the Germanic languages. This work, which in its final edition totalled four volumes, lays out and systematises several insights into the historical development of the Germanic languages as a group. On the strength of their scholarship, both Grimm brothers were elevated later in life into the academic pantheon being constructed in Berlin: they were both made members of the Prussian Academy of the Sciences in 1841, and taught at the University of Berlin.

From our present-day perspective, the diverse scholarship of the Grimm brothers may seem like contributions to rather distinct branches of learning, but it must be remembered that for the Grimms themselves their various undertakings were inextricably intertwined. On their understanding, the law, literature and language were all manifestations of the spirit of a people, the *Volksgeist*. The broader movement that shaped much of the Grimms' outlook and methodology in this respect is historicism. This was a movement which began around the turn of the eighteenth to the nineteenth century and which is closely related to the Romanticism we already encountered in the previous sections. Like Romanticism, historicism was in large part a reaction against the mission of the Enlightenment to remake humanity and human society according to principles derived from pure reason.

Perhaps the best way to understand the Grimms' connection to historicism is to examine their relationship to Friedrich Carl von Savigny (1779–1861), one of the leading legal scholars of the period and lecturer in law to the Grimm brothers in their first undergraduate years at the University of Marburg (see Beiser 2011: chap. 5). The association between the Grimms and Savigny lasted their lifetimes and resulted in a deep mutual influence. Jacob Grimm in fact dedicated his *Deutsche Grammatik* to Savigny, and Grimm's preface to the book is written in the form of an open letter to Savigny.

A prime illustration of Savigny's historicism is the role he played in the so-called codification controversy that flared up in the wake of the Napoleonic Wars. One of the most spectacular careers to be made in the French Revolution was that of Napoleon Bonaparte (1769–1821). After rising to the top of the revolutionary leadership in the 1790s – which culminated in his self-coronation as Emperor of the French in 1804 – Napoleon embarked on the conquest of much of Europe. Many of the German-speaking territories he conquered were organised into the Confederation of the Rhine, a state allied with France which adopted many of the social and legal reforms emanating from the French Revolution.

The French Revolution was infused with the ideals of the Enlightenment and put into practice in many spheres of life the thoroughgoing rationalisation of the world that Enlightenment thinkers advocated. One of these rationalising interventions was the introduction of a single, unified and, above all, explicitly codified system of laws, often referred to as the *Code Napoléon*. The *Code* was intended as a definitive guide to the law in France, in which judges could simply look up the relevant transgression and mechanically apply the appropriate judgment. The *Code* became the basis of the law in many other European countries influenced by revolutionary France, including the Confederation of the Rhine.

But Napoleon was ultimately defeated in 1815, and his conservative opponents across Europe sought to impose the old order on the ruins of his empire. The Confederation of the Rhine was broken up and largely absorbed into Prussia. Although many Napoleonic reforms were in fact quite popular, they were in many cases considered untenable under the new Prussian hegemony. In the case of the law, the question arose as to what would be the best replacement for the *Code Napoléon*. Should the new Prussian provinces develop their own legal code cleansed of its French character? In the rest of Prussia there was already a common legal code in force that was in fact slightly older than the *Code Napoléon*. Or should the states revert to the ancient system of custom, obscure statutes and historical precedent that was in effect in many of these lands before the French conquest?

Savigny emphatically supported the restitution of the old order. He argued that the law was an expression of the particular people that is subject to it, of their *Volksgeist*. According to Savigny, the law cannot be derived from reason in the abstract, set down in a single document and applied universally. The only legitimate way to practise law is to study its evolution over time. This highly conservative principle was brought into the centre of the Prussian intellectual world when Wilhelm von Humboldt arranged for Savigny to become the first professor of law at the new University of Berlin in 1810.

The historicist spirit manifested and propagated by Savigny animated Jacob and Wilhelm Grimm's own scholarship. The idea that a people's law, literature and language are all expressions of its *Volksgeist* is what motivated their studies. Both Grimm brothers also specifically understood their work as a nationalist project directed towards strengthening the self-awareness of the German nation in the face of the division and foreign influence that was felt most acutely during the period of the Napoleonic Wars (see Jendreieck 1975: 22).

The Grimms' study of lexicography and grammar grew out of their work on German myths and legends. In trying to reconstruct the correct, original form of tales, they were led to examine word etymologies. But their first efforts at etymology lacked method; they indulged in a practice that has come to be known as 'wild etymology', where words from different languages and different periods were simply lined up alongside one other, and hypotheses were put forward about the possible etymological links between them. The result was inevitably speculative and scientifically unsatisfying. What was wanted was a set of rigorous principles to constrain etymologies.

Friedrich Schlegel (1808: 6–7) had already highlighted the need for strict principles for identifying the correspondence of sounds in words across languages when devising etymologies. His brother August Wilhelm Schlegel – the wry conscience of the emerging field – wrote a withering review of the Grimms' free-wheeling etymological researches. Jacob Grimm he described as an 'etymological Heraclitus' (Schlegel 1847 [1815]: 403), for whom everything flows, has no fixed form and is in constant chaotic change.

In response to A. W. Schlegel's critique, Jacob Grimm strove for greater rigour in his etymologies. He paid increasing attention to how sounds and grammatical forms change over time without trying to explain these changes by appealing to factors that lie outside the language itself, such as the meanings of words or the culture in which they are embedded (see Ginschel 1989 [1967]: 362). One of the most iconic of the many formal rules he proposed in the historic development of the Germanic languages is that usually referred to in English as 'Grimm's Law'.

Grimm noticed a series of sound correspondences that distinguish the Germanic languages as a group from all other Indo-European languages. Very briefly – and to use modern terminology – where other Indo-European languages have voiceless stops, Germanic languages usually have fricatives. For example, we can see this correspondence when we compare the first sound in the French word *poisson* with the English 'fish'; French *trois*, English 'three'; French *cœur*, English 'heart'. Voiced stops in other Indo-European languages are usually voiceless in the Germanic languages; for example, the first sound in French *dix* compared with English 'ten'. And the aspirated voiced stops of Sanskrit are unaspirated in the Germanic languages, as in Sanskrit *bhrātr* compared with English 'brother'. These patterns are consistent across many words in many different Indo-European languages.

It is as if these consonantal sounds in the Germanic languages have all shifted following a consistent rule. This rule seems to have then applied a second time in southern varieties of German. This can be seen in many words in modern Standard German compared with their English equivalents, since the sound system of modern Standard German is largely based on southern dialects, while English derives historically from northern Germanic varieties. The last sound in the German word *Schiff* is a fricative, while the sound in its English equivalent, 'ship', is a stop. The same correspondence occurs in the middle consonants of the German words *Wasser* and *machen* compared with English 'water' and 'make' (for a detailed description of Grimm's Law as it is understood today, see Campbell 2013 [1998]: 135–9). Grimm's Law therefore describes a regular process of historical change in the sound systems of the Germanic languages. Grimm imagined that this process was a manifestation of the Germanic *Volksgeist*.

Grimm's Law is an example of a 'sound law', a description of a regular change in sounds that has occurred in the history of a group of related languages. The practical application of sound laws, including Grimm's Law, is to guide our etymological reconstructions. For example, we can now say with confidence that French *poisson* and English 'fish' go back to the same word in the parent language because the sound laws tell us the precise steps through which these words have developed into their modern forms. If, on the other hand, we were to propose an etymology that does not accord with the sound laws, then it would have to be rejected as invalid.

We must note that Jacob Grimm was not alone in thinking along these lines. Most notably, the Danish linguist Rasmus Rask (1787–1832), with whom Grimm was in contact, observed many of the same sound correspondences that informed Grimm's Law. But in the preface to the first volume of his *Deutsche Grammatik*, the book in which he first described his law, Grimm said that unfortunately he only came to read Rask's work after his own book was sent off to the printers.

Danish linguists have traditionally been avid historians of the field and have been at pains to rescue Rask's legacy. In particular, Otto Jespersen (1860–1943), a Danish linguist whose work straddled the late nineteenth and early twentieth centuries, highlighted Rask's pioneering insights – and his priority over Grimm – in the potted disciplinary history that opens his 1922 *Language*, a general introduction to the linguistics of the time (Jespersen 1922: 36–40). Rask has been forgotten, Jespersen argued, because he wrote in Danish, a language with limited international currency. But even if we accord Rask the priority, and claim that Grimm and others were inspired by his work, it was Grimm's *Deutsche Grammatik* that was widely read and served as the main point of reference in the new endeavour to discover sound laws.

Through the pioneering work of such scholars as Franz Bopp and Jacob Grimm in the first half of the nineteenth century, comparative-historical grammar started to become a discipline. The field had clear goals and methods, and, crucially, an institutional base. Comparative-historical grammar could enter a period of 'normal science', to use the term introduced by Thomas Kuhn in his 1962 *The Structure of Scientific Revolutions*. That is, a scientific paradigm had solidified in which diligent scholars trained in the field could beaver away on defined tasks. But comparative-historical grammar was not the only approach cultivated in the new academic linguistics: it had an alter ego in the pursuit of language classification, with which it was in many ways intertwined. We turn to language classification in the next chapter.

2.5 Further reading

An excellent secondary source that treats many of the figures and innovations discussed in this chapter is Anna Morpurgo Davies's (1998) *History of Linguistics, Volume IV: Nineteenth-Century Linguistics*. In particular, chapters 3 and 6 of her book cover Sir William Jones, Friedrich Schlegel, Franz Bopp, Jacob Grimm and Rasmus Rask, with great detail on the technical aspects of their work. For an exposition of the comparative method as it is understood today, along with an explanation of Grimm's Law and other sound laws with examples, see chapter 7 of Lyle Campbell's (2020 [1998]) *Historical Linguistics: An Introduction*.

For a comprehensive account of the historicism that informed Jacob Grimm's research, see Frederick Beiser's (2011) *The German Historicist Tradition*. For the story of advances in geology and palaeontology in the nineteenth century, and their role in pioneering new techniques of comparison and reconstruction, see Martin Rudwick's (2005) *Bursting the Limits of Time: The Reconstruction of Geohistory in the Age of Revolution*, in particular chapters 6 and 7.

The best entry point for understanding recent work in postcolonial scholarship remains Edward Said's (2003 [1978]) highly accessible *Orientalism*, which, as we indicated in Section 2.1, played a major role in launching the movement. Thomas Trautmann's (1997) *Aryans and British India* provides a superb overview of the interplay between colonialism, racism, ethnology and linguistic scholarship as it pertains to the notion of 'Indo-European'. Douglas McGetchin's (2009) *Indology, Indomania and Orientalism: Ancient India's Rebirth in Modern Germany* focuses on Sanskrit studies in nineteenth-century Germany.

For a wide-ranging account of the emergence of comparative-historical grammar and linguistics as a discipline – as well as other modern humanities – from the broader field of philology in the nineteenth century, see James Turner's (2014) *Philology: The Forgotten Origins of the Modern Humanities*.

3 Language classification

In the early years of comparative-historical linguistics, there was a widespread belief that each language family exhibits a characteristic grammatical type, and that grammatical types are sufficient evidence for postulating genealogical connections between languages. Received opinion in linguistics today is in stark contrast to this view: most present-day linguists observe a clear distinction between genealogy and typology. Genealogical relationships are recognised only when there are specific similarities in words and grammatical forms that allow putative ancestral forms to be identified or reconstructed. General resemblances in the overall grammatical organisation of languages are believed to have no direct bearing on questions of common descent.

But up into the first half of the nineteenth century, the present-day separation of genealogy and typology did not exist. If we look, for example, at the *Mithridates* of Johann Christoph Adelung (1732–1806), one of the major pre-Boppian comparative compendia of the world's languages (discussed in Section 2.2), we see that Adelung arranged his survey of languages by geographical region and then according to supposedly shared grammatical structure. This conflation of genealogy and typology continued into the era of comparative-historical linguistics proper: Friedrich Schlegel (1772–1829), in introducing his 'comparative grammar', assumed that the Indo-European languages, as the family would soon be called, had a unique grammatical structure that set them apart from all other languages of the world, an idea that was further developed by his brother, August Wilhelm Schlegel (1767–1845), and which became part of the background to comparative grammar.

Alongside the belief in a link between genealogy and typology, it was widely held that there is a necessary relationship between the grammatical structure of a language and the mentality and lifestyle of its speakers. The most influential exponents of this position in nineteenth-century language scholarship were Wilhelm von Humboldt (1767–1835), and his chief interpreter, Heymann Steinthal (1823–1899). In this chapter, we examine this constellation of ideas regarding language structure, language relatedness, and the minds of speakers.

3.1 The Schlegel brothers and the 'inner structure' of languages

In his *Ueber die Sprache und Weisheit der Indier* – a book we introduced in Section 2.2 – Friedrich Schlegel devoted a chapter to what he called the 'inner structure' of Sanskrit and the European languages (Schlegel 1808: chap. 4). Schlegel believed that the Indo-European languages possess an 'organic' (*organisch*) grammatical structure, which distinguishes them from all other languages of the world, whose structure is merely 'mechanical' (*mechanisch*). What makes the Indo-European languages 'organic', according to Schlegel, is their use of inflection.

Inflection is a grammatical process in which the ending of a word changes depending on its role in the sentence. For example, in Latin, *puella* 'girl' is a word form in the nominative case, the case that marks the subject of a sentence. For this word to serve as the direct object of the sentence, it would need to be placed in the accusative case, indicated by a different ending: *puellam*. On this example, it may seem that creating the accusative form is simply a matter of adding the suffix -*m* to the nominative, but inflection is in fact much more complicated than that. There is no single accusative ending; rather, different words inflect in different ways to indicate the accusative. Latin nouns are traditionally divided up into five classes, called 'declensions', each of which is defined by the particular set of inflections exhibited by the nouns it contains – and even within these declensions there remain numerous exceptions and irregularities in the forms of specific nouns. Inflectional endings also tend to fuse with the word root in such a way that it is difficult to tease the ending and root apart. This can be seen in such Latin nouns as *rex* 'king [nominative singular]': *regem* 'king [accusative singular]', where the word root itself changes across the different case forms.

Genuine inflectional structures, Schlegel thought, are found only in Indo-European languages: the apparent inflectional forms of other languages, such as Arabic and its relatives, were taken by Schlegel (1808: 48) to be the product of mixing or 'artificial development'. Although Schlegel exaggerated in making inflection the exclusive property of Indo-European, it is true that the classical Indo-European languages – and indeed many modern members of the family – make extensive use of inflection on nouns, verbs and other major word classes, to the point that it could be said that inflection is characteristic of the family.

The main feature of inflection that inspired Schlegel to describe it as 'organic' is the way in which the word root and ending are interwoven. Inflectional endings, Schlegel (1808: 50–2) argued, seem to grow out of the 'living germ' (*lebendiger Keim*) of the root. By contrast, in the so-called 'mechanical' languages – a negative category in which Schlegel included all non-inflecting languages – words are merely cobbled together out of roots and affixes, without any true integration between the parts. Even worse, some 'mechanical' languages have no affixes at all and simply line up bare word roots to create sentences.

The opposition Schlegel set up between the 'organic' and 'mechanical' draws on a conceptual distinction that was widespread at the time, but which found a particularly influential formulation in the work of the leading Enlightenment philosopher Immanuel Kant (1724–1804). In his discussion of 'teleology', Kant imagined a fundamental difference between living organisms and inanimate, 'mechanical' entities. A living organism, Kant contended, is a *Naturzweck* (natural purpose). This is a complex notion that has inspired over two hundred years of exegesis and debate, but the essential idea is that living organisms are self-directed, self-sustaining, and exist for their own sake. A living organism will both reproduce itself through offspring and maintain itself by taking in nourishment from the environment. Most importantly, an organism is an indivisible whole, whose parts work together as a mutually supporting system to keep the organism alive (as we will see in the following chapters, the conceptualisation of languages as organic systems will play a crucial role in subsequent linguistic scholarship, right up into the twentieth century). Mechanical entities, on the other hand, have no life of their own. They are created and used by external forces to serve ends determined from outside their own being (for further explication of Kant's theory of teleology, see Ginsborg 2019: section 3; Richards 2002a: 64–71).

On one level Schlegel therefore tapped into discourses popular in contemporary philosophy and the aesthetic preferences of the early Romantic movement, with its exaltation of the natural world and suspicion of purely functional human invention (see Richards 2002a). But the love of the 'organic' is also tied in with the scientific justification of Schlegel's project. As we saw in Section 2.1, Schlegel's 'comparative grammar' is constructed on direct analogy with comparative anatomy, and 'organic' inflection is the primary source of data for Schlegel's comparativism: it is the analysis of the shared convolutions and irregularities in the inflectional forms of the Indo-European languages that delivers the proof of their relatedness. The 'mechanical' languages, with their much looser structures, offer less evidence of this kind to work with. The forms of mechanical languages, Schlegel (1808: 51) said, are 'like a heap of atoms, which the wind of chance can easily drive apart or bring together'. That is to say, the mechanical languages allegedly have no forms that remain stable through time and allow us to trace their history.

Friedrich Schlegel's dichotomous classification of languages was taken up and elaborated by his brother August Wilhelm Schlegel, who was also an accomplished Sanskritist, as we saw in Sections 2.1 and 2.2. In his 1818 book *Observations sur la langue et la littérature provençales* (Observations on Provençal language and literature), A. W. Schlegel (1818: 14–17) developed a scheme of language classification with three primary categories. This scheme persists to this day in a genericised form, where the three categories are usually called 'isolating', 'agglutinative' and 'inflectional'.

The prototypical example of an isolating language is Classical Chinese, in which there is virtually no inflection or affixation. Most words have a constant form and information about their grammatical role is conveyed almost entirely through syntax – that is, their position in the sentence relative to other words – or through self-standing grammatical particles. A well-known agglutinative language is Turkish, which makes extensive use of affixation. Although the affixes of Turkish may interact with roots – for example, through vowel harmony, where all vowels across a word must agree in such features as backness and roundedness – the roots and affixes of the Turkish word are clearly separable units, and any variation in form through vowel harmony or similar processes can be stated in terms of simple rules. This is in contrast to the forms of inflectional languages which, as we have discussed, frequently defy neat separation into root and affix, and generally exhibit a high degree of irregularity. The best exemplars of inflectional languages are the classical Indo-European languages.

But if we compare some of the major modern European languages with their classical ancestors, we see that they have lost much of their inflectional character. Modern French, Spanish or Italian, for instance, make much less use of inflection than Latin, and rely much more on syntax to convey grammatical distinctions. It would seem they have changed over time to become more like isolating languages. This historical development led A. W. Schlegel to divide the inflectional class into the older 'synthetic languages' (*les langues synthétiques*) and the younger 'analytic languages' (*les langues analytiques*). As we will see in the following sections, this is another terminological pair that evokes the philosophy of Immanuel Kant.

A. W. Schlegel was more circumspect than his brother in passing judgement on the grammatical types he postulated. He assigned the inflectional languages to the 'top rank' (*le premier rang*) and believed that isolating languages 'present great obstacles to the development of intellectual faculties' (Schlegel 1818: 14–15), but he did not necessarily think that the modern analytic languages were inferior. Despite their moving away from the inflectional ideal and in the direction of the isolating languages, the modern analytic vernaculars are capable of a 'degree of perfection', reflected in their use in great literature (ibid.: 17). A confirmed philologist of the old school (as we saw in Section 2.2), A. W. Schlegel was more interested in the literary feats achieved in a language than in the minutiae of its grammar.

But in the nineteenth-century mind, literature and grammar were not necessarily two separate domains. In the following decades, the question of how the grammatical structure of a language might make it a more or less suitable medium for literature and philosophical thought became a major topic in linguistic scholarship, perhaps best represented in the work of Wilhelm von Humboldt and his followers.

3.2 Wilhelm von Humboldt's 'anti-semiotics'

A common theme running through nineteenth-century language typology was speculation about the possible connections between language structure and the characteristic thought patterns of speakers. A leading figure in this area, who inspired numerous scholars in the nineteenth century and beyond, is Wilhelm von Humboldt.

We already encountered Humboldt in Sections 2.3 and 2.4 for his role in reforming the Prussian education system and founding the University of Berlin, which quickly became the centre of the German academic world. But Humboldt was also a respected scholar, who made innovative contributions to such fields as language research and historiography (see Mueller-Vollmer and Messling 2021). In his scholarship, Humboldt combined elements of contemporary German philosophy of language with empirical data from diverse languages to arrive at key insights into language typology.

Humboldt's assumption of a link between language and thought is a consequence of what the Humboldt scholar Jürgen Trabant (1986) calls his 'anti-semiotics'. To understand what this means, we need to make a short excursion into the philosophy of language. The semiotic doctrines to which Humboldt's ideas are opposed go back to the Ancient Greek philosopher Aristotle (384–322 BC), whose collected writings on logic and language are usually referred to as the *Organon*. The Greek word *organon* means 'tool' or 'instrument' and as the collective title of these texts highlights the fact that Aristotle conceived of language as a tool that we use in reasoning (in Section 13.1, we see the notion of language as an *organon*, in a somewhat different sense, revived in twentieth-century language philosophy).

As a preliminary to his model of language, Aristotle offered the following account of how words mean:

> Spoken signs are representations of impressions in the soul, and written signs are representations of the spoken ones. Just as letters are not the same for all men, so the sounds are not the same either. However, what these signs stand for – the impressions of the soul – are the same for everyone, and the real-world things of which they are the likeness are also the same. (Aristotle, *On Interpretation*, quoted in Law 2003: 28)

That is, words ('spoken signs') are names for concepts ('impressions on the soul'), which we have from our perception of things in the world. Written words are then simply representations of spoken words in a graphic medium. Aristotle acknowledged that different languages have different words ('letters and sounds are not the same for all men') but, crucially, he believed that the concepts represented by the words are universal across languages ('are the same for everyone'). The vocabulary of a language is therefore a kind of nomenclature, a set of conventional labels for pre-existing ideas.

Aristotle's semiotics was transmitted and amplified through Antiquity and the Middle Ages, and became part of the background to discussions of philosophy of language in the Renaissance and Enlightenment. It is the Enlightenment debates that directly informed Humboldt's work. Enlightenment-era thinking about language, the mind, and our sources of knowledge is traditionally divided into two broad camps, the empiricists and the rationalists (on these debates, see Aarsleff 1982). We briefly met representatives of these two camps in Section 2.2 when we talked about John Locke (1632–1704), a leading empiricist, and Gottfried Wilhelm Leibniz (1646–1716), who is usually counted among the rationalists.

Empiricism was popular among many English and French thinkers, although there of course remained diversity of opinion in both those countries. Empiricism held that the mind is essentially a *tabula rasa*, or blank slate. On this view, sense impressions – the sights, sounds, smells and tactile feelings we receive from the world – cause us to form ideas, and we attach words to these ideas in an arbitrary way. The characteristically German position, by contrast, was to say that there is some sort of natural connection between words and ideas. It was this belief that led Leibniz to suggest pursuing etymological research to trace words back to their original, natural sources, as we saw in Section 2.2.

The chief continuers of this debate into the generation after Locke and Leibniz were, on the French side, Étienne Bonnot de Condillac (1714–1780) and, on the

German side, Johann Gottfried von Herder (1744–1803). Condillac developed what is referred to as a 'sensationist' or 'sensualist' account of the origin of language (on Condillac, see Harris and Taylor 1997 [1989]: chap. 11). In his 1746 *Essai sur l'origine des connoissances humaines* (*Essay on the Origin of Human Knowledge*) – which was specifically conceived as a response to Locke's treatise on language and epistemology, *Essay on Human Understanding* – Condillac posited three kinds of sign: accidental, natural and instituted. Accidental signs are things that, through particular recurring circumstances, come to be connected by memory with certain ideas. Condillac offered the example of hunger as the sign of a fruit-laden tree. When we experience hunger pangs, it may cause us to think of a tree bearing fruit from which we have eaten on previous occasions in order to satisfy our hunger. Natural signs are the cries that we produce instinctively, such as the 'oohs' and 'aahs' that issue from us involuntarily when we are emotionally stimulated. Opposed to these first two categories are instituted signs, which are arbitrary. These are signs that we consciously decide to associate with particular things.

In a thought experiment in his *Essay*, Condillac imagined a boy and a girl set out in the world on their own. He hypothesised that they will quickly come to invent language on the basis of instituted signs. In the first step, they will only produce natural signs, crying out automatically whenever gripped by a feeling or sensation. But their inborn empathy for one another will lead them, after repeated occurrences of these natural signs, to gradually associate the signs with the accompanying sensations. Over time, they will come to invoke and manipulate the signs consciously, resulting in the institution of arbitrary human language.

Herder had a different view. In his 1772 *Abhandlung über den Ursprung der Sprache* (*Treatise on the Origin of Language*), he argued that the transition from natural signs to arbitrary language is not a gradual process, as Condillac had assumed, but in fact represents a difference in kind. It is the human ability for 'reflection' (the term Herder used is *Besonnenheit*) that is the qualitative difference that separates humans from animals and makes language possible. Reflection in Herder's sense is essentially the conscious recognition of our own thoughts. Herder offered the example of a human coming to recognise a lamb. The human encounters the lamb on several occasions and receives various sense impressions from it: white, soft, woolly. But one of these impressions will stick out and become the marker on which the human fixates in developing their notion of lamb. The most salient characteristic may, for example, be the lamb's bleating. In the moment of recognition, when the concept of lamb precipitates in the human's mind, they will exclaim, 'Aha! You are the bleating one' (Herder 1772: 55).

In coining their words, Herder argued, different peoples will have focused on different properties of the things named. This means that each language with its characteristic forms will encapsulate a slightly different perspective on the world. As languages are passed on from generation to generation, the differences between them will accumulate, making the languages and the world views they contain more and more distinct. In order to understand the unique perspective of each language, we must trace the forms of words back to their etymological origins. Herder's approach evinces a historicist spirit, in the sense we explored in Section 2.4.

Humboldt developed his 'anti-semiotics' in the midst of these debates about knowledge, reason and the origin of language. He formulated his ideas in a number of places, but his most notable text is *Über die Verschiedenheit des menschlichen Sprachbaues und ihren Einfluß auf die geistige Entwicklung des Menschengeschlechts* (On the difference of human language construction and its influence on the development of humankind), first published posthumously in 1836. Here Humboldt memorably described language as 'the forming organ of thought' (*das bildende Organ des Gedanken*; Humboldt 1836: 50). In opposition to the traditional Aristotelian model of semiotics and in line with the views espoused in Herder's writings, Humboldt argued that it is through the process of articulating our thoughts in words that we synthesise our experiences of the world with our understanding.

In putting forward this formulation Humboldt was drawing on the epistemology – or theory of knowledge – of Immanuel Kant (who we first met in Section 3.1). In his *Critik der reinen Vernunft* (*Critique of Pure Reason*), Kant (1787 [1781]) famously tried to reconcile the two camps of empiricism and rationalism. Kant resisted the extreme empiricist claim that our mind is a *tabula rasa* and everything we know is determined by sense impressions alone, but at the same time he objected to the attempts of the most radical rationalists to discount the outside world and derive all of our knowledge from the workings of our internal cognitive faculties. Kant's solution was to acknowledge that there is a real world out there and that we receive sense impressions from it, but to add that we cannot know this world directly. Rather, our understanding plays an active role in mediating our perception of the world. Through our faculty of sensibility, we receive sense impressions from the outside world, but we then reconstruct these impressions to build our picture of the world using innate categories given by our faculty of understanding.

In Humboldt's adaptation of Kant's philosophy, language is the transcendental medium on which we make this reconstruction of the world: it is in language that the Kantian synthesis of perceptual experience with our internal understanding takes place. For Humboldt, there is a dialectic relation between language and thought, and between speakers of a language. That is to say, there is a continual exchange back and forth between thoughts and words, and between interlocutors: our thoughts shape our words and our words shape our thoughts, and when we speak with others, we influence their way of thinking, and they influence ours. As we see in the next section, this view provided the philosophical framework for Humboldt's approach to the study of the world's languages.

3.3 Humboldt's linguistics of structure and linguistics of character

In outlining a programme for applying his philosophy of language to the study of actual languages, Humboldt divided his project into two dimensions, one concerned with the 'organism' (*Organismus*) or 'structure' (*Bau*) of languages, and another that focused on the development of their 'character' (*Charakter*; Humboldt 1836).

In practice, the linguistics of structure looks at grammatical features. The assumption is that these features emerged in a putative prehistoric period in which languages developed in a largely unconscious way. The linguistics of character, on the other hand, looks at the use made of a language to create literature. The creation of literature, according to Humboldt, is a conscious activity that can only be undertaken once the language has developed a solidified form. The goal of the linguistics of character is to study how the most eloquent speakers and writers have employed the grammatical means provided by a language in order to express themselves.

Humboldt (1905 [1820]: 12–13) described the linguistics of character as the 'keystone' (*Schlussstein*) of language study. Linguistics should not limit itself to the sterile study of grammars and dictionaries, because a language only reveals its true nature through use: 'The study of languages cannot be separated from their literature, since in a grammar book and dictionary only their dead skeleton is visible, but in their works we can see their living structure' (Humboldt 1836: 417). Humboldt's position here is a consequence of his belief that language is in its essence a creative activity and not, as most grammarians and philologists have traditionally assumed, the forms that are produced through this activity. In order to capture this contrast, Humboldt used the Greek words *ergon* (product) and *energeia* (activity):

> Language, understood in its true essence, is something that is constantly and in every moment fleeting. Even the preservation of language in writing is an incomplete and mummified record, which requires us to try and imagine the living recitation. Language itself is not a product (*ergon*) but an activity (*energeia*). (Humboldt 1836: 41)

Humboldt's conceptual pair of *ergon* and *energeia* would have a long life in linguistic theory. As we see in Sections 8.2 and 13.2, parallel ideas appear in the later work of Ferdinand de Saussure (1857–1913) and Karl Bühler (1879–1963), among others.

To try to understand something of the *energeia* that constitutes a language, to understand the spirit that animates it, we need to see how the language has come into full flower in its literature. This is why Humboldt considered the linguistics of character to be the 'keystone' of language study. However, even though Humboldt relegated the linguistics of structure to a subordinate role, he still devoted considerable attention to it – and it was predominantly the linguistics of structure that was pursued by his successors.

In line with his view that language is the medium in which the Kantian synthesis of perceptual experience and our internal understanding takes place, Humboldt saw a word in language as the combination of the physically perceptible sound with a concept. It is only through the combination of these two sides – the sound and the meaning – that each takes on a definite form. Humboldt's linguistics of structure looks at the different grammatical processes through which this synthesis takes place.

In his linguistics of structure, Humboldt more or less elaborated on the classificatory scheme that came from August Wilhelm Schlegel. According to Humboldt – and in line with aesthetic judgements generally in this period, which we saw in Section 3.1 – the most sophisticated grammatical process is inflection. The inflected word combines the concept and its relation to the rest of the proposition – expressed by the root and the inflectional ending respectively – into a single package where the concept retains its individual identity. This is in contrast to isolating and agglutinative structures, where the relation is only loosely associated with the concept or not expressed at all.

Humboldt added a fourth grammatical process to the original tripartite scheme, which he called 'incorporation' (*Einverleibung*). Incorporation – also known as 'polysynthesis' – describes structures in which a single word can reach a level of complexity in which it contains all parts of a sentence. This kind of structure is very common in American languages, to the point that in the nineteenth century incorporation was often taken to be a defining property of the languages of that continent (see Solleveld 2023). Humboldt felt incorporation to be inferior to inflection because he found the fusion it effects excessive. The way in which incorporation compacts the entire sentence into a single whole, argued Humboldt, robs the constituent concepts of their individual identity:

> The Mexican [i.e. the Mexican language Nahuatl] method of incorporation attests to a correct feeling for the formation of the sentence in that it puts the indication of the relations within the sentence directly onto the verb; that is, at the point at which the sentence wraps itself together as a single unit. In this way, this method is distinguished essentially and advantageously from the lack of specification in Chinese [an isolating language], where the verb is not even clearly indicated by its position, but is rather often only materially recognisable through its meaning. [. . .] Sanskrit [an inflectional language] indicates each word as a constitutive part of the sentence in a very simple and natural way. The method of incorporation does not do this, but rather, wherever it cannot put everything together as one, allows indications to emerge from the middle of the sentence, much like arrows, which show the direction in which the individual parts must be sought, according to their relationship to the sentence. (Humboldt 1836: 169)

We should note that Humboldt, in talking about these different language structures, was not positing essentialist types for individual languages, but rather cataloguing grammatical processes that can co-exist in a single language. On Humboldt's understanding, no language is purely isolating, agglutinative, inflectional or incorporating, although one of these processes might predominate. Nevertheless, the preferred approach of the leading linguists in the nineteenth century was to try to identify the type of each language and classify languages according to these purported types. For most of these linguists, Humboldt's theorising, and its philosophical background, was the point of departure and touchstone for their own typological work (see Ringmacher 2001a, 2001b).

3.4 Heymann Steinthal and *Völkerpsychologie*

One of the most prominent exponents of the Humboldtian tradition of language study in the nineteenth century was Heymann Steinthal. Steinthal not only wrote extensively on Humboldt's thought, but also developed his ideas in new directions (see Ringmacher 1996). Inspired by Humboldt's typological writings, Steinthal elaborated his own system of language classification, which interfaced closely with *Völkerpsychologie*, a wide-ranging field of study that Steinthal founded in collaboration with his colleague and friend Moritz Lazarus (1824–1903).

Völkerpsychologie – which means 'psychology of peoples' or 'ethnopsychology' – was an attempt to create an all-encompassing theory of society and culture which touched on topics that today would be considered to belong to such diverse disciplines as anthropology, history, philology and linguistics. But linguistic concerns always occupied a central place: the journal that Lazarus and Steinthal founded in 1859 as the primary organ for the new field was called the *Zeitschrift für Völkerpsychologie und Sprachwissenschaft* (Journal for *Völkerpsychologie* and linguistics). From the mid-nineteenth century, Lazarus and Steinthal's *Völkerpsychologie* attracted numerous scholars working across the fields it covered. Towards the end of the century, the term *Völkerpsychologie* was adopted and repurposed by Wilhelm Wundt (1832–1920), a professor of philosophy at the University of Leipzig and a founding figure of modern experimental psychology. Wundt carried *Völkerpsychologie* in this new form into the early twentieth century (Wundt is a recurring figure in our story, featuring in Chapters 6, 7, 10, 13 and 16). But as the twentieth century progressed, the kind of grand synthesis envisaged in *Völkerpsychologie* went out of fashion, and the approach faded away as the individual disciplines that we recognise today started to assert themselves.

The overarching goal of *Völkerpsychologie* was to characterise the *Volksgeist* of each people; that is, the shared mind or spirit of a people (*Volksgeist* is a term we already encountered in Section 2.4, in the context of the Grimms' historicism). Lazarus and Steinthal's proposal was to take the psychological methods that had been developed to describe the mental goings-on in individual persons and apply these to the study of the supposed shared mentality of entire nations (we explore Steinthal and Lazarus's methods in greater detail in Section 11.1). A *Volk* (a people or nation), they argued, is a voluntary and culturally defined entity: anyone who believes themselves to belong to a particular people and partakes of its culture is a member of that people. Their view was in stark contrast to racialist notions of the time, which sought to reduce each people to biologically defined 'races' (in Section 4.2, we see one of the most extreme examples of this racialist approach in nineteenth-century linguistics when we look at the work of August Schleicher).

Lazarus and Steinthal's *Völkerpsychologie* was intertwined with their political views. Both Lazarus and Steinthal were Jewish and were part of a movement among nineteenth-century Jewish Germans who considered themselves to be first and foremost members of the German nation, but at the same time wanted to maintain their Jewish identity within it. Their voluntarist conception of a people, where membership in a nation is determined by participation in its culture, provides a mechanism for constructing such an identity. Needless to say, Lazarus and Steinthal's views were attacked by anti-Semites of the time who sought to erect essentialist racial definitions of Germanness and Jewishness. But they were also attacked by some people of Jewish background who believed that

Jewish people should renounce their minority identity and simply assimilate to the Christian majority in Germany.

Even though Prussia – the German state in which Lazarus and Steinthal lived, and the most powerful German state of the time – was at a relatively liberal point in its history, both Lazarus and Steinthal suffered from discrimination, more or less overt. A striking example of this is Steinthal's given name. He is usually referred to as 'Heymann' Steinthal, although in contemporary literature and in some library catalogues he is also to be found under the names 'Heinemann' and even 'Hermann' and 'Heinrich'. In his memoirs, Steinthal explained the instability of his given name by the fact that at the time of his birth the Jewish population of his home town was barred from inclusion in the official register of births, deaths and marriages. For this reason, no official version of his name was recorded and, not feeling attached to any particular name, he let variants proliferate (see Belke 1971: 379). Steinthal's own practice in stating his name in his publications was to simply use his initial, 'H.'. Within the Jewish community, Steinthal was known by the name 'Chajim'.

State-sanctioned anti-Semitism declined during Lazarus and Steinthal's lifetimes – with Jewish citizens of Prussia being granted full and equal rights in 1869 – but there remained an unofficial residue of anti-Semitism that continued to impinge on the lives of Jewish Prussians and which created a glass ceiling for many Jewish academics, Lazarus and Steinthal included. Despite their undisputed intellectual prominence, and the importance of their work to German academia, neither Lazarus nor Steinthal ever reached the rank of ordinary professor in Berlin, the ultimate career goal of any German academic of this time.

Lazarus and Steinthal played up the political dimension of their work. In addition to legitimising the place of the Jewish minority in the German nation, they also advertised *Völkerpsychologie* as a means for cultivating the German *Volksgeist* as a preliminary to achieving German unification. In the mid-nineteenth century, Germany as we know it today did not yet exist. The German-speaking lands were divided up into a patchwork of more or less independent states, although there was a widespread desire – especially among academics and intellectuals – to join these states into a single political entity (this is a story that we take up in greater detail in Section 4.2). The understanding of the German *Volksgeist* facilitated by *Völkerpsychologie*, argued Lazarus and Steinthal, would aid this nationalist political project.

3.5 Steinthal's characterisation of languages

According to Lazarus and Steinthal, language is one of the main ways in which the *Volksgeist*, the object of study of *Völkerpsychologie*, manifests itself. This idea led Steinthal, in his linguistic writings, to try to capture and characterise languages. To this end, Steinthal sought to lay bare the respective 'inner form' of each language. 'Inner form' is a term that is usually attributed to Humboldt, although it only appears fleetingly in his writings and without any explicit definition. Steinthal's notion of inner form is to a large extent his own invention, even if he claimed only to have adapted it from Humboldt (see further McElvenny 2016b: 31–3; Borsche 1989).

For Steinthal there is a sense in which all of language is form and nothing else. That is, language is simply a representation of thought, in the same way that a stage play is a representation of some event that might take place in the real world or a portrait is a representation of a person. But there is still a sense in which a language can be a more or less pure representation of thoughts, and this is how Steinthal identifies inner form. There are material parts of language that represent the conceptual elements of thought, and then more purely formal parts that represent the relations between the concepts. Here Steinthal is continuing the distinction between conceptual and relational elements in language that we saw Humboldt make in Section 3.3.

Steinthal insists that we cannot simply read the formal character of a language off its externally visible parts. He does not assume that an isolating language is necessarily devoid of relational elements or that the grammatical affixes of an agglutinative language are necessarily formal, as was implied and even explicitly stated in many other approaches to language typology at the time (see Sections 2.2 and 4.4). Instead, we must look beneath the surface structures to discern the inner form of each language. In order to do this, we need to look to etymology. If a relation is expressed using 'material' words – that is, words that also name concrete concepts – then, on Steinthal's analysis, the language does not have a properly developed inner form. For example, if a language expresses the relation 'behind' with an expression like 'A back B' then this is not properly formal. The etymological origin of the form 'back' is still clear to speakers; it is a transparent metaphor referring to a physical body part. Since the concrete conceptual origin is still apparent, this is a material word being used to represent a formal relation. An expression is only truly formal when the etymology is no longer apparent to speakers (see Steinthal 1855: 366; 1860a: 317–18).

Steinthal's analysis is unfortunately rather slippery. Whether an etymology can be established for a relational element in a language is largely a question of the ingenuity of the linguist and does not really tell us much about the psychological reality of the etymology for speakers of the language. Even if a linguist can construct an etymology, it does not mean that speakers of the language are conscious of it when they use the word. This is a criticism that Steinthal faced from some of his contemporaries (see McElvenny 2016b).

In his 1860 book *Charakteristik der hauptsächlichsten Typen des Sprachbaues* (Characterisation of the main types of language structure), Steinthal turned his analysis of inner form into a system of language classification. Here he recognised a primary division between 'formal languages' (*Formsprachen*), those that possess inner form, and 'formless languages' (*formlose Sprachen*), those that supposedly lack inner form. Steinthal's classification crosscut the existing categories of isolating, agglutinative and inflectional languages, which appealed to the 'outer' – externally visible – forms exhibited in languages. For instance, Steinthal classified the isolating language Chinese as a 'formal language', because Chinese has a highly developed syntax and a large range of purely formal grammatical particles that are not etymologically transparent. According to Steinthal's criteria, these properties mean that the language has real inner form, even though this inner form is not realised as affixes or inflections.

But other isolating languages that superficially seem to have a grammatical structure similar to Chinese, such as many languages of South-East Asia, are not considered by Steinthal to have properly developed inner form. He was unable to identify in these languages the pure particles and syntactic structures that he found in Chinese. The same principle applied to the incorporating languages of the Americas: these were classified by Steinthal as formless because he believed he could identify a clear material origin for all their grammatical elements (see Steinthal 1860a: 312–31). The table in which Steinthal summarised his classification is shown in Figure 3.1. The key terms have been translated in parentheses.

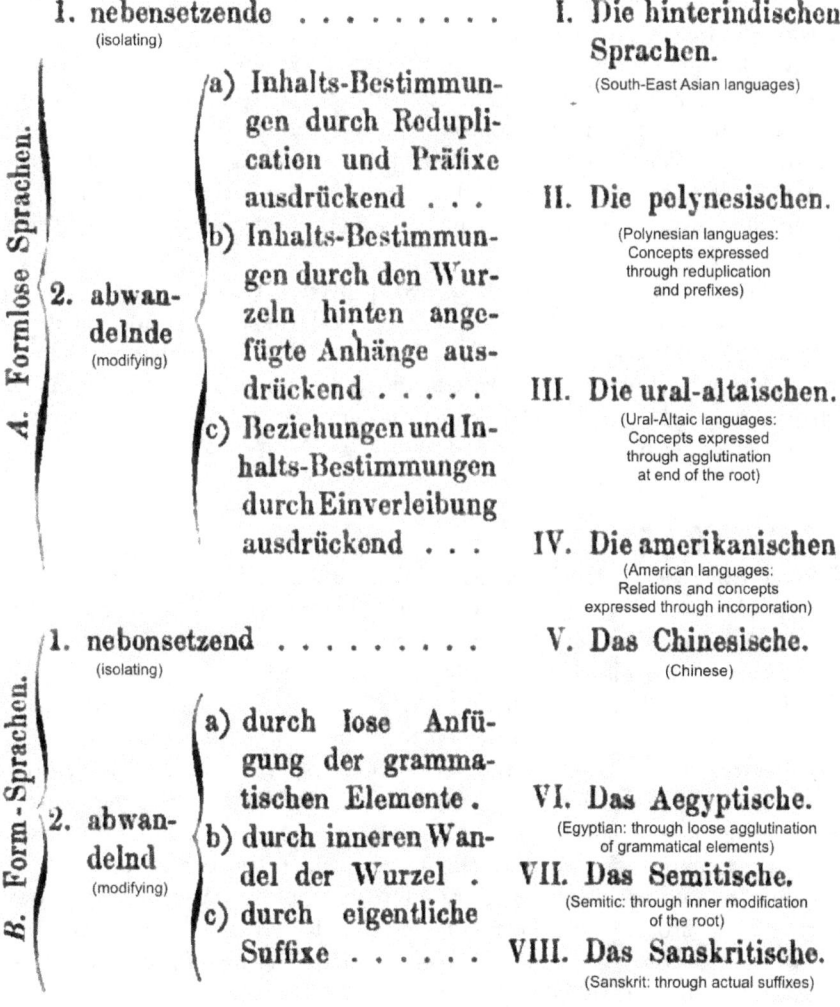

Figure 3.1 Steinthal's (1860a: 327) classification of languages

The slipperiness of Steinthal's classification is on show here. Why could he see inner form in Chinese but not in structurally similar South-East Asian languages? And why does he say there is no inner form in American languages, despite their elaborate incorporating structures? The unfortunate answer to these questions would seem to be that Steinthal's analyses are influenced by his preconceived ideas about which peoples should be considered 'civilised'. On Steinthal's estimation, the Chinese are 'civilised' because they have developed a 'high culture', producing art and literature prized around their region and the world, and living in an ancient, large-scale state. But he had a much lower opinion of the cultural and material life of their South-East Asian neighbours and of the peoples of the Americas.

Steinthal's prejudice becomes even clearer in his discussion of the emergence of the modern Indo-European 'analytic' languages from their 'synthetic' ancestors (a distinction introduced in Section 3.1). Despite the apparent reduction in formal features through their loss of inflection, Steinthal considered the modern analytic languages to be no less formal than their ancestors. Their pronouns and prepositions, he argued, are simply alternative manifestations of the same inner formal principles that motivated the noun and verb inflections of the classical synthetic languages (see Steinthal 1855: 366–7). Once again, Steinthal's analysis would seem to be guided not by the attested grammatical features of the languages under consideration but by his assessments of the alleged level of civilisation of their speakers.

Steinthal's language classification, tied to his and Lazarus's *Völkerpsychologie*, was predicated on the psychological analysis of the supposed shared mentalities of peoples. But this appeal to the intangible mental realm was put into question by philosophical currents that arose in the mid-nineteenth century. In the next chapter, we see how these debates affected linguistic scholarship in the example of August Schleicher.

3.6 Further reading

The best overview of language classification in the nineteenth century and its interconnection with comparative-historical linguistics can be found in Anna Morpurgo Davies's (1998) *History of Linguistics, Volume IV: Nineteenth-Century Linguistics*, in particular in chapters 4, 5 and 8. Her earlier (1975) essay, 'Language classification in the nineteenth century', which goes into greater detail, is also highly recommended. The entries on the history of typology from the eighteenth to the twentieth century, by various authors, in volume 2 of the *History of the Language Sciences* (Auroux et al. 2000–6, vol. 2: 1399–467), provide a chronologically broader perspective on the topic, with a focus on the technical aspects.

Some recent studies that highlight the problematic connections between eighteenth- and nineteenth-century approaches to language typology, racial theory and European colonialism include Joseph Errington's (2008) *Linguistics in a Colonial World: A Story of Language, Meaning, and Power* and Markus Messling's (2016) *Gebeugter Geist. Rassismus und Erkenntnis in der modernen europäischen Philologie*.

A good English-language introduction to Humboldt's thought is James Underhill's (2009) *Humboldt, Worldview and Language*. The best introductory texts, however, are Jürgen Trabant's numerous books on Humboldt, in particular his (1986) *Apeliotes oder der Sinn der Sprache, Wilhelm von Humboldts Sprachbild* and (2012) *Weltansichten: Wilhelm von Humboldts Sprachprojekt*. Neither of these books is available in English translation, although a revised and expanded version of *Apeliotes* is available in French under the title *Humboldt ou le sens du langage* (Trabant 1992).

For an exposition of the Enlightenment-era philosophy of language that informed Humboldt's work, see Hans Aarsleff's (1982) *From Locke to Saussure: Essays on the Study of Language and Intellectual History*. For an introduction to the topics in Kant's philosophy discussed in this chapter, see Nicholas Stang's (2018 [2016]) 'Kant's transcendental idealism' and Hannah Ginsborg's (2019) 'Kant's aesthetics and teleology', both of which are articles in the online *Stanford Encyclopedia of Philosophy*. On classical European philosophy of language, including Aristotle, see Vivien Law's (2003) *The History of Linguistics in Europe: From Plato to 1600*.

For an introduction to *Völkerpsychologie* from Lazarus and Steinthal to Wundt and beyond, see Egbert Klautke's (2013) *The Mind of the Nation: Völkerpsychologie in Germany, 1851–1955*. Céline Trautmann-Waller's (2006) *Aux origines d'une science allemande de la culture: linguistique et psychologie des peuples chez Heymann Steinthal* is a superb study of Steinthal's work, including his linguistics and *Völkerpsychologie*.

4 The consolidation of comparative-historical linguistics

By the middle of the nineteenth century, comparative-historical linguistics – which we introduced in Chapter 2 – had become a firmly established field. The methods pioneered by such figures as Franz Bopp (1791–1867) and Jacob Grimm (1785–1863) had been synthesised and elaborated by their students and followers. A major contribution in this direction was made by August Friedrich Pott (1802–1887), who in his *Etymologische Forschungen auf dem Gebiete der indogermanischen Sprachen* (Etymological researches in the area of Indo-European languages), published in two volumes from 1833 to 1836, married Bopp's comparativism to Grimm's sound laws on the scale of the whole Indo-European family.

Furthermore, the relationships within various Indo-European subgroups received detailed attention in this period. To name just a few of the most prominent examples: from 1836 to 1844, Friedrich Christian Diez (1794–1876) published his comprehensive comparative grammar of the Romance languages in three volumes; from 1852 to 1875, Franz von Miklosich (1813–1891) offered a comparative grammar of the Slavic languages in four volumes; and in 1853, in a relatively modest two volumes, Johann Kaspar Zeuß (1806–1856) set out a comparative grammar of the Celtic languages.

The methods of comparative-historical linguistics were also being applied outside the Indo-European family. Wilhelm Bleek (1827–1875) produced in two volumes, from 1862 to 1869, a comparative grammar of the Bantu family of Sub-Saharan Africa. The Dravidian family, whose languages are spoken predominantly in the southern part of the Indian subcontinent, was sketched by Robert Caldwell (1814–1891) in 1856. The links between Chinese and Tibetan were recognised by Karl Richard Lepsius (1810–1884) in 1861, laying the foundations for the Sino-Tibetan family. Finally, Hans Conon von der Gabelentz (1807–1874) outlined relations between several Melanesian languages of the South Pacific in two publications in 1861 and 1873.

There arose a somewhat excessive zeal in applying the comparative method. A notable example here is the attempt made by Bopp in 1842 to set up a genealogical link between the Indo-European family and the Malayo-Polynesian languages. This attempt was controversial even in Bopp's time and would not be accepted today: the Malayo-Polynesian languages are now considered one of the major groups within the larger Austronesian family, and most present-day linguists would not acknowledge any credible genealogical connection between

Austronesian and Indo-European. In fact, Bopp was only able to suggest such a connection by abandoning his own method: his comparison was based largely on superficial lexical similarities – which are the result of the borrowing of words from Sanskrit into Malay – rather than on underlying parallels in grammatical forms.

Another sign of the maturity of comparative-historical linguistics in this period was the way in which its principles and methods were received outside its immediate disciplinary confines. As the historian of linguistics Anna Morpurgo Davies (1998: 157–60) has observed, if scholars working in such traditional areas as philology, language teaching and dictionary writing wanted to be taken seriously, it became necessary for them to be aware of the advances made in comparative-historical grammar and to integrate its results in their own work.

With comparative-historical linguistics in full bloom, the time was ripe for a consolidation of both the methodology and underlying theory of the field. In the standard narrative of the history of linguistics, the figure usually credited with stepping up to this challenge is August Schleicher (1821–1868). Schleicher built his reputation on refining the methods of comparative grammar and articulating an explicit philosophy of science motivating his project. In the following sections, we look at Schleicher's contributions and the reactions they provoked.

4.1 August Schleicher and realism

As comparative-historical linguistics developed into an institutionalised discipline, it became increasingly narrow and technical in scope, concentrating ever more on the minute details of grammatical forms. Some scholars saw this as a decline into pointless pedantry (we may recall August Wilhelm Schlegel's wry remarks to that effect, quoted in Section 2.3), but most of those working within the emerging field of comparative grammar embraced this narrowness and began to distinguish between traditional philology, with its broader literary and cultural concerns, and linguistics as the scientific study of languages for their own sake. Jacob Grimm, for one, made this distinction (see Grimm 1840 [1819]: xii–xiii).

In one of his earliest comprehensive works, *Die Sprachen Europas in systematischer Uebersicht* (The languages of Europe in systematic overview), August Schleicher (1850: 1–5) sharpened this contrast between philology and linguistics. Linguists should not only be interested in languages for their own sake, he argued, but should also look beyond the peculiarities of individual languages to seek the 'immutable natural laws' governing human language in general. He insisted that linguistics is different from the 'historical' sciences, which trace the development of individual things over time, and should instead be counted among the natural sciences like physics and chemistry, which search for universal laws. Schleicher in effect inverted the perspective of the discipline. Up until this point, comparative linguistics was dominated by a historicist outlook (as discussed in Section 2.4), which emphasised the individuality and uniqueness of each language and its history; now the task was to abstract away from the particular in order to find the universal.

One result of Schleicher's theoretical views is that he became more consequential in his application of sound laws – the descriptions of regular sound changes in the history of languages, such as Grimm's Law, which we met in Section 2.4. Many of Schleicher's contemporaries – including his friend and colleague Georg Curtius (1820–1885), introduced properly in Section 6.1 – were rather resigned about the apparent limits of sound laws: there always seemed to be exceptions to the laws, a remainder of words and grammatical forms that would just not conform to the patterns they described. But Schleicher saw this as a failure of method, not as a problem insoluble in principle. He pushed harder to refine his sound laws in order to eliminate as many exceptions as possible.

A further outcome of Schleicher's approach is that he imbued the analyses of the comparative method with a new degree of reality. For his predecessors the reconstructed forms of the various proto-languages remained more or less on the level of hypothesis. Schleicher, however, took a position that would today be considered a kind of scientific realism: he did not consider the reconstructed forms he worked with to be theoretical posits, but rather entities in the real world. He had enough faith in the reality of his reconstructions to go ahead and write a short fable in Proto-Indo-European, his 1868 'Avis akvāsas ka' (The sheep and the horses):

> Avis, jasmin varnā na ā ast, dadarka akvams, tam, vāgham garum vaghantam, tam, bhā ram magham, tam, manum āku bharantam. Avis akvabhjams ā vavakat: kard aghnutai mai vidanti manum akvams agantam.
>
> Akvāsas ā vavakant: krudhi avai, kard aghnutai vividvant- svas: manus patis varnām avisāms karnauti svabhjam gharmam vastram avibhjams ka varnā na asti.
>
> Tat kukruvants avis agram ā bhugat. (Schleicher 1868: 207)

In presenting this fable, Schleicher (1868: 207) commented that a 'translation is of course superfluous for all who are to some degree at home in Indo-European'. Nevertheless, he offered a German version of his tale for his more ignorant readers. An English translation of Schleicher's German version would be:

> A sheep on which there was no wool (i.e. a shorn sheep) saw horses, one driving a heavy wagon, one carrying a great weight, one carrying a person quickly. The sheep said to the horses: the heart is narrowed in me (I am very/heartily sorry), seeing people driving the horses.
>
> The horses said: Listen sheep, the heart is narrowed in those who have seen (We are very sorry, since we know): people, the lords, make the wool of the sheep into warm clothes for themselves and there is no wool to the sheep (but the sheep have no wool any more, they are shorn; they are even worse off than the horses).
>
> Having heard this, the sheep turned (escaped) into the field (it took to its heels).

This story of interspecies exploitation has a certain artificial quality to it, no doubt because Schleicher used only words and idioms that he felt he could reconstruct with sufficient confidence. It is also interesting to observe the image that Schleicher sought to project of his Indo-European forebears as masters of the beasts of the field, which they oppress for their own personal gain. Schleicher's fable has become a favourite plaything of Indo-Europeanists and has been continually updated to incorporate the latest thinking on the sounds and structures of Proto-Indo-European (see, e.g., Kortland 2010: 47–50).

We should note that Schleicher's exaggerated commitment to realism would seem to have been slightly embarrassing for his contemporaries and, above all, for his students. This is apparent in the preface to the third edition of Schleicher's *Compendium der vergleichenden Grammatik der indogermanischen Sprachen* (Compendium of the comparative grammar of the Indo-European languages), his magnum opus. The third edition was prepared after Schleicher's death by his former students August Leskien (1840–1916) and Johannes Schmidt (1843–1901), two prominent figures in the following generation, who reappear in Chapters 6 and 7. In a footnote, Leskien and Schmidt inserted the disclaimer that in putting forward his very definite reconstructions Schleicher did not necessarily assert that the words once really existed in precisely this form (Schleicher 1871 [1861–2]: 8). We may, however, legitimately ask whether this disclaimer reflects Schleicher's actual views, or is rather an attempt on the part of his disciples to posthumously rescue his reputation.

Schleicher's realism manifested itself also in the way he depicted the relations between languages. As we saw in Chapter 2, the notion that languages could be related to one another in a genealogical sense was the founding insight of comparative-historical linguistics. From the very beginning, this insight was based on an analogy between languages and biological organisms. But Schleicher was the first to popularise the visual representation of language relationships as a family tree, as we would draw to illustrate the pedigree of animals or our own more modest lineages. Figure 4.1 reproduces the diagram Schleicher offered in his *Compendium*. Schleicher's realism in fact went even further. As we see in the next section, Schleicher turned this analogy between languages and biological organisms into a literal equivalence.

4.2 Darwinism and scientific materialism

In 1863, Schleicher published a remarkable pamphlet called *Die Darwinsche Theorie und die Sprachwissenschaft* (The Darwinian theory and linguistics), in which he wrote: 'Languages are organisms of nature; [. . .] they arose, grew and developed according to definite laws; they become old and die out [. . .]' (Schleicher 1863: 7). Schleicher's claim was not that languages are like natural organisms, but that they are literally natural organisms.

Schleicher's pamphlet was inspired by his reading of a German translation of *On the Origin of Species* by Charles Darwin (1809–1882), the first English edition of which appeared in 1859. Darwin's theory of evolution was taking the English-speaking world by storm and was being eagerly promoted in Germany. The goal of Schleicher's pamphlet was to affirm the validity of Darwinian evolution and demonstrate its applicability to the alleged 'natural organisms' that are human languages. Subsequent scholars have generally taken Schleicher's claims at face

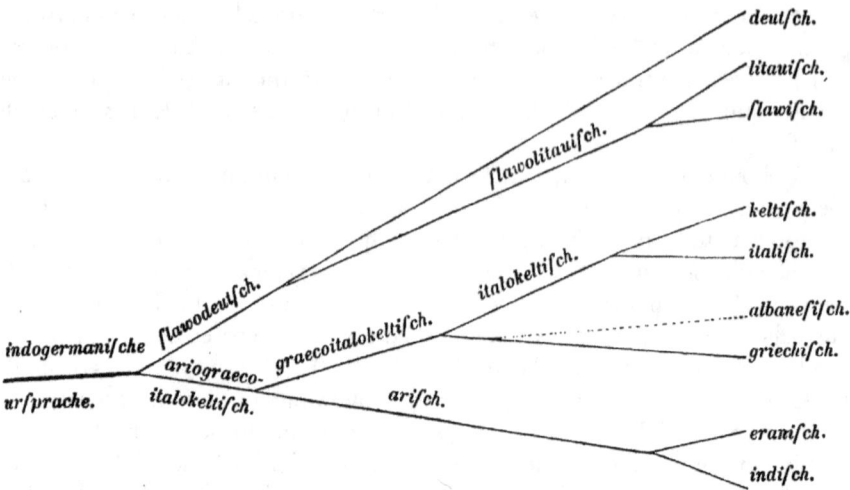

Figure 4.1 Schleicher's (1861–2, vol. 1: 7) family tree showing the main branches of Indo-European

value and talk about his 'Darwinian linguistics'. Actually reading Schleicher's pamphlet, however, reveals a very idiosyncratic understanding of Darwinism on Schleicher's part. It would seem that Schleicher was in fact projecting his own pre-existing ideas onto Darwin.

Among his contemporaries in Germany, Schleicher's work was not so much considered an example of Darwinism as of 'materialism', a word used in a very wide range of senses. The specific form of materialism with which we can identify Schleicher is 'scientific materialism', a doctrine that recognises only physical entities in the world and denies the existence of such things as the mind or the soul. Scientific materialism is distinct from Marxist 'historical materialism' – another materialist conception from this era, much better known today – which appeals to matter as an explanatory rather than an ontological principle. The key idea underlying historical materialism is that developments in the material conditions of production cause changes in social structures.

But the specific sense in which Schleicher's critics used the term 'materialism' is only of secondary importance: in mid-nineteenth-century Germany, 'materialism' was a highly charged word, rarely used by scholars to describe themselves, but more often as a term of abuse. Schleicher rejected this term as a description of his own work, preferring to call his philosophy 'monism' (Schleicher 1863: 8).

Despite these terminological battles, Schleicher was clearly aligned, both personally and intellectually, with the movement of scientific materialism. Scientific materialism had its roots in biology. At the dawn of the nineteenth century, biological theory was dominated by various Romantically inclined approaches often grouped under the title of *Naturphilosophie* (philosophy of nature; see Richards 2002a: 8–11). To our eyes, *Naturphilosophie* may seem to be indistinguishable from mysticism: in order to account for the functioning of living organisms, proponents of *Naturphilosophie* would appeal to such invisible powers as 'vital forces' or the soul. But with the rapid improvement in scientific instruments in the first half of the nineteenth century, in particular microscope technology, it became possible for biologists to directly observe the individual cells that make up organisms and the minute goings-on inside them. It was now possible to conceive of cells as little machines working on the same physical principles that can be observed on a larger scale; appeals to vital forces or the soul now seemed entirely superfluous.

Of course, questioning the existence of the soul and other supernatural powers challenges the business model of some rather powerful social institutions, among them the church. While some scientific materialists trod carefully in this area, the most strident members of the movement weaponised their science and wielded it against religion and the conservative politics with which it was generally allied in this period. The political dimension of scientific materialism was most pronounced around 1848. In this year, simmering social tensions – between the upwardly mobile middle classes, downtrodden workers, and the aristocrats who ruled over them – came to the boil and resulted in revolts across Europe. In Germany – at this time still a loose collection of small states, mostly ruled by aristocrats – a 'pre-parliament' came together in Frankfurt am Main in an effort to unite the various German-speaking lands into a single political entity.

An embarrassingly large proportion of the representatives in the pre-parliament were professors, who for the most part advocated 'liberal' political positions. In this context, liberal politics meant in the first instance a belief in limiting the power of aristocrats and instituting constitutional government. But it also entailed a strong element of nationalism – the goal was after all to unite the German nation, understood as being all those who speak German, and excluding those who do not. We already encountered an expression of this kind of nationalism in Section 2.4, when we looked at the work of the Grimm brothers. In fact, the Grimm brothers were among the representatives who sat in the Frankfurt parliament.

The plans of the Frankfurt parliament were incompatible with the interests and rivalries of the ruling houses across the German-speaking world. The parliament's resolutions were ignored and the revolts put down by military force. It would be another twenty years before German unification would come about, and not from below through democratic agreement, but from above through the overwhelming power of Prussia – and without the participation of Austria, which remained the centre of the multi-ethnic Habsburg Empire.

As a young man, Schleicher moved in radical liberal-patriotic circles. During 1848 and its aftermath, he was a correspondent based in Austria for two German newspapers. His articles evince a clear sympathy for the liberal cause and were considered sufficiently incendiary for him to have had several run-ins with the Austrian authorities. Schleicher's scholarly reading was also very much oriented towards the work of the scientific materialists. In his *Darwinsche Theorie und die Sprachwissenschaft*, Schleicher (1863: 6) names three figures who inspired his understanding of evolutionary theory. These three figures allow us to triangulate Schleicher's position in the contemporary intellectual landscape.

The first two names are Matthias Schleiden (1804–1881) and Carl Vogt (1817–1895). Schleiden was a botanist whose work on cell theory had inspired many scientific materialists, although Schleiden himself shied away from the religious and political implications of his work and later disavowed the materialist movement completely. Vogt, a professor of zoology, was by contrast one of the ringleaders of political scientific materialism. He wrote a series of *Physiologische Briefe* (Physiological letters; Vogt 1846) that were serialised in the *Augsburger Allgemeine Zeitung*, one of the newspapers to which Schleicher contributed as correspondent. Vogt's letters conveyed the latest discoveries in the life sciences to a general audience and over time became increasingly polemical in tone, attacking traditional views about the mind and soul. Vogt was also a representative in the Frankfurt parliament of 1848. His political activities eventually resulted in his being forced to emigrate to Switzerland.

The third name Schleicher mentions is that of Ernst Haeckel (1834–1919), to whom he in fact dedicated his Darwinian pamphlet. As Schleicher (1863) himself explained in the introduction, it was Haeckel who recommended that Schleicher read Darwin's *On the Origin of Species* and thereby prompted him to write the pamphlet. Haeckel was a good friend of Schleicher and was his colleague at the University of Jena, where Haeckel was professor of comparative anatomy. Haeckel was one of the chief promoters of Darwinism in Germany and was also active in liberal politics in the second half of the nineteenth century. He advocated a modern, 'scientific' view of life and the world against traditional religion and conservative political interests, and was frequently cited, by his opponents, as a leading representative of 'materialism' (see Richards 2008).

In concert with Schleicher, Haeckel rejected the term 'materialism' as a description for his philosophy and preferred to describe it as 'monism' (see Haeckel 1899). Both Schleicher and Haeckel – and other like-minded thinkers in this period – insisted that they did not seek to reduce everything to matter, but instead that there is only one kind of substance that is neither matter, mind nor soul but rather all of these at once. This is why they called their approach 'monism': there is supposed to be only one kind of thing.

Schleicher was steeped in this thought emanating from such figures as Schleiden and Vogt and continued by Haeckel. In this context, Schleicher's claim that languages are literally natural organisms becomes more understandable: it is a move designed to align linguistics with his materialist or monistic philosophy of science, which is reinforced by his liberal political views.

In the last years of his life, Schleicher doubled down on his materialism. In his 1865 essay *Über die Bedeutung der Sprache für die Naturgeschichte des Menschen* (On the significance of language for the natural history of humankind), essentially the sequel to his 1863 Darwinian pamphlet, Schleicher explicitly collapsed language onto a single material plane: 'Language is the symptom perceptible through the ear of the activity of a complex of material relations in the formation of the brain and the language organs with their nerves, bones, muscles and so on' (Schleicher 1865a: 8). Schleicher's statement is reminiscent of a scandalous observation that Vogt had made in his *Physiologische Briefe*:

[A]ll those abilities that we conceive of as activities of the soul are merely functions of the brain substance; or, to put it somewhat crudely, thoughts have the same relationship to the brain as bile to the liver or urine to the kidneys. (Vogt 1846: 206)

4.3 Morphology of languages

As we saw in Chapter 3, in its earliest days comparative-historical linguistics was closely intertwined with language typology. Over the course of the nineteenth century, however, these two strands of research became increasingly decoupled. Schleicher exemplifies this trend: although he devoted himself in equal measure to both typological and comparative-historical work, Schleicher struck a very modern note in distinguishing between typology and genealogy. Genealogically related languages, Schleicher (1859: 37–8; 1860: 30) wrote, can belong to different typological classes; there is no necessary coincidence between the two. But Schleicher's typology came with other baggage: it was bound up with his beliefs about the evolution of human language.

The name Schleicher gave to his typological project was 'morphology', a term that in linguistics has since become the generic label for grammatical processes that occur at the level of the word – such as compounding, affixation, inflection, and so on – and their study. In the intellectual environment in which Schleicher was writing, Germany in the mid-nineteenth century, the term 'morphology' was associated above all with the biological writings of the great German poet and polymath Johann Wolfgang von Goethe (1749–1832).

Goethe's morphology was a theory of the development of biological organisms, in terms of both ontogenesis, the development of individuals over their own lifetimes, and phylogenesis, the evolution of species. Goethe's theory has many points of contact with the contributions to comparative anatomy of such figures as Johann Friedrich Blumenbach (1752–1840) and Georges Cuvier (1769–1832), which we discussed in Section 2.2. Goethe worked out his theory of morphology over several decades, but the central publication in which it is expounded is his *Zur Morphologie* (On morphology), published in six parts from 1817 to 1824 (Goethe 1877 [1817–24]). The paper in which Schleicher first put forward his linguistic morphology is the 1859 'Zur Morphologie der Sprache' (On the morphology of language), the title of which clearly echoes the title of Goethe's work.

The fundamental aim of Goethe's morphology was to identify the archetypal forms underlying each organism, on both the individual ontogenetic level and the species-wide phylogenetic level. The phylogenetic aspect of Goethe's theory is perhaps the most comprehensible from our present-day perspective. By comparing the structures of plants and animals, Goethe hoped to identify their commonalities and through this process abstract away their differences to discover the *Urpflanze* (proto-plant) and the *Urtier* (proto-animal). That is to say, Goethe believed that it was possible to find the essential or archetypal forms underlying all plants and animals. This concept of the *Urpflanze* or *Urtier* may be congenial to us because it can be assimilated to current ideas about evolution: the *Urpflanze* or *Urtier* can be understood as the common ancestor from which the plants and creatures in the world today have descended. In fact, Charles Darwin, in a brief historical sketch of his predecessors added to the third edition of *On the Origin of Species*, supported such an interpretation of Goethe's theory (Darwin 1861 [1859]: xiv).

On the ontogenetic level, Goethe imagined that there is an underlying archetype for each part of a living thing, which then grows into all of its diversified organs. On this theory, there is, for example, an archetypal leaf that grows into all the parts of a plant: the stem, the leaves, the petals of a flower, its stamens, and so on. In the animal world, Goethe sought an archetypal bone that underlies all the parts of the skeleton; this he identified in the vertebra of the spine.

One feature of Goethe's theory that is rather different from our present-day conceptions, however, is that he believed the growth of organisms to be a teleological or goal-directed process. In Goethe's mind, the growth of an organism is motivated and guided by the *Bildungstrieb* (drive to formation), a notion he adopted from Blumenbach. The *Bildungstrieb* is in turn related to the Kantian idea that living things are 'natural purposes', which we discussed in Section 3.1 – although Kant himself was uneasy about positing the real existence of such drives, preferring to see them as heuristic devices that merely aid our understanding (see Richards 2002a: 64–7). Needless to say, the *Bildungstrieb* is one of these mysterious forces of *Naturphilosophie* that were attacked by the scientific materialists. The materialists felt that such forces belonged not to the realm of science but to superstition.

There were, however, many who sought to bridge the gap, to retain the insights of the earlier *Naturphilosophie* while making it compatible with the metaphysics of modern science. One of the most prominent of these figures was Ernst Haeckel, Schleicher's friend and intellectual ally in Jena, who we met in the previous section. In his 1866 *Generelle Morphologie* (General morphology), Haeckel developed a theory combining Goethe's insights on ontogenesis and phylogenesis with Darwinian doctrine. Haeckel – citing Schleicher as one of his sources of inspiration (see Richards 2002b) – allowed that there is indeed a directed process of growth in individual organisms, and a direction in species evolution. But he denied that these are the product of mysterious non-material forces. Instead, he treated them as the emergent outcomes of recognisable mechanical forces interacting with one another. For example, the increasing 'fitness' to their environment that organisms seem to develop over generations is not due to the intervention of God, but is simply the result of variation within the population coupled with natural selection (see Richards 2008: chap. 5).

Schleicher's linguistic morphology aimed to do for languages what Goethe's and Haeckel's various versions of morphology did for the biological world: it sought to describe the building blocks and structures of all the world's languages and, in addition, to fit these into an evolutionary framework. Schleicher sketched his ideas in a number of publications, although he was most explicit in his 1860 *Die Deutsche Sprache* (The German language). Drawing in particular on Wilhelm von Humboldt's (1767–1835) discussion of grammatical processes across languages – which we saw in Section 3.3 – Schleicher's (1860: 33–7) evolutionary scheme posits isolation as the most 'primitive' state of language. In this state, a language consists of nothing but an agglomeration of word roots. Agglutinative structures then emerge from isolation as a differentiation of linguistic forms takes place: word roots come to represent concepts and affixes to represent the relations between those concepts. Finally, agglutination gives way to inflection, as word roots and endings merge into integrated packages combining concepts and relations. Humboldt (1905 [1822]) had suggested a similar evolutionary scheme in his paper 'Über das Entstehen der grammatischen Formen und ihren Einfluss auf die Ideenentwicklung' (On the emergence of grammatical forms and their influence on the development of ideas), although he was not quite so committed to the idea as Schleicher.

Both Humboldt and Schleicher assumed that the ascension of languages up this morphological ladder occurred in prehistoric times, and ceased once the speakers of the language entered the historical age. Schleicher went one step further than Humboldt and stated that languages begin to decline once their speakers enter the historical period: this explains the development of the modern 'analytic' languages from their 'synthetic' ancestors (which we discussed in Section 3.1). The degree of decline of a language, according to Schleicher (1860: 35), is directly proportional to the involvement of its speakers in world history. For example, commented Schleicher, English is the most degenerate of the Germanic languages – having lost almost all of its inflectional morphology – since the English as a nation are so deeply involved in international affairs.

The division of language evolution into prehistoric and historic periods reflects a trope of Romanticism in which an imagined prehistoric era is contrasted to contemporary 'civilised' life. On this account, prehistoric humans – and 'uncivilised' peoples today – live in a 'primitive' state of nature, while those of us in the modern world have supposedly reached a higher level of mental and cultural development. But civilisation is both a blessing and curse: our effete existence ultimately dooms us to depravity and degeneration. This view is classically associated with such thinkers as Jean-Jacques Rousseau (1712–1778), but became so widespread as to be a cliché. Schleicher's vision of prehistoric language growth and historical decline, based on his reading of Humboldt, is essentially a projection of this attitude onto language (see McElvenny 2021).

Schleicher was not the only scholar to paint such a picture of language evolution. Franz Bopp, in his *Vergleichende Grammatik* (1833–52), imagined a similar scheme. Bopp's approach, which came to be known as the 'agglutination theory', was advanced in opposition to the absolute dichotomy of 'organic' and 'mechanical' languages of Friedrich Schlegel, which we introduced in Section 3.1. Bopp used the agglutination theory to argue for a fluid transition between different linguistic types. This fluidity licensed his analyses of verb conjugations as originally compounded forms which, over time, gradually became ever more closely bound, eventually developing the character of inflections (see Section 2.3). Agglutination theory was rediscovered and claimed towards the end of the twentieth century by practitioners of the new subfield of grammaticalisation (see, e.g., Lehmann 2015 [1982]: 1–9).

4.4 Inner and outer form

In his morphology of languages, August Schleicher (1859: 1) focused exclusively on the 'outer phonetic form' of words. This was in contrast to the typological work of Heymann Steinthal (1823–1899), which, as we saw in Section 3.5, revolved around the 'inner form' of languages, a concept that Steinthal developed from his reading of Wilhelm von Humboldt. Schleicher was prevented from penetrating below the visible surface of languages by his painstaking empirical philosophy of science: given the current state of knowledge, argued Schleicher (1859: 1), it is inevitably speculative to make pronouncements on inner form. He did, however, allow for the possibility that future advances may make inner form amenable to scientific investigation.

But just a few years later Schleicher's position hardened. In his 1865 *Unterscheidung von Nomen und Verbum in der lautlichen Form* (Differentiation of noun and verb in the phonetic form) – published in the same year as the sequel to his Darwinian pamphlet (Schleicher 1865a) – Schleicher drew the consequences of his materialist metaphysics for language research:

> The linguistic sound, the phonetic form of language, is the body, the phenomenon of the function, of the content of language. Neither appears separate from the other, they are always inseparably bound to one another. They are identical, even if of course not of the same kind. We have no right to assume functions where they are not indicated by sounds. Even in language the mind, the function, does not run independently of its body, the sound, but is always only really present in and through the latter. Our view of language is not dualistic, but rather monistic and we can consider only this [view] justified. (Schleicher 1865b: 502)

Schleicher concluded:

> We therefore maintain the conviction that nothing occurs in the speaker that is not expressed phonetically; that the sound is a fully valid and indeed the only witness of the function and that therefore a language only has those functions that it indicates phonetically. (Schleicher: 505–6)

That is, there is no inner life of language that is not immediately perceptible in its outer phonetic shell.

Steinthal could not accept Schleicher's banishment of inner form. The most direct and succinct formulations of Steinthal's opposition appear in his reviews of Schleicher's successive writings. The core issue in Steinthal's critique was that Schleicher reduced the study of language, in both the data he was prepared to countenance and the limits of his explanatory horizons, to the 'barest outer appearance [. . .] the empty shell of language', as Steinthal (1860b: 434) wrote in his review of Schleicher's 'Zur Morphologie der Sprache'. In his review of Schleicher's *Unterscheidung von Nomen und Verbum in der lautlichen Form*, Steinthal (1865: 506) insisted that the outer form of language does not stand for itself; there is indeed much that goes on in the minds of speakers which finds no phonetic expression. The linguist's task is to interpret the outer form in order to discover the inner form.

Steinthal illustrated his point with several German idioms, including 'Heute rot, morgen tot'. This phrase means literally 'Red today, dead tomorrow', and has the idiomatic sense that even though someone may be quite healthy today, they could suddenly fall ill and die tomorrow. Steinthal pointed out that the logical connection between the two parts of the idiom, 'red today' and 'dead tomorrow', is not spelt out in the outer linguistic form. There is no explicit conjunction between these two parts; we must infer the contrast that is implied. Here Steinthal (1865: 506) noted: 'So some things do indeed occur in the mind that are not expressed in the sound, but which the sound prompts the mind [to think of], since they are indeed included in that which the sound indicates.'

Furthermore, Steinthal objected to the deterministic scheme of language evolution assumed in Schleicher's morphology. As we saw in the previous section, Schleicher claimed that the typological classes of isolation, agglutination and inflection represent successive stages in the evolutionary development of languages. In opposition to Schleicher's universalist view of development, Steinthal (1860b) asserted a kind of historical particularism, in which every individual form has a unique identity that is the product of a complex developmental history, involving the interaction of numerous internal and external factors. On Steinthal's view, it is impossible to consider a single form in any language as an instance of some pre-existing type. This dispute between Steinthal and Schleicher is yet another example of the tension, which we first encountered in Section 2.2, between the desire to account for the development of all languages in terms of a single set of universal laws and the historicist belief that each language must be treated as an individual with its own unique story.

We must note that Steinthal's objections to Schleicher are concerned specifically with Schleicher's materialism and search for universal laws. Steinthal was not opposed to the analogy between languages and biological organisms, which had been a mainstay of nineteenth-century linguistics since at least Friedrich Schlegel's first proposals for comparative grammar. In fact, Steinthal even appealed to biological analogy himself in critiquing Schleicher: he cited the *Allgemeine Physiologie* (General physiology; 1851) of the German philosopher Hermann Lotze (1817–1881). Lotze argued that biological organisms do not simply develop according to a predetermined scheme, as Goethe's morphology and related theories postulated, but that their development is also shaped by external factors. In support of this position, Lotze cited Wilhelm von Humboldt's writings, thereby completing the feedback loop between linguistics and biology (see Lotze 1851: 324; McElvenny 2018b: 138).

Steinthal's penchant for biological analogy is on show also in his own typological system: we will recall from Section 3.5 that the top-level division in his 1860 *Charakteristik* was between *Formsprachen* (formal languages) and *formlose Sprachen* (formless languages). These labels clearly evoke the German terms for vertebrate and invertebrate animals: *Wirbeltiere* and *wirbellose Tiere*.

But many contemporary language scholars found both Steinthal's and Schleicher's ideas to be incurably speculative and metaphysical, and language typology more generally became an increasingly marginal topic in linguistics towards the end of the nineteenth century (see McElvenny 2023c). In the next chapter, we meet one of the most outspoken – even curmudgeonly – critics of Steinthal and Schleicher, the American linguist William Dwight Whitney (1827–1894).

4.5 Further reading

For a succinct overview of the consolidation of comparative-historical linguistics in the mid-nineteenth century and the associated theoretical debates, see chapters 7 and 8 of Anna Morpurgo Davies's (1998) *History of Linguistics, Volume IV: Nineteenth-Century Linguistics*.

A masterful exposition of the history of biology in the nineteenth century, with its connections to Romanticism, *Naturphilosophie* and the materialism controversy can be found in Robert Richards's books *The Romantic Conception of Life: Science and Philosophy in the Age of Goethe* (2002a) and *The Tragic Sense of Life: Ernst Haeckel and the Struggle over Evolutionary Thought* (2008), the former of which deals with the Romantic period of the early nineteenth century and the latter with Ernst Haeckel and evolutionary theory. Appendix 1 of *The Tragic Sense of Life* offers an excellent summary of theories of 'morphology' in biology from Goethe to Haeckel and beyond. Stephen G. Alter's (1999) *Darwinism and the Linguistic Image: Language, Race, and Natural Theology in the Nineteenth Century* reveals how ideas emanating from linguistics influenced Darwinian evolutionary theory and then fed back into language study.

For a detailed account of scientific materialism, see Frederick Gregory's (1977) *Scientific Materialism in Nineteenth-Century Germany* and chapter 2 of Frederick Beiser's (2014) *After Hegel*. For discussion of Schleicher's materialist position, see my article 'August Schleicher and materialism in 19th-century linguistics' in *Historiographia Linguistica* (McElvenny 2018b).

5 The pragmatic turn of the mid-nineteenth century

In the previous chapters, we met two major conceptions of language current in the mid-nineteenth century. The first of these – which we encountered in Section 3.5 – is that advanced principally by Heymann Steinthal (1823–1899). Building on his interpretation of Wilhelm von Humboldt (1767–1835) and his own theory of *Völkerpsychologie*, Steinthal saw language as a window onto the workings of the human mind. Under this view, the peculiarities of each individual language are treated as a key to the *Volksgeist*, or shared mentality, of its speakers. The second conception – which we examined in Section 4.2 – is the materialist or monist view of August Schleicher (1821–1868), which saw languages as something akin to biological organisms that grow and develop according to natural laws.

In this chapter, we meet the third major conception of this era, which understood languages first and foremost as a means of communication between people. We can describe this position as 'pragmatic' in character, since it was concerned with how language is used. The pragmatic conception was put forward most forcefully by the American Sanskritist and general linguist William Dwight Whitney (1827–1894), who presented it in opposition to the views of Steinthal, Schleicher and others.

Whitney was a vigorous polemicist. That is to say, he was not shy about criticising other scholars. But he was not merely a scold: amid his polemics, Whitney set out his alternative views on language, which would prove to be influential on the next generation of linguists. While his critiques may have caused much consternation at the time, they provide an excellent starting point for us today to explore what was at stake in nineteenth-century philosophical debates in linguistics.

5.1 William Dwight Whitney and his enemies

In a number of essays, lectures and books from the 1860s to the early 1870s, Whitney went into battle against what he called respectively the 'psychological' and 'physical' theories of language. Both theories, he argued, fundamentally misconceive the true nature of language. Whitney identified the 'psychological' theory primarily with Steinthal and Humboldt, whose ideas he more or less conflated. In his chief polemic against Steinthal, 'Steinthal and the psychological theory of language', Whitney commented:

> [Steinthal] has been, in particular, the disciple, interpreter, and continuer of Wilhelm von Humboldt, a man whom it is nowadays the fashion to praise highly, without understanding or even reading him; Steinthal is *the* man in Germany, perhaps the world, who penetrates the mysteries, unravels the inconsistencies, and expounds the dark sayings, of that ingenious and profound, but unclear and wholly unpractical thinker. (Whitney 1873 [1872]: 333; Whitney's italics)

Whitney accused Steinthal and Humboldt of being back to front in their approach to language. The starting point for the linguist, according to Whitney, should be solid facts established through observation; from this empirical foundation, the linguist can then proceed to ask philosophical questions. But Steinthal and Humboldt begin with philosophical speculation and then look for evidence to support their conjectures. Whitney accepted that we might one day be in a position to pose philosophical questions and answer them profitably, but first we need to get the facts straight.

Whitney's critique of Steinthal and Humboldt reflects a common ambivalence about philosophy among linguists of the time. We saw in Section 4.3, for example, that Schleicher's commitment to materialism drove him to confine his analyses to the directly visible surface forms of languages and declare the 'inner form' off limits. But Whitney found Schleicher's views to be equally suspect for their metaphysical excesses. Schleicher was for Whitney the principal representative of the 'physical' theory of language. In his main polemic against Schleicher, 'Schleicher and the physical theory of language', Whitney (1873 [1871]: 299) described Schleicher's views as 'wholly superficial, or even preposterous and absurd'. Elsewhere, in his 1867 *Language and the Study of Language*, a volume based on lectures he had originally given to a general audience at the Smithsonian Institution in Washington DC, Whitney criticised the assimilation of language to natural organisms as a metaphor run amok:

> [W]e see, I think, from our examination of the manner in which language is learned and taught, in which its life is kept up, what is meant when we speak and write of it as having an independent or objective existence, as being an organism or possessing an organic structure, as having laws of growth, as feeling tendencies, as developing, as adapting itself to our needs, and so on. All these are figurative expressions, the language of trope and metaphor, not of plain fact; they are wholly unobjectionable when consciously employed in their proper character, for the sake of brevity and liveliness of delineation; they are only harmful when we allow them to blind us to the real nature of the truths they represent. (Whitney 1867: 35)

Whitney's critique here is directed not only at Schleicher but also at Friedrich Max Müller (1823–1900). Max Müller, who was born and educated in Germany, became a professor at the University of Oxford in 1850, and from this prestigious perch quickly acquired the reputation of being the chief representative of the German science of comparative-historical grammar in the English-speaking world, a reputation he solidified through his popular *Lectures on the Science of Language* to the Royal Institution in London. The first series of these lectures was delivered and subsequently published in 1861, followed by a second series delivered in 1863, and published in 1864. Whitney and Müller were therefore rivals for the attention and admiration of the English-speaking public (on the rivalry between Whitney and Müller, see Alter 2005).

Max Müller opposed materialism, in the sense we met in Section 4.2, as a soulless metaphysical doctrine. He also opposed the suggestion – supported by Darwin, and elaborated most fully in Darwin's 1871 *Descent of Man* – that human language evolved gradually from animal cries. Invoking the Herderian idea that language is inseparable from a uniquely human capacity for conceptual thought (which we discussed in Section 3.2), Müller insisted that human language and animal communication are of fundamentally different kinds. In a highly memorable passage in his *Lectures on the Science of Language*, Müller wrote:

> [T]he one great barrier between the brute and man is *Language*. Man speaks, and no brute has ever uttered a word. Language is our Rubicon, and no brute will dare to cross it. This is our matter-of-fact answer to those who speak of development, who think they discover the rudiments of at least all human faculties in apes, and who would fain keep open the possibility that man is only a more favoured beast, the triumphant conqueror in the primeval struggle for life. Language is something more palpable than a fold of the brain or an angle of the skull. It admits of no cavilling, and no process of natural selection will ever distil significant words out of the notes of birds or the cries of beasts. (Müller 1861: 367; Müller's italics)

Nevertheless, Müller still considered linguistics to be a 'physical science', because it deals with the 'works of God' as opposed to the 'works of man' (Müller 1861: 22). That is to say, Müller saw language not as a human creation but as part of the natural world: languages are not mere tools fashioned by humans for the purposes of communication but natural entities that develop according to their own inherent laws. For this reason, Müller (1870) later endorsed Schleicher's importation of Darwinian evolution into linguistics. In a review of the English translation of Schleicher's (1863) pamphlet on Darwinian linguistics, Müller wrote:

> It is by supplying a new point of view for the consideration of these world-old problems [of necessity vs free will], that Darwin's book 'On the Origin of Species' has exercised an influence far beyond the sphere for which it was originally intended. The two technical terms of 'Natural Selection' and 'Struggle for Life,' which are in reality but two aspects of the same process, are the very categories which were wanted to enable us to grasp [. . .] the inevitable limitation of spontaneous action by the controlling influences of social life. (Müller 1870: 256)

What Müller is endorsing here is the use of Darwinian principles to explain language change. The historical changes in words, pronunciations and grammatical forms that interest the comparative grammarian, argued Müller, occur without the conscious intervention of speakers – and even against speakers' efforts to constrain those changes. The course of language change would seem to follow natural laws, just like those that apply in the biological realm.

Even though Müller had dispensed with the most outlandish metaphysical claims of Schleicher's materialism, Whitney could still not countenance Müller's efforts to assimilate language to the natural world. Language change, insisted Whitney, is not a 'natural' process but the product of human will and action. In the next section, we will see how Whitney imagined that speakers do indeed control and direct their language.

5.2 Language as an 'institution'

In opposition to the 'psychological' and 'physical' conceptions of language against which we saw him polemicise in the previous section, Whitney advocated an alternative view of language as an 'institution'. He wrote:

> Language is, in fact, an institution – the word may seem an awkward one, but we can find none better or more truly descriptive – the work of those whose wants it subserves; it is in their sole keeping and control; it has been by them adapted to their circumstances and wants, and is still everywhere undergoing at their hands such adaptation; every separate item of which it is composed is, in its present form – for we are not yet ready for a discussion of the ultimate origin of human speech – the product of a series of changes, effected by the will and consent of men, working themselves out under historical conditions, and conditions of man's nature, and by the impulse of motives, which are, in the main, distinctly traceable, and form a legitimate subject of scientific investigation. (Whitney 1867: 48)

What Whitney means by 'institution' is that language is a set of conventions for the purpose of communication which speakers have inherited and continually add to through successive interactions. On Whitney's account, change in language comes about through the accretion of new forms that users have created in an effort to make themselves understood.

But it would seem difficult to accept Whitney's contention that change in language is 'effected by the will and consent of men', that it is a voluntary process. On the contrary, as we observed in the previous section, language change seems to proceed following rules inherent to the language, which have nothing to do with the wishes of speakers. The story of comparative-historical linguistics up to this point has largely been about identifying and describing these speaker-independent rules. Schleicher's 'Darwinian' theory – and Müller's selective adaptation of it – takes such rules as its starting point and assumes that they represent the real, autonomous life of languages. Steinthal's psychological approach – although it treats each language much more as an individual (see Section 4.4) – locates the apparently speaker-independent forces shaping a language in the mental rather than the physical realm.

Whitney, by contrast, insisted that languages are indeed shaped by the individual actions of their users. This process is not immediately perceptible, however, because speakers do not necessarily perform these actions consciously, and the changes that result are gradual and therefore noticeable only in the long term. Whitney (1867: 45) pointed out that speakers innovate in their language all the time by creating new words or new senses of words. But individual speakers do not have the power or the right to determine whether these innovations will be taken up. Whether a new word or word sense ultimately becomes part of the language is a decision that is made – unconsciously – by the entire speech community. Some individuals, however, might have more influence on this process, because they hold a position of authority or their words may be considered particularly apposite or eloquent.

When a new form finds recognition in the community and is reproduced, it gradually comes to be considered a normal part of the language. In this case, we can say language change has taken place. Whitney believed that this principle applies not only to words, the most tangible components of language for us as speakers, but also to more subtle features of language, such as grammar and phonology. Some speakers may innovate new grammatical constructions or pronunciations, and these may then be adopted by the wider speech community.

Whitney's conception of language as an institution led him to apply new methods to study language change. He introduced what we might describe from a present-day perspective as a variationist approach to sound change, the central topic of comparative-historical linguistics. He was conscious of the fact that there is always diversity in the speech community, that speakers will produce slightly different forms and sounds, and these variant forms will, in a sense, be in competition with one another. On this model, sound change takes place when some sounds come to be used more frequently and others less so. In order to gather empirical data in support of this hypothesis, Whitney tabulated the frequencies of sounds in corpora of various Indo-European languages, from Sanskrit to historical varieties of Germanic, to Modern English. An example of this undertaking can be seen in Figure 5.1, reproduced from Whitney's essay 'The elements of English pronunciation'.

From his frequency tables, Whitney hypothesised various 'tendencies' in the historical development of sounds. He saw, for example, a tendency in the history of Indo-European languages to gradually reduce the openness of vowels (Whitney 1874: 205–7). Sanskrit and the older Indo-European languages, so claimed Whitney, have a much higher occurrence of the vowel [a], pronounced with the mouth fully open. According to Whitney's statistics, in Sanskrit this vowel occurs 70 per cent of the time in comparison with other vowel sounds, and 30 per cent in comparison with both vowels and consonants. In the oldest Germanic language this rate of occurrence falls to 14 per cent of all sounds, in German to 5 per cent, and in Whitney's dialect of American English to 0.5 per cent. In his own speech, commented Whitney, [a] is the rarest of all vowel sounds.

This observed tendency to reduce vowel openness, argued Whitney, is a manifestation of a more general 'tendency to economy', which he saw as driving all historical change in language. Speakers always want to expend the least amount of effort in expressing themselves, and this leads to the gradual reduction of linguistic forms. In the case of Indo-European vowel sounds, articulating closed vowels in preference to open vowels represents a reduction in effort because the speaker does not have to open their mouth as wide. But this reduction of forms also leads to the renewal of grammar. As collocations – that is, frequent sequences of words – and compound words are reduced, they are compacted into new affixes and inflections (see Whitney 1875: 53). Here Whitney is essentially

SCALE AND RATE OF FREQUENCY OF ENGLISH SOUNDS.

Consonant.	Vowel.	Per Cent.	Per Cent.	Minimum.		Maximum.	
r	..	7.44	..	VI.	5.4	VIII.	9.3
n	..	6.76	..	III.	5.7	IX.	7.9
t	..	5.93	..	VI.	4.6	II.	8.9
..	ĭ	..	5.90	VI.	4.7	VII.	7.4
..	ə	..	5.66	II.	4.3	I., VII.	6.9
d	..	4.94	..	I.	4.0	V.	5.8
s	..	4.69	..	III., VIII.	3.7	I., II.	5.8
l	..	3.84	..	I., VII.	2.5	III.	6.2
dh	..	3.83	..	VIII.	2.4	III.	5.1
..	ĕ	..	3.34	I.–III.	2.6	IX.	4.7
..	œ	..	3.32	III.	2.4	VIII.	4.0
m	..	3.06	..	VIII.	1.8	I.	4.1
z	..	2.92	..	VI.	2.2	I.	4.3
..	ī	..	2.80	VII., IX.	1.5	VI.	4.8
..	ă	..	2.59	IV., IX.	1.8	VII.	4.2
v	..	2.37	..	I.	1.4	VII.	3.5
h	..	2.34	..	IX.	1.2	V.	3.1
w	..	2.31	..	III.	1.6	VIII.	3.0
k	..	2.17	..	II.	1.1	X.	3.1
f	..	2.06	..	IV., VII.	1.2	II.	2.8
..	ŭ	..	2.00	VI.	1.1	I.	3.5
..	ai	..	1.91	IX.	.9	VI.	4.8
..	ä	..	1.85	I.	.9	VIII.	2.5
..	ŏ	..	1.76	X.	.9	III.	2.6
p	..	1.71	..	V.	1.0	VII.	2.6
b	..	1.64	..	IX.	1.0	I.	3.4
..	ē	..	1.61	I.	.5	X.	2.7
..	A	..	1.54	X.	.8	II.	2.2
sh	..	.86	..	II.	.1	IV.	1.8
..	au	..	.83	X.	.3	III., IV.	1.3
g	..	.79	..	VII., IX.	.3	VIII.	1.6
ng	..	.79	..	I.	.1	III., VIII.	1.4
y	..	.66	..	IX.	.3	IV.	1.1
th	..	.58	..	VIII.	.2	IV.	1.0
..	a	..	.56	VIII., X.	.1	IX.	1.2
ch	..	.53	..	I., II.	.1	VIII.	1.2
..	æ	..	.47	VII.	.0	III.	1.4
j	..	.47	..	VI.	.1	IX.	.9
..	ū	..	.44	IX., X.	.2	VIII.	1.2
..	ḷ	..	.35	VII.	.1	I.	.7
..	ṇ	..	.16	I., III., X.	.0	II., VII., IX.	.3
..	ȧi	..	.12	I., II., VIII.	.0	III.–VI., IX.	.2
..	ō	..	.08	II., IV., VI., VII.	.0	I., III.	.2
zh	..	.02	..	I.–VIII.	.0	IX., X.	.1
		62.71	37.29				

Figure 5.1 Whitney's (1874: 274) table of the frequency of English sounds

describing the process treated by 'agglutination theory', which we discussed in Section 4.3, and offering a general explanation for why it takes place (on this point, see also McElvenny 2016a, 2020).

The mechanisms of language change to which Whitney appealed – variation within the speech community accompanied by selection of variants for further propagation – sound very much like the principles of Darwinian evolution, and in fact would seem to be more in tune with Darwin's work than Schleicher's self-professed 'Darwinian' linguistics. Whitney was not opposed to Darwinism in principle. He even cautiously cultivated an alliance with Darwin against Max Müller's attacks on the *Descent of Man* (see Alter 2005: 181–92). Whitney's objection to the biological analogy was merely that it ignored the role of human agency in language change. For Whitney, change in language is not a blind process that takes place according to inevitable natural laws but something that results from the exigencies of human communicative interaction.

Whitney had shown a way in which both sound change and the development of grammatical forms can be accounted for as the product of gradually accreted modifications arising from language use, without the need to appeal to psychological or physical laws. He also pioneered a method for capturing this process using statistics. As we see in Section 6.3, Whitney's new pragmatic conception would be quite influential in linguistic scholarship of the latter half of the nineteenth century. His statistical methods, however, did not enjoy immediate uptake in the field; it would not be until the twentieth century that statistics found widespread application in linguistics (see Section 7.1; McElvenny 2023c).

5.3 Common Sense philosophy

Whitney's conception of language as an 'institution' would seem to be rather out of step with the mainstream linguistics of his time. In accounting for his very different perspective on language, Whitney's biographer Stephen G. Alter (2005) argues that his views are essentially the result of the lasting influence of Enlightenment-era empiricism.

Whitney was an American from New England. As the name suggests, this region in the north-east of the United States is the centre of English-speaking colonial civilisation in the New World. As Alter (2005: 71–6) points out, the default philosophical position that permeated school and university education in New England during Whitney's youth was a form of the empiricism that had dominated English-speaking philosophy in the Enlightenment. Specifically, Alter identifies this position as a variety of Scottish 'Common Sense' realism. Leading Common Sense philosophers include such figures as Thomas Reid (1710–1796) and Dugald Stewart (1753–1828), although the treatment of language within this school is due mostly to the less well-known figures Hugh Blair (1718–1800) and George Campbell (1719–1796).

As we saw in Section 3.2, the English philosopher John Locke (1632–1704) asserted the arbitrary nature of language. He believed that there is no necessary connection between words and their meanings; rather, speakers of a language simply associate words with certain meanings depending on their individual experiences.

But the typical German view that arose in response to empiricist claims of this kind was to insist that there is at base some sort of necessary connection between words and their meanings. In the nineteenth century, this view became part of the general philosophical background to academic linguistics in Germany.

The Scottish Common Sense philosophers upheld the empiricist claim that language is essentially arbitrary, but added the further qualification that language is also conventional. On this view, even though there is no necessary connection between words and their meanings, we still agree as members of a speech community to associate the same words with the same meanings. By inserting the pressure of convention, the Common Sense philosophers were able to rescue arbitrary language from the danger Locke envisaged, that every speaker might attach different meanings to their words. Whitney's conception of language as an 'institution' encapsulates this Common Sense view of language as arbitrary and conventional.

Although Common Sense philosophy – and indeed other forms of empiricism more generally – formed the background to Whitney's education, it was often seen as rather unsophisticated in Germany, and even went out of fashion in the English-speaking countries during the course of the nineteenth century. In 1875, Steinthal responded to the critiques Whitney levelled against his 'psychological' theory of language – which we saw in Section 5.1 – and used this occasion to criticise Whitney's underlying philosophy. Steinthal (1875) was not impressed by Whitney's theorising: he charged that Whitney was merely a naïve and simple-minded American who did not understand the epistemological and metaphysical depths of German philosophy.

Steinthal's impugning of Whitney's philosophical sophistication may not have been entirely fair. Like many highly educated Americans of his day, Whitney had in fact studied in Germany where, among other things, he attended courses given by Bopp and Steinthal in Berlin. Whitney had most certainly made an effort to enter the exalted intellectual world of mid-century German linguistics, with all its philosophical flourishes, although the sobering influence of empiricism was clearly stronger. But the controversy between Whitney and Steinthal was not simply a matter of philosophical differences. There was a very real element of personal antipathy in their exchange. Steinthal closed his response to Whitney with a further *ad hominem* attack:

> Whitney has nothing at all to do with Common Sense, Induction, natural science or history; these are only shields held up to cover his haughty vanity [. . . W]e are dealing here with a snobbish and pretentious individual of unrestrained pride. (Steinthal 1875: 234; translation quoted from Nerlich 1990: 36)

5.4 Uniformitarianism

While the philosophical basis of Whitney's understanding of language as arbitrary and conventional can be traced back to older currents in Enlightenment-era empiricism, the mechanisms he invoked to explain the processes of language change owed much to recent innovations in the natural sciences.

As we saw in Section 4.3, Schleicher imagined distinct stages in the life of languages: a prehistoric period in which languages supposedly come into being and grow, and the historical period in which they decline. Schleicher was not alone in this contention: in the work of Wilhelm von Humboldt, for one, we find similar suggestions. Whitney, however, banished this kind of speculation in favour of constant principles. From Section 5.2, we will recall Whitney (1867: 48) insisted that 'we are not yet ready for a discussion of the ultimate origin of human speech', but that the conditions shaping language in its 'present form' are 'distinctly traceable'.

Whitney's approach here represents an adaptation of the doctrine of uniformitarianism, which had its origins in geology (see Christy 1983). Whitney was well versed in the theory and practice of geology through his educational and family background: his schooling included many courses in the natural sciences, and his elder brother Josiah Dwight Whitney (1819–1896) was a geologist who worked for various government-backed geological surveys across the United States, and later became Professor of Geology at Harvard University. Whitney accompanied his brother on some of his survey expeditions and participated in the collection of scientific data.

Uniformitarianism had long been in the air, but became definitively established when the Scottish geologist Charles Lyell (1797–1875) published his *Principles of Geology* in three volumes from 1830 to 1833. Uniformitarian theory holds that changes we see in the earth's features are best explained by appealing to constant forces that have been acting in the same way since the beginning of time. These forces act gradually, so much so that the changes which are continually taking place in the earth's crust are imperceptible to us on a day-to-day basis. Over the course of millions of years, however, they create the mountains and valleys, seas and deserts that we know in the world.

Uniformitarianism was put forward in opposition to catastrophism, the idea that individual high-impact events – catastrophes – bring about sudden changes in the form of the earth; for example, volcanic eruptions that might bring islands into existence, or earthquakes and tsunamis that reshape terrain. As a scientific principle, uniformitarianism has the great advantages of being grounded in empirical observation and induction, and of being explanatorily parsimonious. We can extrapolate from the phenomena we observe in the world today to explain the past; we do not need to invent otherwise unknown and unproven forces to account for the changes attested in the historical record.

Catastrophism fits well with the traditional biblical narrative of the history of the earth, which is laced with dramatic events – like Noah's flood – in which the world is changed from one day to the next. This mode of telling the story of the earth also accords well with biblical chronology, because it allows us to assume that changes could have happened very rapidly at some points, more rapidly than they happen now. This means that the world could have reached its current state in only 6,000 years, as is sometimes claimed on the basis of biblical sources.

But catastrophism does not simply represent subservience to biblical scholarship. Even as European scientists weaned themselves off traditional interpretations of Christian scripture, many of the assumptions underlying older accounts were recast in a modern mould. One prominent supporter of catastrophism who was also a renowned modern scientist is Georges Cuvier (1769–1832), who – as we discussed in Section 2.2 – was a leading representative of comparative anatomy and an inspiration to the first comparative-historical grammarians. Catastrophism still has a place in geological theory today: a widely accepted account of the great extinction at the end of the Cretaceous period, which killed off the dinosaurs, holds that the extinction was triggered by a massive asteroid impact. This is of course a catastrophic event by any measure.

Whitney's adaptation of uniformitarianism to linguistics is visible in the way he imagined language change as proceeding from the gradual accumulation of linguistic material that in turn issues from individual communicative acts governed by constant laws of human interaction. Whitney could not accept the existence of a distinct prehistoric period, with its own unique principles, in which language came into being; rather, there was for Whitney a sense in which language is constantly being invented, because when we use language we are always negotiating our communication with one another using the linguistic means available to us.

Charles Lyell had in fact already made a similar adaptation of uniformitarian ideas to the study of language, which would seem to have inspired Whitney's approach (see Nerlich 1990: 43–5). Chapter 23 of Lyell's 1863 book *The Geological Evidences of the Antiquity of Man* discusses the 'Origin and Development of languages and species compared'. Here Lyell wrote:

> Although speakers may be unconscious that any great fluctuation is going on in their language,—although when we observe the manner in which new words and phrases are thrown out, as if at random or in sport, while others get into vogue, we may think the process of change to be the result of mere chance,—there are nevertheless fixed laws in action, by which, in the general struggle for existence, some terms and dialects gain the victory over others. The slightest advantage attached to some new mode of pronouncing or spelling, from considerations of brevity or euphony, may turn the scale, or more powerful causes of selection may decide which of two or more rivals shall triumph and which succumb. Among these are fashion, or the influence of aristocracy, whether of birth or education, popular writers, orators, preachers,—a centralised government organising its schools expressly to promote uniformity of diction, and to get the better of provincialisms and local dialects. (Lyell 1863: 463–4)

In this passage we see not only uniformitarianism being applied to language – 'fixed laws in action' – but also Darwinian principles: 'struggle for existence', 'causes of selection'. Lyell's invocation of Darwinism is much more in line with Whitney's account of language change than those of Schleicher or Max Müller (which we saw Whitney criticise in Section 5.1). The 'causes of selection' named by Lyell are predominantly social in character – fashion, the influence of various agents in society, and government policy – and not the mysterious 'laws of nature' called upon by Schleicher and Müller. Whitney (1867: 47) described Lyell's position as 'a lucid and able analogical argument bearing on the Darwinian theory of the mutation of species', while Schleicher's approach overlooks 'the fact that the relation between the two classes of phenomena [language and biological species] is one of analogy only, not of essential agreement'.

Among linguists, Whitney was not alone in his adherence to uniformitarianism. In fact, both Max Müller and Steinthal espoused uniformitarian principles in some aspects of their work: even though they allowed themselves to speculate about the ultimate origins language, both Müller and Steinthal still insisted that we must concentrate on constant factors when trying to account for language change in the historical period (see Christy 1983; Nerlich 1990). But, as we see in the next chapter, the dogmatic empiricism and rejection of any form of speculation that characterised Whitney's writings reflected a growing sentiment in the field, even in Germany.

5.5 Further reading

Stephen G. Alter's (2005) intellectual biography of Whitney, *William Dwight Whitney and the Science of Language*, covers many of the topics dealt with in this chapter, including Whitney's contributions to nineteenth-century linguistic theory, the background to his thought, and the various controversies in which he became embroiled. John Joseph's (2002) *From Whitney to Chomsky: Essays on the History of American Linguistics* is another excellent guide to Whitney's work and ideas in historical context. See in particular chapter 2. Whitney's own writings – such as his 1867 *Language and the Study of Language: Twelve Lectures on the Principles of Linguistic Science*, and his 1875 *The Life and Growth of Language* – remain highly accessible to the present-day reader. The same is true of Friedrich Max Müller's *Lectures on the Science of Language* (1861, 1864).

For an overview of the many manifestations of uniformitarianism in nineteenth-century linguistics, see Craig Christy's (1983) *Uniformitarianism in Linguistics*. For discussion of the pragmatic turn in the linguistics of the mid-nineteenth century, with a focus on the work of Whitney, but also Michel Bréal (1832–1915) and Philipp Wegener (1848–1916), who we will meet properly in Chapters 8 and 11, see Brigitte Nerlich's (1990) *Change in Language: Whitney, Bréal, and Wegener*.

6 Neogrammarian doctrine

By the last decades of the nineteenth century, comparative-historical linguistics had become a firmly established field. All major universities in Germany had at least one professor specialising in Indo-European, and the comparative method was a core part of the curriculum across language departments, for languages both within and outside the Indo-European family. In other countries – in Europe, America and the Europeanised colonial world – scholars followed the latest advances coming out of Germany and contributed new impulses to the field (see Morpurgo Davies 1998: 226–9).

In this chapter, we look at the dominant school in this period, the Neogrammarians, who had their centre of gravity at the University of Leipzig. The Neogrammarians brought the technical side of comparative-historical linguistics to a new level of sophistication and at the same time put forward a precise and yet austere philosophy of science underlying their endeavour. The Neogrammarians are also interesting from a sociological point of view, since it is probably fair to say that they were the first group of linguists who consciously conceived of themselves as forming a movement. Up until now we have mostly examined the work of individual scholars. The most prominent of these passed on their views and methods to their students and in this way founded schools, but the Neogrammarians were the first collective of peers who were bound together by an explicitly articulated set of doctrines.

6.1 Young Turks

Who exactly counts as a Neogrammarian and who does not are questions that do not have any definite answers. There were several ringleaders who we can uncontroversially identify as Neogrammarians, but there was also a much broader periphery of those who were more or less involved – or who sympathised – with the movement. The term 'ringleader' to describe the movement's core members is chosen consciously here for its connotations of rebelliousness. The Neogrammarians had a reputation for being a group of punk scholars who were disrespectful of their elders and who sought to instigate a revolution in linguistics.

The Neogrammarians' attitude is often portrayed as a manifestation of generational conflict. As the historian of linguistics Olga Amsterdamska (1987: chap. 5) pointed out, the 1870s was a period of generational change in academic linguistics: the old guard from the period of consolidation in the mid-nineteenth century – which we discussed in Chapter 4 – was gradually dying out and the next generation of scholars was rising up to take their place. The Neogrammarians' perceived disrespect for their elders was perhaps the result of their desire to assert their claims as the new stewards of the discipline.

The English term 'Neogrammarian' is a not entirely satisfactory rendering of the name that was used for them in Germany, the *Junggrammatiker*, literally the 'Young Grammarians'. This designation was originally applied from outside the group by the philologist Friedrich Zarncke (1825–1891) and was intended to be an ironic play on the name of various intellectual and political movements of the time (see Morpurgo Davies 1998: 229). The 'Young Hegelians' (*Junghegelianer*) of the mid-nineteenth century, for example, were a group of radical students of the German idealist philosopher G. W. F. Hegel (1770–1831), who further developed their master's ideas but turned them against the conservative political positions that he had supported. Outside Germany and towards the end of the nineteenth century there emerged in the Ottoman Empire a group of young radicals who were given the moniker of the 'Young Turks' for their uncompromising efforts to push through their modernising reforms. 'Young Turk' remains today, in a number of languages, a generic term to describe young, zealous revolutionaries.

An anecdote at the foundation of the Neogrammarian movement may help to illustrate why they had this reputation. The core clique of the Neogrammarians were students and young scholars in the orbit of Georg Curtius (1820–1885), a professor of classics at the University of Leipzig. One day in 1876, Curtius went away travelling and left his pupil Karl Brugman (1849–1919; Brugman's name is also often spelt 'Brugmann') in charge of his journal *Studien zur griechischen und lateinischen Grammatik* (Studies on Greek and Latin grammar). In the nineteenth century, it was common for scientific journals to be personally identified with their editors, such was the importance of the editor in defining the direction and character of a journal. This journal was often referred to simply as the 'Curtius-Studien' (Curtius studies). While the master, Curtius, was away, Brugman published in the journal two articles (Brugman 1876a, 1876b) that proposed radically different reconstructions in Indo-European from those accepted by Curtius and the older generation. In addition, Brugman repeatedly criticised the methodology of his seniors. When Curtius returned from his travels, he was absolutely horrified. He wrote a small afterword (Curtius 1876) to the journal in which he discounted responsibility for its contents, and with the next issue cancelled the further publication of the journal altogether.

Brugman's rather aggressive performance in Curtius's journal is generally considered one of the first clear expressions of the Neogrammarian movement, and is representative of its pugnacious character and the irritation it caused to the generation of the elders. In 1878, Brugman teamed up with his colleague Hermann Osthoff (1847–1909) to launch a new journal, the *Morphologische Untersuchungen* (Morphological investigations). From the beginning, this journal was intended as an organ for the emerging movement. The first issue contains a preface penned by Osthoff and Brugman in which they set out a manifesto for this new direction in language study, and in which they claimed the designation *Junggrammatiker* for themselves, which up until that point had only been used facetiously by those outside the movement.

The central theoretical claim of Osthoff and Brugman's manifesto is that previous research in comparative-historical linguistics lacked a proper scientific foundation. They accused their predecessors of having only looked at languages, without trying to establish underlying principles. In contrast to this, the Neogrammarians wanted to base their investigations on a solid foundation that accounts for how human language actually functions in the minds and mouths of speakers. This is how Osthoff and Brugman described their position in the manifesto:

> The older language research, no one can deny, approached its object of study, the Indo-European languages, without having a clear idea of how human language lives and develops, what factors are active in speaking and how working together these factors cause the progress and re-forming of the material of language. Languages were eagerly studied, but the speaking human was studied too little. (Osthoff and Brugman 1878: 3; English translation in Lehmann 1967: 197)

Osthoff and Brugman went on to say that linguists need to turn away from their fixation on analysing the lifeless words of ancient languages that exist only on the page. Instead, linguists should look to modern languages to gain a clearer idea of the processes active in language change. In particular, linguists should examine the minority forms we find in non-standard dialects, since these show all the subtle shades of variation possible in language. Contemporary dialects give us direct access to the real living language: we do not have to puzzle out obscure inscriptions in dead tongues, how they may have been pronounced and precisely what they may have meant.

But among the theoretical claims put forward in Osthoff and Brugman's manifesto, the signature idea for which the Neogrammarians became known was their insistence on the exceptionless nature of sound laws, which we explore in the next section.

6.2 Sound laws and analogy

The entire edifice of Neogrammarian scholarship is often reduced to a single slogan: that sound laws admit no exception. The classic formulation of this position is found in Osthoff and Brugman's (1878) manifesto, where they wrote:

> [E]very sound change, inasmuch as it occurs mechanically, takes place according to laws that admit no exception. That is, the direction of the sound shift is always the same for all the members of a linguistic community except where a split into dialects occurs; and all words in which the sound subjected to the change appears in the same relationship are affected by the change without exception. (Osthoff and Brugman 1878: 13; English translation in Lehmann 1967: 204)

The central claim here is that normal sound change should be absolutely regular; that is, a sound found in the same phonetic environment across words should always change in the same way, and this change should be the same for all speakers. The only case in which this principle would not apply is when there is a dialect split, with the result that separate dialects emerge, each with its own independent sound laws governing its further historical development.

But why was this claim considered so revolutionary? In order to answer this question, we have to first appreciate some of the difficulties with which linguistics was faced in this period. The story of comparative-historical linguistics from Bopp to Grimm to Schleicher – which we have traced in the previous chapters – is one of increasing precision in working out the historical changes that have occurred in languages and in formulating the 'laws' governing those changes. But, as we have observed on several occasions throughout this book, there was always an annoying remainder of forms that just seemed to be completely irregular and could not be made subject to the sound laws.

In the 1870s, however, comparative grammarians made a series of technical breakthroughs that solved many long-standing problems and reinforced the regularity of sound change (see Morpurgo Davies 1998: 239–45). One classic example, which served as a source of inspiration to the Neogrammarian movement, was the solution to a persistent exception to Grimm's Law that was first published in 1877 (although already discovered in 1875) by the Danish linguist Karl Verner (1846–1896). Grimm's Law, as we saw in Section 2.4, was an account of a series of regular sound changes that distinguished the Germanic languages as a group from the rest of the Indo-European family.

The problem with Grimm's Law, as it was originally formulated, was that there are several common words across the Germanic languages that simply do not obey it. The most glaring examples are perhaps the words for 'mother' and 'father'. If Grimm's Law worked perfectly, we would expect to be able to reconstruct in Proto-Germanic the forms *môþar and *faþar, with a fricative as the middle consonant, but the evidence in the earliest attested Germanic languages points instead to different reconstructions: *môdar and *fadar, with stops in this middle position. It was a puzzle for linguists as to why Grimm's Law had failed in these cases. Other words with the same phonetic structure – and even belonging to the same semantic domain – did behave as expected. We can, for example, reconstruct the form *brôþar with a middle fricative as the Proto-Germanic word for 'brother'.

Karl Verner's breakthrough was to look in greater detail at these problematic words and find a subtle difference in their phonetic structure which conditioned the divergent sound changes. Proto-Indo-European had a free and movable accent; that is, in polysyllabic words the stress could fall in different places. This movable accent was preserved in Sanskrit but had already been lost in Proto-Germanic, which had a fixed accent on the first syllable. Verner noticed that in the Sanskrit words *mātár-* 'mother' and *pitár-* 'father' the stress was on the second syllable, but in the word *bhrā́tar-* 'brother' on the first syllable. With this additional phonetic information to hand, Verner was able to add a further clause to Grimm's Law stipulating that in Proto-Germanic stops became voiced when they were not word initial and the following syllable had been stressed: this is what happened to the words for 'mother' and 'father' (Verner 1877: 117). But when the stressed syllable had preceded the middle consonants, Grimm's Law applied as expected – as occurred in the word for 'brother' – creating the fricatives predicted in Proto-Germanic. All that was required in order to save Grimm's Law was to refine it. Once the law was elaborated to include greater phonetic detail, the apparent exceptions disappeared.

Verner's achievement, which was soon highlighted by the leaders of the Neogrammarian movement, was to stick to his science. Verner showed that there were in principle no exceptions – and no limits to the comparative-historical method – if the linguist simply does not give up and works away uncompromisingly on the data. But even the Neogrammarians could not make all the exceptions disappear – or even account for all of the changes in form and meaning that occur in the history of languages – using sound laws alone. This is the reason for Osthoff and Brugman's disclaimer 'every sound change, *inasmuch as it occurs mechanically*, takes place according to laws that admit no exception'. To deal with other kinds of language change and push back against the pesky exceptions, they introduced a second basic principle to their theory, the principle of 'analogy' (Osthoff and Brugman 1878: 13; English translation in Lehmann 1967: 204).

Analogy was an existing concept with a range of senses, but for the Neogrammarians it meant the creation of new linguistic forms by generalising from one form to another. An example of analogy in this sense is the plural form of the word 'cow' in present-day English. The plural is of course 'cows', which is formed by adding an -*s* to the root of the word. This is the pattern used by the vast majority of nouns in Modern English, but up until the seventeenth century, the more common plural for 'cow' was 'kine'. At this time, the word 'cow' belonged to the same inflectional paradigm as such words as 'brother', with the plural 'brethren', and 'child', plural 'children'. But through the process of analogy, 'cow' was attracted to the larger class of nouns with a plural formed with -*s* and the plural became 'cows'.

Citing the inspiration they had received from the analyses of their colleague August Leskien (1840–1916) in his 1876 book *Die Declination im Slavisch-Lithauischen und Germanischen* (The declension in Slavic-Lithuanian and Germanic), Osthoff and Brugman (1878: 12–14) set up an opposition between analogy and sound laws as counteracting processes. In Neogrammarian doctrine, analogy not only became a cover term for any kind of change that fell outside the purview of the sound laws, but was also deployed to dispense with any apparent exceptions to them. If sound change had not occurred as expected, a common explanation among the Neogrammarians was to say that an analogical change had got in the way and interfered with the normal operation of the sound laws. As we see in Section 7.1, the Neogrammarians were widely criticised for being too lax in their application of analogy. It was said that for the Neogrammarians analogy was a *deus ex machina*, brought out whenever the sound laws broke down.

A further interesting aspect of analogy as treated by Osthoff and Brugman is that it illustrates the Neogrammarian adherence to uniformitarianism, in the sense we explored in Section 5.4. In introducing analogy in their manifesto, Osthoff and Brugman (1878: 13) observed that it 'plays a very important role in the life of the more recent languages' and should therefore 'be recognised without hesitation for older periods too, and even for the oldest'. That is, since analogy is known to be a force of language change today, it should be assumed to have always been active in shaping languages, even in the deep past.

For Osthoff and Brugman, sound laws and analogy were not only counteracting processes, but also manifestations of the two sides of language in the speaker, the physical and the mental. Although they hedged in putting forward their position, Osthoff and Brugman claimed that sound laws are motivated above all by the physical – or physiological – facts of articulation and hearing: sound laws were thought to be the product of the natural action of the mouth, larynx, ears, and so on. Analogy, on the other hand, was understood to be a mental process, the 'association of forms' (Osthoff and Brugman 1878: 13) in the mind. We explore this aspect of Neogrammarian theory further in the next section.

6.3 Hermann Paul's science of principles

While Osthoff and Brugman provided the Neogrammarians with their manifesto, the definitive statement of Neogrammarian theory came from their colleague Hermann Paul (1846–1921). Paul's book *Principien der Sprachgeschichte* (Principles of language history) was widely cited as the clearest and most influential outline of Neogrammarian theory, to the point that it was often referred to as the 'Neogrammarian Bible'. The book first appeared in 1880 and went through five editions up until 1920, one year before Paul's death (later editions bore the title *Prinzipien der Sprachgeschichte*, with a 'z', following an orthography reform in Germany). This timespan covers the heyday of the Neogrammarian movement.

The central contribution of Paul's work was to sketch what he called a 'science of principles' (*Prinzipienwissenschaft*) that deals with the functioning of human language (see Morpurgo Davies 1998: 244–51). In line with the existing Neogrammarian consensus, Paul argued that language is a complex phenomenon: it is the product of individual people interacting with one other in order to exchange their ideas in the medium of speech. To capture this multifaceted phenomenon, we need to draw on the results of several different sciences. On the one hand, we need psychology in order to be able to understand the processes active in people's minds as they formulate their speech and comprehend the speech of others, and on the other, we need physiology and physics to be able to understand how people articulate and perceive speech. The 'science of principles' that Paul proposed was intended to be an umbrella science stating the higher order principles in action when the elements of these other sciences come together.

In the previous section, we saw that Osthoff and Brugman also acknowledged the importance of psychology to studying language, in particular in the 'association of forms' that underlies the process of analogical change. Somewhat surprisingly, Osthoff and Brugman (1878: 4) cited Steinthal as paving the way for the psychological investigation of language. This is surprising because, as we will recall from Section 3.4, Steinthal was co-founder of the field of *Völkerpsychologie*, which sought to study the collective mentality of entire peoples. Such a notion would seem to be incompatible with the pragmatic view the Neogrammarians advocated, which located language in the interactions between individual persons. But Osthoff and Brugman praised Steinthal because they felt he was the first linguist to properly consider psychology: earlier linguists, so they claimed, had looked only to physiological causes in explaining sound change. However, Osthoff and Brugman's praise extended only to Steinthal's account of psychological processes in individuals; they disregarded his discussion of the supposed shared psychology of whole peoples.

The separation of individual psychology from the psychology of peoples was even more explicit in Paul's (1880) *Principien*, which opened with a long refutation of *Völkerpsychologie* and its supposition that there could be a shared mind of the people (ibid.: 9–23). Paul was quite clear about recognising psychological processes only in the minds of individual speakers of a language and rejecting any shared mentality (see Klautke 2013: 30–2):

> All psychological processes take place in individual minds and nowhere else. Neither the mind of the people [*Volksgeist*] nor elements of the mind of the people – such as art, religion, etc. – have a concrete existence and therefore there can be nothing that happens in them or between them. For this reason: Away with these abstractions! For 'Away with these abstractions' must be our slogan if we want to try to find somewhere the factors of real occurrences. (Paul 1880: 13)

In like measure, Paul (1880: 13) rejected the materialist or monist position of Schleicher, without naming him, when he dismissed those 'researchers of culture' who 'talk in Darwinian similes'. All study of culture, under which he subsumed language, must be a study of society, Paul (ibid.: 8) insisted. The goal must be to ascertain how physical and mental factors operating in and between individual members of a community come together to produce the results we see. Even the notion of a language is an illusion. There is no language that exists independently of its speakers; rather, there is just a language norm (*Sprachusus*), which individual speakers more or less conform to when they produce their utterances. In later editions of the *Principien*, Paul summarised the task of language science as being to examine how the individual usage of speakers relates to the norm and how feedback mechanisms determine changes in the norm:

> [T]he whole body of principles [*Prinzipienlehre*] of language history concentrates on the question: What is the relation between the language norm [*Sprachusus*] and individual speech [*individuelle Sprechtätigkeit*]? How is individual speech determined by the norm, and how does individual speech have an effect back on the norm? (Paul 1920 [1880]: 33)

The Neogrammarian scepticism towards *Völkerpsychologie* and visions of superordinate mental entities continued as *Völkerpsychologie* was developed in new directions by Wilhelm Wundt (1832–1920). As we observed in Section 3.4, Wundt adopted the term *Völkerpsychologie* from Lazarus and Steinthal and reconfigured it to suit his own theoretical purposes. From 1900 to 1920, he published a comprehensive, ten-volume exposition of *Völkerpsychologie* as he understood it. The first of these volumes dealt with language, which maintained its central importance for Wundt. As a founding figure of modern experimental psychology, Wundt had similar realist sympathies to the Neogrammarians and, as a result, was wary of the metaphysical implications of positing a 'national mind'. Nevertheless, he contended that it is possible to scientifically investigate a *Volksseele* (national soul), a shared mentality of the people manifested in its language and other cultural products (see Wundt 1900: 7–18).

Paul felt that Wundt was stricken by more or less the same metaphysical confusion as Lazarus and Steinthal before him and, in the 1909 fourth edition of his *Prinzipien*, extended his critique to Wundt's version of *Völkerpsychologie*. Other Neogrammarians and their supporters, such as Berthold Delbrück (1842–1922; 1901) and Ludwig Sütterlin (1863–1934; 1902), essentially joined Paul in this critique of Wundt's *Völkerpsychologie*, even if they were less direct. Like Osthoff and Brugman's treatment of Steinthal in their manifesto some twenty-five years earlier, Delbrück and Sütterlin preferred to simply ignore Wundt's claims about the national soul and discussed only his individual psychology (see Klautke 2013: 70–1).

The Neogrammarians' pragmatic approach to language might remind us of the views of William Dwight Whitney (1827–1894), which we saw in the previous chapter. The Neogrammarians and Whitney did indeed have a very close relationship: Whitney was a personal friend of many of the Neogrammarians and visited them on his trips to Germany in the 1870s. August Leskien directly contributed to the spreading of Whitney's ideas in Germany through his 1876 German translation of Whitney's *Life and Growth of Language*. Although Osthoff and Brugman did not mention Whitney by name in their manifesto, Brugman did later write a contribution to an 1894 conference dedicated to the memory of Whitney, who had died earlier that year. Here Brugman (1897 [1894]: 75) highlighted Whitney's pioneering achievements in studying the 'foundational questions of the life of language', as he put it, and the influence Whitney's thinking had on the development of the Neogrammarian movement. In contrasting the inspiration that they derived from Steinthal and Whitney, Berthold Delbrück came to the conclusion:

> If Steinthal was a difficult to understand philosopher, who was most at home at the height of abstraction, then his contemporary William Dwight Whitney was the true embodiment of a calm and clear understanding directed towards the tangible. (Delbrück 1919 [1880]: 111)

In Neogrammarian doctrine there is a visible shift in the temperament of German language science. As we saw in Section 5.3, Steinthal (1875) sought to deflect Whitney's critiques by accusing Whitney of not understanding the depths of German philosophy. But only a few years later, Paul (1880: 1) was able to write, on the first page of his *Principien*, that 'our unphilosophical age' is suspicious of anything that smells of the metaphysical speculation of earlier philosophy. Empiricist 'Common Sense', as represented by Whitney, had taken hold of German linguistics.

We see then that the Neogrammarian movement was characterised by a revolutionary spirit that strove for uncompromising methodological precision and aimed to sweep away the perceived theoretical confusions of the previous generations. In a way, these assertions of revolution seem to be a simple recapitulation of a pattern we have repeatedly observed right from the initial establishment of linguistics as a discipline: in almost every generation, linguists believed they were starting anew and righting the wrongs of their predecessors.

6.4 Further reading

As the culmination of nineteenth-century comparative-historical grammar, the Neogrammarians occupy a prominent place in all histories of nineteenth-century linguistics. Anna Morpurgo Davies (1998) examines the Neogrammarians and their work extensively in chapter 9 of her *History of Linguistics, Volume IV: Nineteenth-Century Linguistics*. Olga Amsterdamska's (1987) *Schools of Thought: The Development of Linguistics from Bopp to Saussure*, a history of nineteenth-century linguistics written from the perspective of the sociology of science, is at its most perceptive when treating the Neogrammarians. See in particular chapters 4 and 5.

For an exposition of Verner's Law and the notion of analogical change as they are understood today, see chapters 4 and 5 of Lyle Campbell's (2020 [1998]) *Historical Linguistics: An Introduction*. For a detailed discussion of the technical problems faced in mid-nineteenth comparative-historical linguistics and the solutions arrived at by the Neogrammarians, see Kurt Jankowsky's (2001) article 'The crisis of historical-comparative linguistics in the 1860s' in volume 2 of the handbook *History of the Language Sciences*.

7 Critiques of Neogrammarian doctrine

From the mid-1870s until the early twentieth century, academic linguistics was overcome with Neogrammarian fever. In many ways, the Neogrammarian movement came to define the field: linguists either counted themselves as Neogrammarians – or at least as sympathisers – or they joined the ranks of their vociferous critics. In this chapter, we look at some of the various directions from which the Neogrammarians were criticised, and how these critiques influenced the further development of linguistics.

The most sweeping critique was to say that the Neogrammarians, with their focus on historical sound change in Indo-European, had embraced an excessively narrow and technical conception of linguistic scholarship. There was a longing – even nostalgia – among many linguists for the broader questions that had animated the field in earlier decades. One of the most succinct expressions of this sentiment came from Georg von der Gabelentz (1840–1893), a professor of Chinese and general linguistics, first at the Neogrammarian stronghold of the University of Leipzig, and later at the University of Berlin, the centre of the German academic world (see Vogel and McElvenny 2019; McElvenny 2017). We meet Gabelentz again in Section 8.3, for his supposed role in ushering in the structuralist era in modern linguistics.

Gabelentz not only complained of what he saw as Neogrammarian tunnel vision in the way they restricted themselves to the task of working out genealogical relations through sound changes, but also objected to how they dismissed other approaches to language study as insufficiently scientific. In his 1891 magnum opus, *Die Sprachwissenschaft, ihre Aufgaben, Methoden, und bisherigen Ergebnisse* (Linguistics, its tasks, methods, and results to date), Gabelentz wrote:

> Most of us linguists have limited [our] work to the investigation of one or another language family, and the genealogical-historical school [represented at this time chiefly by the Neogrammarians] has shown such amazing progress that they deserve a certain degree of self-satisfaction. It seemed reasonable to say: Progress in linguistics occurs only in this school. Others might call themselves philologists, language philosophers, or even language experts or polyglots, or whatever they like, but they shouldn't claim to be linguists and what they do to be linguistics. But whoever says this confuses the little field that they plough with the commons of a large community, or if I may put it in terms of a common Chinese saying, passes

judgement like someone who sits at the bottom of a well and says the sky is small. (Gabelentz 2016 [1891]: 12)

We should note, however, that Gabelentz did acknowledge the theoretical contributions of some Neogrammarians, even if he was generally unimpressed by what he saw as the narrowness and closed-mindedness of most adherents of the movement. Gabelentz (2016 [1891]: 143) cited, for example, Hermann Paul's (1880) *Principien der Sprachgeschichte* – the 'Neogrammarian Bible', which we introduced in Section 6.3 – as a guide to the 'general basic principles' of language. He mentioned Paul's book in the same sentence as William Dwight Whitney's (1875) *The Life and Growth of Language*.

Beyond the general discontent in many quarters of linguistics with the narrow technical nature of Neogrammarian scholarship and their totalising pretensions, there were many critiques that targeted the substance of Neogrammarian doctrine. The central point around which most critiques revolved was the claim, which we examined in Section 6.2, that 'every sound change, inasmuch as it occurs mechanically, takes place according to laws that admit no exception' (Osthoff and Brugman 1878: 13; English translation in Lehmann 1967: 204). This claim was just one principle – albeit a very important principle – in the edifice of Neogrammarian theory, but it came to be considered by many as the defining feature of the movement.

In the Neogrammarian manifesto, Hermann Osthoff (1847–1909) and Karl Brugman (1849–1919) had emphasised the centrality of sound laws to their project: 'Only those who hold tightly on to the sound laws, those pillars of our whole science, have solid ground under their feet' (Osthoff and Brugman 1878: 14). The implication was that their predecessors, and contemporaries outside their camp, had wavered in their commitment to rigorous, absolute sound laws. But among the critics of the Neogrammarians were many who felt that the Neogrammarians were wrong to claim novelty or uniqueness for their approach.

From Section 4.1, we will recall that one of the main achievements of which August Schleicher (1821–1868) could boast, and on which his reputation was based, was his thoroughness and rigour in formulating accounts of historical sound changes in Indo-European languages. He followed through on sound laws and elevated them to a level equivalent to the laws of the natural sciences. Johannes Schmidt (1843–1901), a former student of Schleicher's, argued that the Neogrammarians were merely continuing down the path pioneered by his teacher (Schmidt 1887): Schleicher's (1850: 1–5) 'immutable natural laws' became the Neogrammarians' sound laws that 'admit no exception'. Leading Neogrammarians did have a direct Schleicherian genealogy. August Leskien (1840–1916), for example, who first set up the Neogrammarian opposition of sound laws and analogy, had also been a student of Schleicher's.

But the more trenchant critiques of the Neogrammarians attacked their very concept of law. In the following sections, we examine a number of theoretical and empirical arguments levelled against the Neogrammarians, and alternative proposals that grew out of these arguments.

7.1 Schuchardt, Gabelentz and Whitney on the limits of sound laws

One of the most comprehensive – and best-known – critiques of Neogrammarian sound laws was that launched by the Romanist Hugo Schuchardt (1842–1927) in his 1885 essay *Über die Lautgesetze. Gegen die Junggrammatiker* (On the sound laws. Against the Neogrammarians; Schuchardt 1928 [1885]). The essence of Schuchardt's critique was to say that the Neogrammarians' talk of laws was a feeble attempt to cast their discipline in the mould of the natural sciences. Schuchardt was another of Schleicher's former students, but he had not acquired his teacher's fetish for the supposedly strict, incontrovertible laws of the natural sciences. According to Schuchardt, the equivalence between natural and linguistic laws does not hold. A law in physics, for example, is supposed to have universal validity, but so-called sound laws are restricted in a number of seemingly arbitrary ways:

> When a natural scientist hears for the first time about the exceptionless character of sound laws, he will probably think of sound laws that are valid all the time and everywhere. Such laws are not only possible when the basic conditions of the activity of speaking are the same, but we should also expect them. Why does sound change not – at least for the most part – maintain the same direction, so that voiced stops always develop from the voiceless stops, monophthongs from diphthongs, and not the other way round? If we inform this naïve scientist that such general sound laws have not yet been discovered, that in fact all sound laws known so far have a relatively narrow spatial and temporal validity, then he will find that absolute necessity that is required for exceptionless laws to be lacking. (Schuchardt 1928 [1885]: 58)

Sound laws do not operate in the same way in all languages, but are restricted to certain dialects and to specific time periods within those dialects. If we take the example of Grimm's Law – which we discussed in Sections 2.4 and 6.2 – we see that it applies only in the Germanic languages. Indeed, its utility for the linguist comes from the fact that it is restricted to the Germanic languages: the sound changes it describes are what set the Germanic languages apart from the rest of Indo-European and thereby define the Germanic languages as a group. Grimm's Law – and all other sound laws – therefore say nothing about the universal functioning of human language but merely describe specific, local occurrences. Even within this specific context, they have a temporally limited operation. Grimm's Law, for example, describes a historical process that has supposedly gone to completion, meaning that the sound changes it describes are no longer happening.

On Schuchardt's (1928 [1885]: 66–7) estimation, this temporally bound concept of law has the further undesirable consequence of supporting a teleological view of language change. It assumes that there are final states towards which languages strive. These specific sound laws require us to imagine a period before a sound change, a period in which it is taking place, and a final stage when it is completed. But this is not the case: in reality, all languages are in a constant state of flux. Every period in the history of a language is in fact an intermediate period. There is no final endpoint that languages seek to reach.

The restriction of sound laws to distinct dialects is also empirically untenable, argued Schuchardt (ibid.: 67). If we examine the way people actually talk, we find that sound changes do not proceed in the regular way that sound laws would suggest. Sound changes seem to propagate unevenly through different words in a single dialect. Even the notion of self-contained dialects is problematic: the boundaries between one dialect and the next are often unclear, a point that we explore further in the next section, when we look at the 'wave theory'.

Not everyone saw the limited applicability of Neogrammarian sound laws as a fault. In this period, towards the end of the nineteenth century, statistical techniques were being adopted across the sciences. This was true even in such fields as physics, traditionally held up as the very home of scientific rigour, where statistical methods were being used to render thermodynamic processes tractable. The philosopher and founding figure of experimental psychology Wilhelm Wundt (1832–1920), who we have met on several occasions in this book, attempted to introduce a statistical and probabilistic perspective into the debates surrounding sound laws. The Neogrammarians' claim of 'exceptionless' sound laws, Wundt argued, is an exaggeration: what they really mean is generally valid laws (see Formigari 2018). Wundt (e.g. 1886; 1908 [1883]: 124–45) recognised a hierarchy of laws based on the scope of their validity: the more generally applicable a law, the fewer the factors that can interfere with its operation and cause apparent exceptions. The level of generality of a law, and therefore its place in the hierarchy, is to be determined by statistical investigation of the phenomena in which the law is manifested (Wundt 1908 [1883]: 138; see also McElvenny 2023c).

Georg von der Gabelentz – who, as we saw in the opening of this chapter, was also a critic of the Neogrammarians – tried independently to apply statistical methods to comparative-historical research, specifically in order to tackle the question of whether there is a genealogical link between the Basque language of Europe and the Berber languages of North Africa. Most linguists today would not recognise such a link between these languages – Basque is usually taken to be an isolate and Berber a subgroup within the Afro-Asiatic family – but in Gabelentz's time this question was still controversial. In an effort to prove a genealogical link, Gabelentz (1893, 1894) drew up tables of probable sound correspondences between Basque and Berber. These correspondences, argued Gabelentz (1893: 606), are not absolute, as in Indo-European, but probabilistic, since these are languages 'at a lower cultural level' that allow a much greater variation in pronunciation. A probabilistic proof should therefore suffice to establish the relationship.

In making this argument, Gabelentz was drawing on tropes, widespread in the language scholarship of the time, about the alleged greater variability of so-called 'primitive' languages, a topic to which we return in Section 14.3 (see also McElvenny 2019b). While most present-day linguists would be unimpressed by Gabelentz's arguments, there are elements of his concept of phonological variation that have stood the test of time. Among the many sound alternations Gabelentz observed are those that today would be classed as allophonic variation (a concept introduced in Chapter 9). But most linguists today would recognise allophonic variation as a regular process in all languages, whereas Gabelentz suggested that 'primitive' languages were less constrained in the degree of variation they permit. For his part, Schuchardt was not swayed at all by Gabelentz's arguments: he rejected Gabelentz's work as incurably dilettantish, criticising him for his apparent ignorance of the grammatical principles of the languages studied, his cavalier treatment of the linguistic data, and his general laxness of method (see Schuchardt 1893; Hurch and Purgay 2019).

Schuchardt (1928 [1885]: 53–8) not only attacked the empirical adequacy of the Neogrammarians' approach, but also questioned the underlying apparatus of their explanatory model. He accused the Neogrammarians of setting up an overly simplistic antithesis between physiologically based, exceptionless sound laws and psychologically based, unpredictable analogies. The Neogrammarians, he said, try to explain away any apparent exception to a sound law by pulling an analogy out of a hat. But the relationships between regular sound change and analogy are complex and open to numerous different analyses and interpretations. In addition, analogy is not simply a spontaneous, capricious process, but often has its own logic, and can therefore be studied systematically.

The summary Schuchardt offers of Neogrammarian theory is something of a caricature. As we saw in Sections 6.2 and 6.3, the Neogrammarians painted a more nuanced picture of language and its functioning, and always hedged and acknowledged that processes in the real world are more complex than the idealisations they were putting forward. However, Schuchardt's critique did perhaps point to problems in Neogrammarian practice, the shortcuts they took when they came to apply their carefully articulated theory to the actual study of languages.

Ultimately, argued Schuchardt (1928 [1885]: 80–3), the Neogrammarians' conception of sound laws is scientifically empty. The Neogrammarians often accuse their opponents of just collecting isolated facts without establishing any causal principles that explain them, as the sound laws allegedly do. But, Schuchardt countered, the sound laws are just descriptions of patchwork phenomena that have no explanatory value. In fact, insisting on sound laws only serves to shut down discussion and hinder science in finding deeper explanatory principles. What the Neogrammarians have done, according to Schuchardt, is to hypostasise their laws: they have turned their descriptions of observed regularities into something that is supposed to have a real existence. The reason for the Neogrammarians' success is simply that they have been able to distil their approach into a mechanical method that can be applied easily, without any thought or talent: '[T]he so-called "mechanisation of methods" reduces the demands on independent thought to a minimum and thereby allows the participation of an extraordinary number of those who are actually incompetent in the "scientific" work' (Schuchardt 1928 [1885]: 83).

As an alternative to hypostasised sound laws and erratic analogy, Schuchardt (1928 [1885]: 63) preferred to think of change in language as being similar to fashion: it is a matter of conscious or semi-conscious imitation. Innovations in a language spread because people imitate one another's ways of speaking. He cited the example of the pronunciation of 'r' in French and German as a uvular fricative [ʁ]. Detailed studies show that the uvular realisation of this sound 'has been becoming more and more fashionable for a long time' (ibid.) and in this way is displacing the older pronunciation as an apical trill [r] in many people's speech throughout the French- and German-speaking countries. Furthermore, as we see in more detail in the next section, if we trace the propagation of sound changes like this, we find that they proceed gradually across individual words. It is demonstrably not the case that the change from the trill to the uvular pronunciation has occurred suddenly and consistently according to a 'blind' law.

Schuchardt's description of language change as a matter of innovation and propagation will remind us of William Dwight Whitney's ideas, which we examined in Section 5.2. Even though – as we saw in Section 6.3 – the Neogrammarians appealed to Whitney's work as providing a foundation for their own views, Whitney himself remained somewhat sceptical of their positions. Deploying similar arguments to Schuchardt, Whitney objected to the Neogrammarians' notion of law: the term 'law' should be reserved for principles that have universal validity, he said, but what we see in sound changes are merely 'tendencies' (see Alter 2005: chap. 9). But Whitney only made these arguments in a few obscure talks and in his private correspondence with Georg Curtius (1820–1885), the academic elder who suffered so much from the Neogrammarians' revolutionary zeal (as we saw in Section 6.2). The muteness of Whitney's criticism is perhaps surprising, considering the intensity of his polemics against others. We might speculate that he did not want to offend his younger Neogrammarian colleagues, who held him and his work in such high regard.

7.2 Schmidt, Schuchardt and the wave theory

An interesting aspect of Hugo Schuchardt's illustration of the propagation of sound change, which we saw towards the end of the previous section, is that it reveals the porous nature of linguistic boundaries. The spread of uvular [ʁ] is not a spontaneous sound change contained within a single dialect, a single language, or even a single genealogical subgroup. It is a change that carried across the distinct languages of French and German, which belong to two separate branches of Indo-European, Romance and Germanic respectively.

The impossibility of staking out definite boundaries of dialects, languages, and even entire language families invited theoretical innovation on the part of Schuchardt and other like-minded linguists. The clear splitting of a parent language into independent child dialects postulated by the family tree model cannot be found in the wild. Instead, we find only cases of overlapping sound changes across sibling dialects. A comprehensive, empirical demonstration of this problem came in the 1870s with the detailed description made by the German dialectologist Georg Wenker (1852–1911) of the so-called Rhenish Fan (see Putschke 2001).

Wenker sent out questionnaires to trusted locals – predominantly school teachers – in towns and villages across the Rhineland, the region of western Germany that borders France, Luxemburg, Belgium and the Netherlands. The questionnaires asked for transcriptions into the local dialects of various phrases, which Wenker then used to identify diverging pronunciations of words. When he compiled the questionnaires and charted the results on maps, Wenker (1877) observed that the sound changes we would expect based on Grimm's Law – which we discussed in Section 2.4 – were staggered from south to north. That is to say, the second Germanic sound shift had not proceeded evenly across these dialects. The clear boundary between southern and northern German dialects hypothesised by Grimm's Law simply did not exist in reality.

To the south of the Rhineland, the second Germanic sound shift had gone to completion. Dialects in those areas had forms like Standard German *Apfel* (apple), *das* (that) and *auf* ('on', cognate to English 'up'). In the middle of the Rhineland, however, this sound shift had not occurred in these words. There people said *Appel*, *dat* and *op*. But in this same region people did say *Dorf* ('village', cognate to English 'thorpe') and *mache* (make). These are forms in which the expected sound shift has occurred. But further north, even these words had not been affected by the sound change. There the forms were *Dorp* and *make*. A map charting the dialects Wenker identified in his 1877 *Das Rheinische Platt* (The Rhenish Dialect), which exhibited these various stages of the second Germanic sound shift, can be seen in Figure 7.1.

Schuchardt had already observed the permeability of dialect boundaries in an 1870 speech, 'Über die Klassifikation der romanischen Mundarten' (On the classification of Romance dialects), which he delivered in Leipzig on the conferral of his habilitation, a postdoctoral qualification required in Germany to become a professor (Schuchardt 1928 [1870]). In this speech, Schuchardt highlighted the phenomenon of overlapping dialect features. If we were to walk from the middle of Italy up into France, he said, stopping in each town and village along the way, we would notice that the dialects would gradually become less like Standard Italian and more like Standard French. But at no point would there be a clear boundary where we could definitively say that on this side people speak Italian and on the other they speak French.

The problem, argued Schuchardt (1928 [1870]: 172–80), is that the fundamental premises of the family tree model do not accord with reality. It is not the case that we start with a homogeneous speech community that then splits neatly into separate groups. Rather, there has always been diversity within every speech community, and as the community spreads out, it does not divide neatly but is made up of small groups that continue to be in contact and to influence one another's ways of speaking. Against the family tree model, in which linguistic features develop independently inside autonomous dialects, Schuchardt (ibid.: 181–4) proposed an alternative model where changes begin in one place and radiate out to surrounding varieties. This means that dialects that are located near one another geographically will generally share more features than those that are further apart.

Figure 7.1 Insert map of dialects in the Rhineland from Wenker (1877)

Johannes Schmidt sketched similar ideas at the scale of the whole Indo-European family in his 1872 book *Die Verwandtschaftsverhältnisse der indogermanischen Sprachen* (The genealogical relations of the Indo-European languages). He observed, for example, that languages in the Slavic and Indo-Iranian groups have common features that they do not share with other Indo-European languages. But everything else we know about the Slavic and Indo-Iranian languages tells us that they belong to distinct branches of the Indo-European family and so do not have a direct common ancestor from which they could have inherited these shared features. However, the speakers of these languages have long lived in contiguous geographical regions and throughout this time were in continued contact with one another. A similar state of affairs – shared linguistic features and continued contact – can be observed across the Celtic and Romance languages.

To explain this spreading of changes over geographical regions, Schmidt conjured up the image of successive waves of changes washing across speaker communities. For this reason, the model he proposed is often referred to as the 'wave theory'. Schmidt put his wave theory forward as an alternative to the traditional family tree model:

> If we want now to represent the relationships of the Indo-European languages in a picture that illustrates the origin of their diversity, then we must completely abandon the idea of a family tree. I would like to put a picture of a wave in its place, which diffuses concentrically with the distance from the mid-point in ever weaker rings. (Schmidt 1872: 27)

Schmidt later provided an illustration of this image in the 1875 second volume of his *Zur Geschichte des indogermanischen Vocalismus* (On the history of Indo-European vocalism; Schmidt 1871–5), reproduced in Figure 7.2. Each segment of the circle is supposed to show a different prehistoric Slavic dialect group, and each radius in the circle indicates a sound change that propagated over the adjacent dialect groups (on Schmidt's imagery, see further Kaplan 2019).

There could very well have been a single Indo-European proto-language, admitted Schmidt (1872: 29–30), but the scientific tools we have available to us today do not allow us to penetrate that far back into the past. Our reconstructed Proto-Indo-European is nothing more than a 'scientific fiction' (ibid.: 31). It furthers our research to hazard a reconstruction, but we should not mistake this reconstruction for a real historical entity. For their part, such Neogrammarians as August Leskien (1876) and Karl Brugman (1884) acknowledged the challenge thrown down by Schmidt, but they maintained that the family tree and wave models were complementary theories, which needed to be used in tandem to tease out the history of languages (see Jankowsky 2001: 1329–30; Morpurgo Davies 1998: 284–7).

7.3 Karl Vossler and idealism in linguistics

The criticisms of Neogrammarian doctrine that we have seen in the previous sections more or less stayed within the standard epistemological and methodological confines of disciplinary linguistics. But there were several much more radical critiques of the Neogrammarians at the time, the most notable of which is perhaps that put forward by the Romance philologist Karl Vossler (1872–1949). Starting with two short books, the 1904 *Positivismus und Idealismus in der Sprachwissenschaft*

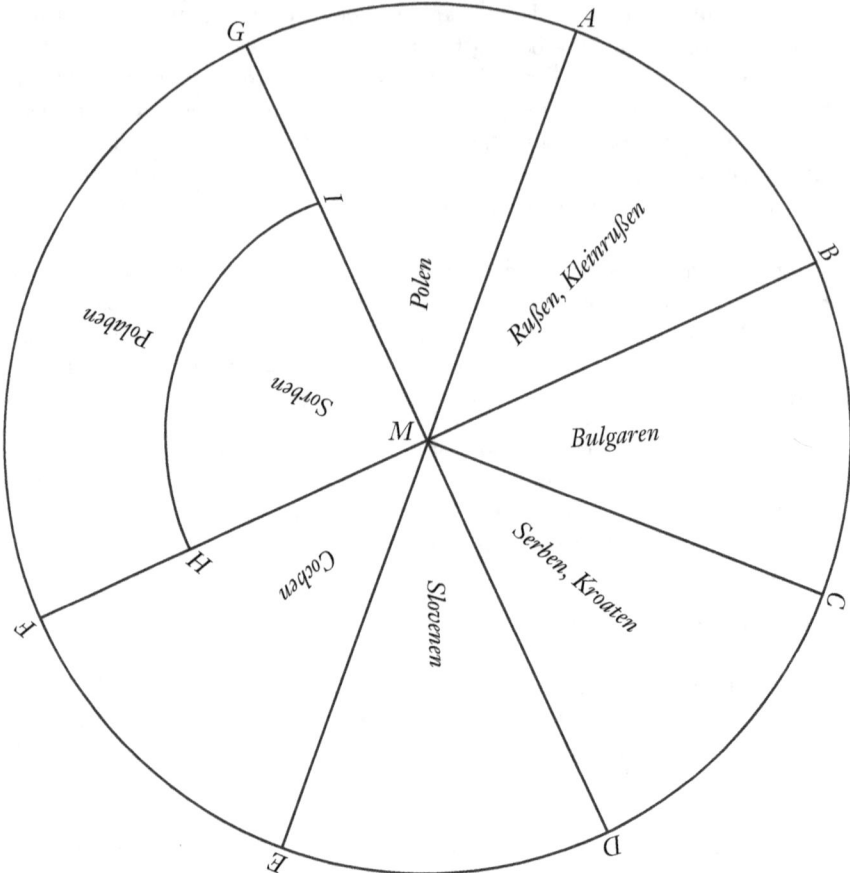

Figure 7.2 Schmidt's (1871–5, vol. 2: 199) diagram of the wave model

(Positivism and idealism in linguistics) and the 1905 *Sprache als Schöpfung und Entwicklung* (Language as creation and development), Vossler pitted his own view of 'idealism' in linguistics against what he called the Neogrammarians' 'positivism'.

The heart of Vossler's position was to argue that the Neogrammarians, in their sound laws and analogies, had developed a very useful method for identifying and tracing changes in language, but that they had then made the mistake of treating this as the end of their task. The Neogrammarians, stated Vossler (1904: 1–5), have fallen victim to 'metaphysical positivism': they have assumed – incorrectly – that a useful empirical method delivers deeper insights explaining the causes of language change. In explaining language change, we must look to the 'reason' of speakers and not try to find the causes in the material of language itself: 'The idealist seeks the principle of causation in human reason, the positivist seeks it in the things, in the phenomena themselves' (ibid.: 3).

We should pause for a moment to consider what exactly Vossler meant by 'positivism'. This term was coined by the French philosopher Auguste Comte (1798–1857) in the first half of the nineteenth century to name the body of philosophical doctrines he developed (see Bourdeau 2018). In very broad terms, Comte held up the empirically based natural sciences as the perfect paradigm for human knowledge. In studying the human world of society and culture, Comte argued, we should emulate the approach of the natural sciences. Comte's positivism had an unmistakable kinship with scientific materialism, which we met in Section 4.2. Vossler (1904: 4), for his part, lumped positivism and materialism together: 'No one gets on better than materialists, positivists, mystics, and swindlers.'

But Comte was in fact quite critical of materialism in its various guises: he found materialism to be too reductive in its desire to assimilate all of life and mind to physical principles. Despite these differences, Comte's positivism and scientific materialism shared an overarching commitment to the natural scientific mindset and were similarly well received among progressive audiences. Positivism and materialism had the further shared characteristic of both being refashioned as generic terms of abuse. This is the sense in which Vossler uses 'positivism': he is not referring specifically to Comte's positivism or any other clearly defined doctrine, but rather simply to what he sees as the unreflected worship of the natural sciences on the part of his colleagues in linguistics.

The term 'idealism', which Vossler contrasts to 'positivism', is similarly non-specific. Many different but related doctrines throughout the nineteenth century were described as 'idealist'. German idealism is classically identified with the philosophy of such figures as Immanuel Kant (1724–1804) and G. W. F. Hegel (1770–1831), who we have encountered at several points in this book. For his own part, Vossler saw his idealism as stemming from the work of Wilhelm von Humboldt, as mediated by the Italian philosopher Benedetto Croce (1866–1952).

Vossler held that human language is ultimately the result of individuals' efforts to express themselves and, as such, it is the product of individual mental activity. This means that in accounting for language change we cannot simply look at attested words, as the positivist would do, but that we must dig deeper to uncover the underlying thoughts; this is what the idealist does. Instead of trying to cut language up into sounds, words and sentences, we need to examine individual instances of expression, preferably as found in literature, and ask why one way of saying something was chosen over others. Linguistics, says Vossler, should really just be stylistics, the study of the style of individual speakers:

> But when the idealist principle of causation is really recognised in language, all phenomena recorded and described by the lower disciplines – phonetics, the study of inflection and word formation, and syntax – must find their true explanation in the highest discipline; that is, stylistics. So-called grammar must be completely dissolved in the aesthetic view of language. (Vossler 1904: 10)

On one level, the opposition Vossler sets up between 'positivism' and 'idealism' in linguistics is a continuation of debates – which we have seen repeatedly in previous chapters – about the place of linguistics among the sciences of nature and those that study the human world. These debates were not confined to linguistics, but involved also history, psychology, ethnography, and so on. Towards the end of the nineteenth century, the demarcation of the natural sciences and humanities became a central topic in German philosophy – we explore this issue in greater detail in Section 11.2.

But there is also a social dimension to this conflict between 'positivism' and 'idealism'. The positivism that Vossler complained about, the obsession with the meticulous ordering and classification of facts to the exclusion of deeper and more speculative questions, was in many ways characteristic of academic thought in Germany from the 1870s to the 1890s, the heyday of the Neogrammarian school. In this period, German academia as a whole was gripped by a conservatism inspired by the broader political environment (see Ringer 1969; Maaß 2003).

In 1871, after a resounding victory against the French in the Franco-Prussian War, Germany was finally united as a single empire under Prussian hegemony. The next twenty years were a period of the pragmatic but authoritarian rule of Otto von Bismarck (1815–1898), who systematically built up the power of the German imperial state, both internally and externally. Academia largely toed the line in Bismarck's Germany and embraced its role of educator of civil servants for the empire. This role demanded training that privileged the inculcation of rote technical skills over the cultivation of the sort of creative and speculative talents that had been prized in the Romantic era just a few generations before, in which the modern German universities were founded. Concerns about the professionalisation and technicisation of academic life were one of the factors driving debates about the nature of education and the humanities in which scholars and intellectuals were engaged.

In 1890, Bismarck was forced out of his role as Reichskanzler after serious differences of opinion with the new Kaiser, Wilhelm II. This marked the beginning of a new era, which was characterised above all by the virulent militarism that ultimately sparked World War I. But Wilhelm's reign was also a period of great economic expansion and, in many ways, liberalisation of German society and politics, a liberalisation that was reflected in the arts and academia. Vossler's idealist turn midway through the Wilhelmine period could be seen as a tiny example of this liberalisation. The Neogrammarians had brought academic linguistics to the peak of technicisation, but Vossler, in the new, comparatively liberal environment, sought to reintroduce something of the old Romanticism.

7.4 Further reading

The key secondary sources on the Neogrammarian movement recommended in the last chapter also treat the opposition they faced. Chapter 9 of Anna Morpurgo Davies's (1998) *History of Linguistics, Volume IV: Nineteenth-Century Linguistics* simultaneously introduces Neogrammarian work and the critiques levelled against it. Chapter 10, the concluding chapter of the book, discusses the wave theory. Olga Amsterdamska's (1987) *Schools of Thought: The Development of*

Linguistics from Bopp to Saussure examines Karl Vossler's 'idealist' critique of the Neogrammarians in detail. See in particular chapter 6.

Wolfgang Putschke's (2001) essay 'Die Dialektologie, ihr Beitrag zur historischen Sprachwissenschaft im 19. Jahrhundert und ihre Kritik am junggrammatischen Programm', in volume 2 of the handbook *History of the Language Sciences*, offers an excellent outline of the challenges that dialectology presented to Neogrammarian orthodoxy.

For discussion of the increasing importance of statistical reasoning to the sciences in the nineteenth century, see Theodore Porter's (1986) *The Rise of Statistical Thinking, 1820–1900*. The classic account of the mutual validation and support that obtained between the German state and German academia around the turn of the twentieth century – and its eventual demise in the Weimar era – is Fritz Ringer's (1969) *The Decline of the German Mandarins: The German Academic Community, 1890–1933*.

8 Language as a system

With the mounting objections to the work of the Neogrammarians around the turn of the nineteenth to the twentieth century – which we surveyed in the previous chapter – the time was ripe for yet another revolution in linguistics. This revolution swept away Neogrammarian doctrine and introduced in its place structuralism, a cluster of theories and approaches that not only had a major impact on linguistics, but influenced scholarship across the humanities and social sciences. In this chapter, we meet the chief folk hero of structuralism, the Genevan linguist Ferdinand de Saussure (1857–1913).

In the modern linguistic imagination, Saussure is a cultish figure who, in the mythologising mode of history, is sometimes credited with single-handedly bringing about the structuralist revolution through his conception of languages as internally coherent synchronic systems. But 'structuralism' is a term that Saussure never used himself. In fact, in his own lifetime, Saussure was widely considered to have been a Neogrammarian, and many of the innovations he proposed were claimed as contributions to Neogrammarian scholarship. It is only in retrospect – in the polemicising, eclipsing narrative of the early structuralists, which we recount in Chapter 10 – that Saussure became a revolutionary who broke definitively with the Neogrammarian past and ushered in the structuralist era. But before we can explore the narratives later built around Saussure, we have to examine his work in its immediate context. That is the task we turn to in the following sections.

8.1 Ferdinand de Saussure, Neogrammarian extraordinaire

As the scion of an aristocratic family from Geneva, whose members had distinguished themselves over generations in the sciences and arts, Saussure enjoyed a very broad education, and pursued a number of different scholarly interests right up into his first years at university in Geneva. But during his undergraduate studies, his focus began to sharpen, and he decided to devote himself to the study of language. At this time, in the mid-1870s, the world centre of linguistic scholarship was Leipzig, and so it was for Leipzig that Saussure departed in 1876 in order to undertake his doctorate in linguistics.

As we saw in Section 6.1, 1876 was a fateful year for linguistics in Leipzig: this is the year in which Karl Brugman (1849–1919) went on a rampage in Georg Curtius's (1820–1885) journal, criticising the work of his academic elders and putting forward radically new reconstructions of Proto-Indo-European, a moment generally considered the first public appearance of the Neogrammarian movement. Saussure therefore came to Leipzig just as the Neogrammarians were beginning the assault that would launch them to the forefront of the field.

However, as Saussure's biographer John Joseph (2012: 184–99) argues, Saussure never really became enamoured of Leipzig and the scholarship that went on there. The older generation, represented primarily by Curtius, he found rather uninspiring. But neither was he impressed by the younger Neogrammarians, such as Brugman and Hermann Osthoff (1847–1909), whose courses he also attended. Saussure could not escape the feeling that many of the discoveries the Neogrammarians were celebrating as great breakthroughs were obvious insights into the history of Indo-European which he had independently arrived at back in Geneva, before he had been exposed to the latest currents of Neogrammarian scholarship in Leipzig.

An episode from Saussure's time in Leipzig illustrates this point. While still only a doctoral student, Saussure struck out on his own to publish his first book, the 1879 *Mémoire sur le système primitif des voyelles dans les langues indo-européennes* (Dissertation on the original system of Indo-European vowels; on the *Mémoire*, see Joseph 2012: chap. 7). Convinced that he had solved fundamental problems in Indo-European linguistics – and perhaps worried that he would be scooped by his teachers in Leipzig – Saussure wrote at a feverish pace and had each section of the book printed as it was completed. The result is a somewhat confusing work in which Saussure modifies his analyses on the fly. Later chapters of the book sometimes even alter and correct claims made in earlier chapters, which had already been printed and so could not be revised.

The *Mémoire* offered a radically simpler reconstruction of the vowel system of Proto-Indo-European than was generally accepted at the time. Saussure argued that Proto-Indo-European probably had only one basic vowel in stressed syllables, although this vowel would have had a phonetically conditioned variant in some environments. Originally, speakers would not have been consciously aware of these variants. Over time, however, the variants would have impressed themselves upon speakers and, as a result, would be reinterpreted as indicating differences in meaning, such as signalling different tenses of verbs. In addition to the basic vowel in its variant forms, Saussure also posited diphthongs in Proto-Indo-European that were formed through the combination of the vowel with what Saussure called 'sonant coefficients' (*coefficients sonantiques*), sounds like [m], [n], [l], [j] and [w], which could both serve as the nucleus of a syllable or form a diphthong with the basic vowel.

On Saussure's view, the many different vowel sounds that we find in the oldest attested Indo-European languages have come about through the later evolution of the variants of the basic vowel and the diphthongs. In some Indo-European languages, the sonant coefficients have disappeared from the diphthongs but have left behind a main vowel that is somehow modified, such as having a different quality, stress or length. In other cases, it is the vowel that has disappeared, leaving just the sonant coefficient behind to act as the nucleus of the syllable.

Outside Germany, the reconstructions Saussure presented in his *Mémoire* were widely praised as a brilliant new analysis of Proto-Indo-European. Within Germany, however, Saussure's book was met with much less enthusiasm. His Neogrammarian teachers in Leipzig felt that it merely repeated points they had already made. The most innovative aspect of Saussure's analysis was the way in which he reconstructed Proto-Indo-European vowels in terms of a 'system': rather than focusing on the properties of individual vowel sounds, Saussure imagined how all the sounds would fit together to create a whole. This notion of 'system' would become one of Saussure's signature doctrines and is taken to be one of his chief contributions to the foundation of structuralism.

But a similar system-oriented approach was a feature of the reconstructions Brugman (1876a, 1876b) had published in Curtius's journal in the inaugural assault of the Neogrammarian movement three years earlier. In his reconstructions, Brugman used a kind of algebraic notation to indicate the vowels he posited in Proto-Indo-European without specifying their precise properties. In Brugman's approach, these unspecified symbols served as placeholders in a system rather than standing for concrete vowels.

Saussure did not cite this earlier Neogrammarian work, which led to the criticism that he had failed to adequately acknowledge his sources, and even to the much more serious charge that he may have plagiarised his teachers. Looking back on this dispute, Saussure's defenders say that no plagiarism was intended: Saussure was merely treating the analyses and examples first published by his teachers as common knowledge in the field.

The advantages of thinking in terms of a system later received empirical reinforcement. Saussure had direct evidence for most of the sonant coefficients that he reconstructed for the Proto-Indo-European vowel system, but he also hypothesised the existence of two additional sonant coefficients for which there was no direct evidence in any of the attested Indo-European languages. In 1880, the year after the publication of Saussure's *Mémoire*, the Danish linguist Hermann Möller (1850–1923) proposed that the two hypothetical sonant coefficients in Saussure's system might correspond to the so-called laryngeal consonants – sounds like [h] or the glottal stop – that Möller postulated in Proto-Indo-European (see Möller 1880).

The most exciting twist in the story comes after 1911, when inscriptions in the archaic Anatolian language Hittite were finally deciphered. It became clear that Hittite was an Indo-European language, and that it had some unusual sounds not found in other Indo-European languages. In 1927, the Polish linguist Jerzy Kuryłowicz (1895–1978) demonstrated that the distribution of these unusual sounds in Hittite corresponded to the laryngeals proposed by Möller, which Möller tied to Saussure's hypothetical sonant coefficients.

The legendary retelling of this story is to say that Saussure predicted the existence of laryngeals in Proto-Indo-European and that his prediction was later borne out by concrete evidence from Hittite. What in fact happened is that Möller's hypothesis, which he tied to Saussure's system, received empirical confirmation. But still we see that this new emphasis on the analysis of languages as systems increased the predicative capacity of linguistics. The ability to make accurate predictions is often invoked as a measure of the validity of the hard sciences: the startling appearance of empirical evidence demonstrating the existence of a hypothesised structure therefore significantly raised the prestige of linguistics as a serious science.

The conception of languages as systems remained a fundamental aspect of Saussure's thinking, which he elaborated in later work and gave a classic formulation in his *Cours de linguistique générale* (*Course in general linguistics*). We examine this text in the next section.

8.2 The Course in General Linguistics

After receiving his doctorate from the University of Leipzig in 1880 – with a thesis on the genitive absolute in Sanskrit, a topic completely unrelated to his notorious *Mémoire* – Saussure taught in Paris for a decade, until he was offered a professorship back in his home town of Geneva in 1891. It is for his teaching in Geneva that Saussure is chiefly remembered today. In 1907, and again in the academic years 1908 to 1909 and 1910 to 1911, Saussure offered a 'course in general linguistics'. What has come down to us from this course is a short book with the title *Cours de linguistique générale* (*Course in General Linguistics*), first published in 1916, three years after Saussure's death (cited here from the second revised edition, Saussure 1922 [1916]). This text is widely venerated as the foundational scripture of structuralism.

Crucially, Saussure did not write the published version of the *Cours* himself. Rather, it is derived from notes Saussure made in preparation for his lectures, supplemented by notes of students who attended the lectures. These various sources were edited into book form by two of Saussure's younger colleagues in Geneva, Charles Bally (1865–1947) and Albert Sechehaye (1870–1946). In the latter part of his career, Saussure published almost nothing, but instead constantly reworked manuscripts in an effort to capture the perfect representation of his ideas. We might speculate that his caution in later life was a response to the backlash he faced in his younger years, when he had rushed his *Mémoire* into print, to a rather mixed reception, as we observed in the previous section.

Saussure's *Cours* is a short, suggestive text that leaves a lot of room for interpretation and the fleshing out of the ideas it presents. Given the way in which it was composed – compiled posthumously by two colleagues from lecture notes – it is also a text that is open to challenge. We can always dispute whether that really is what Saussure said: indeed, there is a veritable cottage industry in the history of linguistics that produces competing interpretations of Saussurean doctrine. Whatever the details of Saussure's *Cours*, we can say that it puts forward a series of elegant conceptual distinctions that have become part of the general background to linguistic scholarship and continue to play a role in how linguists think about language today. In the rest of this section, we take a brief tour through the *Cours* and some of the key ideas it introduced.

Perhaps the most fundamental distinction introduced in the *Cours*, on which much of its conceptual apparatus is built, is that between *la langue* and *la parole* (see Saussure 1922 [1916]: 36–9). These terms are generally used in their original French form in linguistic texts written in English, but a rough translation would be 'the language' and 'speech'. Essentially, *la langue* names the abstract system of a language to which all members of a speech community have access: it is the common possession that makes it possible for them to communicate with one another. *La parole*, on the other hand, is the application of *la langue* in specific instances to create utterances. Saussure also spoke of the general language faculty that all humans possess, which allows them to make use of a particular language. He usually referred to this as the 'faculty of language' (*faculté de langage*), but he made no consistent, systematic distinction here: he sometimes used *la langue* to mean language generally, as an attribute of all humans.

In the *Cours*, Saussure focused most heavily on exploring the nature of *la langue* and had comparatively little to say about *la parole*. It has become a matter of controversy as to whether Saussure felt that the scientific study of language should concern itself only with *la langue*, or whether *la parole* was also amenable to such treatment. Whatever Saussure's intentions, we can say that it is Saussure's concept of *la langue* that has had the most impact on subsequent scholarship in linguistics: the majority of linguists have understood their task to be the investigation of *la langue* and its workings, variously conceived.

The constituent elements of *la langue* are signs. A Saussurean sign (*signe*) has two sides, the signifier (*signifiant*) and the signified (*signifié*). The signifier is the mental image we have of the sound of the sign, and the signified is the idea contained in the sign (see Saussure 1922 [1916]: 97–100). Saussure opposed his conception of the sign to the notion of a nomenclature. In a nomenclature, words are simply labels that name pre-existing concepts. The Saussurean sign, by contrast, exists only in the conjunction of sound and concept; the two sides, the signifier and the signified, cannot exist independently of one another. He illustrated his notion of the sign with the diagram reproduced in Figure 8.1.

Saussurean signs are distinguished from one another in the system of a language through their respective 'value' (*valeur*), another of the key concepts introduced in the *Cours*. Saussure (1922 [1916]: 159) stated: 'Language [*la langue*] is a system of interdependent terms in which the value of each term results solely from the simultaneous presence of the others' (English translation in Saussure 1959 [1916]: 114). The principle is that the limits of the signifier and the signified – the two sides of the sign – are defined by their differences to all other signifiers and signifieds in the system of *la langue*.

In the case of signifieds, there is no simple thing in the world named by the word. Saussure (1922 [1916]: 160) gave the example of the French word *mouton* contrasted with the English word 'sheep'. When a French speaker says 'mouton' they could be referring to a live member of the species *Ovis aries* or they could be referring to its meat. The English speaker, on the other hand, when they say 'sheep', can only mean the live animal. They would have to use a different word, such as 'mutton', to refer to its meat. The point is that the different conceptual boundaries of these two words in French and English – *mouton* and 'sheep' – are part of the respective language systems and not facts given in the world.

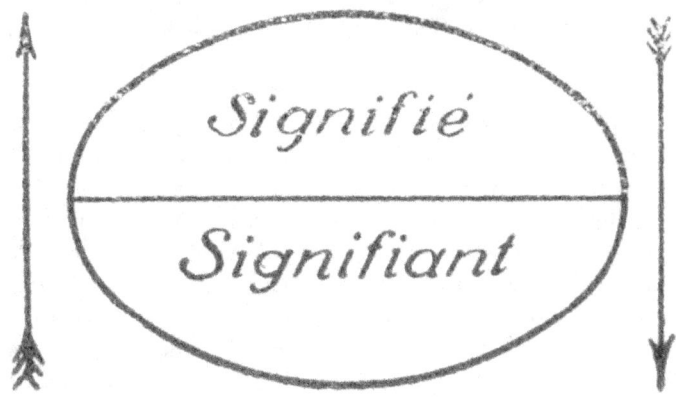

Figure 8.1 The sign according to Saussure (1922 [1916]: 158)

On the side of the signifiers, Saussure (1922 [1916]: 164–5) offered the example of the sound written in French with the letter 'r'. This sound can be pronounced in a range of different ways and yet still be recognised as the same sound. For example, the French word *roi* (king) can be pronounced with a uvular fricative as [ʁ] or with an apical trill as [r], or even as a velar fricative [x], and yet it is still taken to be the same sound as long as it remains distinct from the [m] sound in *moi* (me) or the [d] in *doigt* (finger). But the range of variability permitted in pronouncing a sound depends on the respective language. While 'r' can be pronounced as a velar fricative in French, this is not possible in German. In German, 'r' is usually pronounced as a uvular fricative, as in French, but the velar fricative is a completely different sound, generally written with the letters 'ch'. These sounds have different values in French and German; that is, they occupy different places in the system of each language. The mutually delimiting character of signs is illustrated by Saussure with the diagram in Figure 8.2.

'Value' is a purely negative concept: each item's place in the system of its respective language is determined by what it is not. There is no positive correlation between an element in the system and an absolute in the outside world, such as a particular sound or a particular 'meaning'. However, a specific sign, which

Figure 8.2 Saussure's (1922 [1916]: 159) illustration of 'value', the mutually delimiting character of signs

consists in the unity of a certain signifier and signified, is a positive term, and is concrete rather than abstract. This principle is described in the following way in the *Cours*:

> [I]n a language [*dans la langue*] there are only differences *without positive terms*. Whether we take the signified or the signifier, the language contains neither ideas nor sounds that pre-exist the linguistic system, but only conceptual differences and phonic differences issuing from this system. [. . .] But the statement that everything in language is negative is true only if the signified and the signifier are considered separately; when we consider the sign in its totality, we have something that is positive in its own class. [. . .] Although both the signified and the signifier are purely differential and negative when considered separately, their combination is a positive fact [. . .] (Saussure 1922 [1916]: 166; English translation in Saussure 1959 [1916]: 120–1)

An important property of the system of *la langue* is that it exists at a particular point in time. That is to say, the relative arrangement of all the parts in the system – the values of each part of the system – holds only at a certain point in time. The modification of any one value through change in sound or meaning leads to a reconfiguration of the whole system, resulting in a new *langue* (Saussure 1922 [1916]: 124–7). In order to capture the state of a language at a specific point in time, the linguist must engage in 'synchronic' (*synchronique*) linguistics, to use the term that Saussure introduced, and which quickly gained currency.

Once the linguist has described a series of synchronic states of the language, they can then compare these to see changes through time, thereby doing 'diachronic' (*diachronique*) linguistics, also a term introduced by Saussure. We see that on Saussure's account synchronic linguistics precedes diachronic linguistics. This position would seem to reverse the traditional orientation of the field from the predominantly historical outlook of the nineteenth century – with its overwhelming concern for change in languages – to the focus on describing specific synchronic states of languages from the structuralist era onwards.

Saussure's notion of value is part of his broader doctrine of the arbitrariness of the sign, the idea that signs are entirely self-sufficient and not determined by anything in the external world. Even onomatopoeia, argued Saussure (1922 [1916]: 100–2), the classical case of words that appear not to be arbitrary but rather motivated by the sound of the thing they name, proves on closer inspection to be deceptive. Truly onomatopoeic forms are always to a certain degree conventional, in that they have to conform to the sound system of the language. But even these truly onomatopoeic cases are very rare: most forms that appear to be onomatopoeia are just as arbitrary as any other word in the language. To repeat the example in the *Cours*, the French word for whip, *fouet*, might seem to imitate the sound of a whip, but if we look at the etymology of this word we see that it is just a matter of chance. *Fouet* has developed by regular sound change from Latin *fāgus* (beech), since historically strips of beech wood were used as whips.

Saussure (1922 [1916]: 180–4) did acknowledge, however, that different aspects of language can be motivated to different degrees. For example, the word *vingt* (twenty) is wholly arbitrary, but the word *dix-neuf* (nineteen) is not quite so arbitrary because it is composed of recognisable parts, namely *dix* (ten) and *neuf* (nine): it is ten plus nine. Its construction is part of a regular pattern that occurs in other words with a related meaning, such as *vingt-neuf* (twenty-nine). This principle applies also to grammatical aspects of a language, such as word inflection. The plural form 'ships' follows a common pattern with such words as 'flags', 'birds', 'books', and so on, although there are also less motivated forms, such as the plurals 'men' and 'sheep', which do not conform to such widespread patterns.

The central idea arising out of the various distinctions Saussure put forward in his *Cours de linguistique générale* is the notion of *la langue* as a synchronic system of arbitrary values, a concept fundamental to later structuralism. But even though Saussure provided the classical articulation of this notion, he did not create it from nothing. We saw in the previous section, for example, that the system-oriented thinking that underlies Saussure's *langue* was already present in the work of his Neogrammarian teachers. In the next section, we trace a number of other sources from which Saussure drew inspiration.

8.3 Saussure's sources

Many of the signature doctrines of Saussure's *Cours* – praised by later linguists as revolutionary innovations – may actually seem rather familiar to us from previous chapters. The arbitrariness of the sign, the nature of languages as systems, and even the emphasis on synchrony all have clear antecedents in Saussure's intellectual milieu.

As we saw in Section 3.2, the arbitrary character of linguistic signs was a major topic of debate in Enlightenment-era philosophy, and had roots extending back to Antiquity. Saussure's biographer John Joseph (2012: 88–9) shows that Saussure would have been exposed to these ideas in his schooling in Geneva. Even though nineteenth-century disciplinary linguistics, dominated as it was by German language philosophy, moved away from the traditional arbitrary conception of the sign, there were those who eagerly tried to reintroduce it into linguistics, such as William Dwight Whitney (1827–1894), as we saw in Section 5.2. Saussure (1922 [1916]: 26, 110) in fact cited Whitney favourably in the *Cours* in relation to the arbitrariness of the sign and, in a private note he scrawled in 1894, he commented that Whitney demonstrates 'that language is nothing more than a particular case of the sign' (quoted in Joseph 2012: 89).

Whitney was not alone in reviving older ideas about language in opposition to German language philosophy. Michel Bréal (1832–1915) – Saussure's senior colleague in Paris, who we meet again in Section 11.2 – was propagating a similar conception of the sign in his writings in the second half of the nineteenth century. Bréal's research culminated in his 1897 book *Essai de sémantique* (Essay on semantics), the work that established the term 'semantics' as the name for the field of study that deals with meaning. In this book, Bréal sketched a series of laws governing meaning change in language. The arbitrariness of linguistic signs was one of the fundamental principles on which his laws rested, a principle that he advanced against the materialist linguistics of August Schleicher (see Section 4.2):

> Our forefathers of the school of Condillac [. . .] were less far from the truth when they said, in simple and honest fashion, that words are signs. [. . .] Words are signs: they have no more existence than the signals of the semaphore, or than the dots and dashes of Morse telegraphy. To say that Language is an organism is but to darken counsel and sow a seed of error in the minds of men. (Bréal 1897: 277; English translation in Bréal 1900 [1897]: 249)

To find the immediate antecedents of Saussure's focus on the synchronic systems of languages we need look no further than the Neogrammarians. As we observed in Section 8.1, the methodological breakthrough underlying Saussure's reconstruction of the original vowel system of Proto-Indo-European in his 1879 *Mémoire* was precisely the fact that he treated the sounds of the language as constituting a system. Brugman had already employed a similar system-oriented approach, in prior work that Saussure was accused of copying.

Saussure and his Neogrammarian teachers alike owed a debt to traditional Indian linguistic scholarship, in particular the *Aṣṭādhyāyī* (Eight chapters) attributed to Pāṇini (we introduced this work in Section 2.3). As Joseph (2012: 83–4) points out, Saussure's analysis in the *Mémoire* actually dissolved some of the rules laid down by Pāṇini which had long been accepted by Sanskritists. But Saussure could not have arrived at his insights if he had not internalised Pāṇini's system and, above all, the abstract approach that underlay it.

More broadly, appreciation of the systemic character of languages permeated scholarship throughout nineteenth-century linguistics. This is one of the main insights contained in the common metaphorical description of languages as 'organisms', which we have encountered at several points in the preceding chapters. There were linguists – such as Schleicher, as we saw in the quotation from Bréal above – who took this metaphor literally and claimed that languages are in fact biological organisms, a view for which he was severely criticised, including by Saussure (1922 [1916]: 317). Nevertheless, Saussure maintained the non-biological usage of 'organism' (*organisme*) in the *Cours*, employing it as a synonym of 'system' (*système*; e.g. ibid.: 40–2; see also Kohrt and Kucharczik 2001).

In the mid-twentieth century, the Romanist Eugenio Coseriu (1921–2002) claimed that key elements of Saussure's *Cours* had been anticipated by the German sinologist and general linguist Georg von der Gabelentz (1840–1893) – who we first met in Chapter 7 – in his 1891 magnum opus *Die Sprachwissenschaft* (Linguistics *or* The science of language). Coseriu (1967) attempted to assimilate several key terms of Saussure's *Cours* to similar German terms in Gabelentz's *Sprachwissenschaft*, in particular the core concepts of Saussure's *langage* and Gabelentz's *Sprachvermögen* (language faculty), *langue* and *Einzelsprache* (individual language), and *parole* and *Rede* (speech). In addition, Coseriu observed how Gabelentz's circumscription of linguistics as a science, its internal subdivisions and its place among other sciences seemed to be echoed by the now classical definitions in the *Cours* (a sentiment also expressed by Morpurgo Davies 1998: 299–300).

Against Coseriu's claims for Gabelentz's priority, the historian of linguistics Konrad Koerner (1939–2022) argued that the views Gabelentz and Saussure appear to share were to a certain extent commonplaces in their contemporary scholarly environment (Koerner 1978 [1974]). Furthermore, the available textual and biographical evidence makes it difficult to maintain a direct influence of Gabelentz on Saussure. A much more plausible direct source for Saussure, on Koerner's (2008) reckoning, is the *Principien der Sprachgeschichte* (Principles of language history) of the Neogrammarian Hermann Paul (1846–1921), which we examined in detail in Section 6.3.

Despite his famous assertion that the only scientific way to study language is to take a historical approach (Paul 1920 [1880]: 20), Paul made it clear that such historical research must rest on a 'description of states' – that is, on descriptions of the successive synchronic stages through which a language has passed in the course of its history. These states have an 'organic' character – 'organic' in the sense of forming a system. In a passage already present in the 1886 second edition of his *Prinzipien*, Paul wrote:

> The linguist will not be able to do without the description of states, since what he has to deal with is large complexes of elements that simultaneously lie next to each other. If this description is going to be a truly usable basis for historical observation then it has to stick to the real objects, that is to the psychic organisms that have just been described. (Paul 1920 [1880]: 29; cf. Koerner 2008: 113)

There is, however, an important difference in the metaphysical status accorded to these states of language by Paul and Saussure. We will recall that Paul did not believe in the existence of a language as such: all the linguist has to work with is the language norm (*Sprachusus*), an artificial abstraction created by the linguist for the purposes of analysis. Saussure, by contrast, described *la langue* as a 'social fact' (*fait social*; e.g. 1922 [1916]: 21, 112). This is a term introduced by the French sociologist Émile Durkheim (1858–1917) to describe entities that have an independent existence in society, beyond the level of individual persons. In his choice of terminology, we see that Saussure was prepared to entertain the real existence of abstract entities, an approach that was anathema to Paul and the other Neogrammarians, who had fought so strongly against the abstractions of *Völkerpsychologie*.

Saussure was undoubtedly a very original and insightful linguist, but he was not the lone genius that some admirers in later generations have made him out to be. We might agree with the assessment of Leonard Bloomfield (1887–1949), a leading American linguist from the structuralist era, who we meet properly in Chapter 16. Reviewing the second edition of Saussure's *Cours*, Bloomfield concluded:

> The value of the *Cours* lies in its clear and rigorous demonstration of fundamental principles. Most of what the author says has long been 'in the air' and has been here and there fragmentarily expressed; the systematization is his own. (Bloomfield 1924: 318)

8.4 Further reading

As a legendary figure who is often credited with laying the theoretical foundations of structuralism and, by extension, much of linguistics and the other human sciences in the twentieth century, Saussure is the subject of a vast secondary literature, of varying quality. The best starting point would have to be John Joseph's (2012) *Saussure*, a comprehensive biography that weaves Saussure's life, work and thought into a single narrative. A summary of the key aspects of Saussure's life and work can be found in Joseph's (2017) article 'Ferdinand de Saussure' in the online *Oxford Research Encyclopedia of Linguistics*.

Saussure's major work, the *Cours de linguistique générale*, first published posthumously in 1916, is quite readable today, even if it may be obscure in parts. There are numerous editions of this text, but the most reliable version is perhaps the 1922 second edition edited by Charles Bally and Albert Sechehaye. The best English translation is that by Wade Baskin (Saussure 1959 [1916]).

9 The phoneme

A basic concept occupying a central place in much of linguistic theory and analysis in the twentieth century is that of the 'phoneme'. In this chapter, we trace the emergence of the phoneme concept in the last decades of the nineteenth century, and show how the successive developments it underwent reflect the broader transitions in linguistics around the turn of the century.

Before we embark on the historical discussion, we should briefly review what 'phoneme' means to most present-day linguists. The phoneme remains an important concept in linguistics today, and phonemic analysis of one stripe or another is among the earliest topics taught in any introductory linguistics course. The core idea behind the phoneme is that, while there might be a huge number of sounds which the human mouth can articulate and which the human ear can perceive, each language uses only a restricted subset of these sounds to distinguish words. Even more importantly, the sounds used in a language vary in a way that is both regular, in the sense that we can formulate rules describing this variation, and arbitrary, in that the variation is not directly determined by any external facts of articulation or auditory perception, but is simply a fact about the structure of the sound system of each language.

For example, we can say that in English there are two phonemes, /p/ and /b/, which we usually write with the letters 'p' and 'b'. These are distinct phonemes because they contrast with one another and can be used to distinguish words. The only difference in sound between the words 'park', a grassy space with trees, and 'bark', the skin of one of those trees, is the first phoneme of the respective words, /p/ and /b/. On a phonetic level, the /p/ phoneme is voiceless – that is, it is produced without vibration of the vocal folds – while /b/ is voiced, articulated with vibration of the vocal folds. But the /p/ phoneme is not always pronounced in the same way. When we say 'park', the /p/ is aspirated – that is, released with a puff of air; symbolised as [pʰ] – but when we say 'spark', there is no aspiration: [p].

This is a consistent pattern in the sound system of English: when a voiceless stop follows /s/ at the beginning of a word, the stop is always unaspirated. Unaspirated [p] and aspirated [pʰ] never contrast with one another in English to distinguish words. For this reason, we can say that they are two variant realisations of a single phoneme. In modern linguistic parlance these variants are usually referred to as 'allophones'. This variation is part of the largely subconscious structure of the English language: most native English speakers who have not taken an introductory linguistics course would probably not even be aware of this consistent difference in pronunciation.

But this pattern in the English sound system is not a universal fact of human language. In a language like Hindi, for example, there is a contrast between aspirated and unaspirated voiceless stops, so [p] and [pʰ] constitute two separate phonemes, /p/ and /pʰ/, as in the Hindi words *pal* 'moment' vs *pʰal* 'fruit'. Indeed, in Hindi there is also an aspirated voiced /bʰ/ which contrasts with unaspirated voiced /b/, as in /baːp/ 'father' vs /bʰaːp/ 'steam'. This [bʰ] is a sound that does not occur in English at all. In Hindi there are therefore four distinct phonemes in a phonetic space out of which English carves only two phonemes.

This present-day conception of the phoneme did not appear all at once. In the following sections, we survey the gradual process – spread out over several decades – in which the concept of the phoneme took on the characteristics that define it today.

9.1 The first steps towards theorisation

Despite its technical appearance, imparted through its pseudo-Greek form, the term 'phoneme' was in circulation before it was associated with any clear theoretical notion. According to the historian of linguistics Joachim Mugdan (1985, 2011, 2014), the term is first attested in the writings of the French linguist Antoni Dufriche-Desgenettes (1804–1878), and gained some currency in discussions and publications of the Société de Linguistique de Paris in the 1870s. In these discussions, 'phoneme' was simply used to refer to sounds in language without any explicit definition. But it is from here that the term was taken up and filled out with theoretical content.

The first steps towards theorisation came with Ferdinand de Saussure's (1857–1913) use of the term in his 1879 *Mémoire* on the original sound system of Indo-European vowels, a text we introduced in Section 8.1. In this work, on which his reputation in his own lifetime largely rested, Saussure presented a brilliant reconstruction of the Proto-Indo-European vowel system. The great methodological breakthrough underlying Saussure's approach was to treat the reconstructed vowels as abstract units in a system rather than as concrete sounds. One name Saussure used to refer to these reconstructed forms was *phonème*, perhaps because this term existed as a suggestive neologism but was still not aligned with any particular theoretical position. The term allowed Saussure to indicate that he was talking about some sort of hypothetical construct without specifying precisely what it was.

Saussure's analysis in the *Mémoire* inspired many other scholars working at the time, in particular two Polish linguists: Jan Baudouin de Courtenay (1845–1929) and his student Mikołaj Kruszewski (1851–1887). Baudouin de Courtenay and Kruszewski were both ethnic Poles but subjects of the Russian Tsar. In the period in which they worked together, in the 1870s and 80s, there was no Polish state: the country had been divided up at the end of the eighteenth century between Russia, Prussia and Austria, and only regained its independence at the end of World War I. Baudouin de Courtenay and Kruszewski both came from Polish territories that had been incorporated into the Russian Empire. They worked together deep in the empire, at the University of Kazan, in the capital of the Russian region of Tartarstan, where Baudouin was professor from 1875 to 1883. We might add that Baudouin de Courtenay could trace his ancestry to the French aristocracy, even though his family had been settled in Poland for several generations: this is the reason for his remarkable Gallic surname.

In his lectures throughout the 1870s, Baudouin de Courtenay recognised two perspectives on the study of sounds in language: sounds can be examined from an articulatory and acoustic point of view, or they can treated as psychological entities that carry meaning and distinguish forms in language. He noted that from the psychological perspective the sounds of every language constitute a system that is peculiar to that language, much like the tones of a musical scale (see Jakobson 1971 [1960]: 400). In his Program of Lectures for 1876 to 1877, a syllabus for his university course, Baudouin wrote: 'Physiologically identical sounds of different languages have a distinctive value depending on (their place within) the entire sound system, and their relation to other sounds. [. . .] Comparison with the tones of music' (Baudouin de Courtenay 1972 [1877]: 94).

This statement from Baudouin looks very much like a formulation of the central insight of present-day phonemic theory: that every language has its own arbitrary sound system which configures concrete sounds in different ways. But we have to be careful not to read too much into it. This statement appears in the section of Baudouin's course dedicated to comparative-historical reconstruction and is best understood in the context of the latest Neogrammarian work, which also made a distinction between physiological and psychological aspects of sound change – as we discussed in Sections 6.2 and 6.3 – and which already used algebraic placeholders to represent hypothetical sounds in reconstructed sound systems. We will recall from Section 8.1 that when Saussure's *Mémoire* appeared, he was accused by his Neogrammarian teachers of plagiarism. Whatever the merits of those specific claims, we can definitely say that system-oriented thinking was widespread in 1870s linguistic scholarship.

Furthermore, Baudouin de Courtenay did not use the term 'phoneme' in these lectures. Of the two Polish linguists, it was Kruszewski who first used the term in print, in his master's thesis, published in 1881. The topic of Kruszewski's thesis was what he called 'sound alternations', the regular variation in the sounds of a language. But Kruszewski's sound alternation went far beyond the allophonic variation we discussed in the introduction to this chapter: his alternations mixed synchronic and diachronic considerations, and were not strictly phonological in character, but included also morphological alternations.

In his 1881 thesis, Kruszewski used the term 'phoneme' (фонема in Russian; *Phonem* in Kruszewski's own German translation) to designate the psychological sound under consideration as opposed to the physical sound that is actually produced, following the distinction between the psychological and physical that Baudouin de Courtenay was already making. According to Baudouin de Courtenay's later testimony (see Jakobson 1971 [1960]: 405), Kruszewski was inspired to call this psychological unit the 'phoneme' because of Saussure's usage of this term in his *Mémoire*.

From the 1880s onwards, Baudouin de Courtenay also began using the term 'phoneme' to name the 'psychological equivalent of a speech sound' (Baudouin de Courtenay 1895: 9; English translation in Baudouin de Courtenay 1972 [1895]: 152). This is how 'phoneme' is defined in his 1895 book *Versuch einer Theorie phonetischer Alternationen* (Attempt at a theory of phonetic alternations). But the precise concept that he attached to the term 'phoneme' was still not identical to our present-day notion. In particular, Baudouin de Courtenay's phoneme continued to be tied up with morphological considerations. Around the beginning of the 1880s, he introduced another term that he coined on the model of phoneme: 'morpheme'. Baudouin de Courtenay's 'morpheme' did mean more or less what this term means today. In his 1895 book, he defines 'morpheme' as the minimal meaning-bearing unit of a word, subsuming the concepts of root, affix, and so on (Baudouin de Courtenay 1895: 10; English translation in Baudouin de Courtenay 1972 [1895]: 153).

Saussure took notice of Baudouin de Courtenay and Kruszewski's work on sound alternations and their conceptual and terminological innovations. We know this from notes Saussure made to himself which have survived among his private papers. *Phonème* is a term that Saussure (1922 [1916]) took up again in his *Cours de linguistique générale* – which we introduced in Section 8.2 – where he used it to name the abstract units into which language speakers divide the stream of speech (see Joseph 2012: 495–500). In the published version of the *Cours* we can read: '[A] phoneme is the sum of auditory impressions and articulatory movements, the unit heard and the unit spoken, each conditioning the other' (Saussure 1922 [1916]: 65; English translation in Saussure 1959 [1916]: 40).

On Saussure's definition in the *Cours*, the phoneme is something that has to do with the production and perception of speech. For this reason, Saussure considered the phoneme – somewhat surprisingly – to be an entity that belongs to *la parole* and not *la langue*. This is surprising because key elements of our current concept of phoneme are in a sense built into Saussure's notion of *la langue*. We will recall from Section 8.2 Saussure's (1922 [1916]: 166) statement that 'in a language [*dans la langue*] there are only differences *without positive terms*' (English translation in Saussure 1959 [1916]: 120). The differences – whether in meaning or in sound images – are inherent features of *la langue*. Saussure therefore maintained the idea that the significant differences which distinguish one sound image from another are part of the abstract and arbitrary system of a language, but he did not use the term 'phoneme' in this connection.

By the beginning of the twentieth century, the term 'phoneme' was already used in a number of different senses, but none of these corresponds exactly to the concept of phoneme as it is generally understood in present-day linguistics. The main steps towards theorisation of the concept came from the work of Baudouin de Courtenay and Kruszewski in Russia, which was absorbed back into scholarship in the German- and French-speaking worlds. But, as we see in the next section, there is another line of research that helped to shape the modern concept of the phoneme: the development of systems of phonetic transcription.

9.2 Phonetic alphabets

In his discussion of 'phonemes' as elements of *la parole*, which we saw at the end of the last section, Saussure observed that phonemes are the units of writing into which a perfectly functioning alphabet will break up words. He cited the early Greek alphabet – which he no doubt idealised to some extent – as the best illustration of this principle. In the earliest stages of the Greek alphabet, so Saussure (1922 [1916]: 39) claimed, each simple sound is always represented by a single graphic sign and each graphic sign always stands for the same simple sound.

Saussure is making an insightful point here: the alphabet essentially represents a pre-theoretical phonemic analysis of the language that it writes. But this is an ideal that is rarely realised in practice. When alphabets are adapted to previously unwritten languages, there are often sounds that escape easy transcription with the letters available. This difficulty is clearly observable in the case of the Roman alphabet, which has been adapted to transcribe and provide orthographies for languages from all over the world. When new sounds not anticipated by the Roman alphabet are encountered, the approach usually taken is not to create new letters to represent these sounds, but to add diacritics or to combine existing letters into digraphs. The mismatch of sound and spelling is frequently compounded by conservative or etymologically minded orthographies that further interfere with the principle of one sound to one letter. The way a slightly modified Roman alphabet is used to write present-day English exemplifies all these problems.

Nevertheless, the alphabet seems to embody the principles underlying the phoneme. We might even prefer to say that the modern notion of the phoneme merely represents a conscious theorisation of the alphabet, as it has been used for several thousand years. Indeed, the development of the phoneme concept received significant impetus from efforts to adapt the Roman alphabet in a systematic way to the writing of languages in the wider world, to turn it into a philosophically sound universal alphabet. European explorers, philologists and Christian missionaries had been using the Roman alphabet for centuries in a more or less ad hoc fashion to transcribe words from the languages they encountered around the world. Missionaries, in particular, frequently sought to devise orthographies for the languages they worked with as a foundation for the translation of the Bible and other Christian texts.

Philologists and other academic language scholars increasingly called for a more systematic approach. One notable effort in this direction was the 'Alphabetical Conferences' organised in London in 1854 by the Prussian ambassador to England and amateur Egyptologist Christian Karl Josias Bunsen (1791–1860; see Bunsen 1854: 377–488). At this meeting the German Egyptologist Karl Richard Lepsius (1810–1884) presented his 'Standard Alphabet', outlines of which were subsequently published in 1855 in both German and English editions. Lepsius's alphabet, in various versions, found widespread adoption in nineteenth-century philological works. It was endorsed by the Church Missionary Society, the chief Anglican missionary organisation, which paid for the printing and dissemination of later editions of Lepsius's book – the title page of the 1863 English edition states proudly: 'recommended for adoption by the Church Missionary Society'.

Friedrich Max Müller (1823–1900) – who we met in Section 5.1 as a foe of William Dwight Whitney – was another keen participant in the Alphabetical Conferences, where he presented his own scheme. For his part, Whitney was commissioned to devise an alphabet for writing American languages by the US government Bureau of American Ethnology (see McElvenny 2019b: 39).

The nineteenth century also witnessed great advances in phonetics, the scientific study of the articulatory and perceptual basis of sounds in language. While these advances informed the various adaptations of the Roman alphabet proposed in this period, many phoneticians sought to liberate themselves from the cumbersome cultural heritage of the Roman alphabet, with its arbitrary and illogical forms, and develop entirely new scripts that adhered to the principles of phonetic science. Perhaps the most famous phonetic script of this era built around a priori written forms is the 'Visible Speech' of Alexander Melville Bell (1819–1905), the father of Alexander Graham Bell (1847–1922), who is often credited as the inventor of the telephone. The symbols of Alexander Melville Bell's (1867) Visible Speech – which can be seen in Figure 9.1 – were intended to represent the position of the articulatory organs in making each sound.

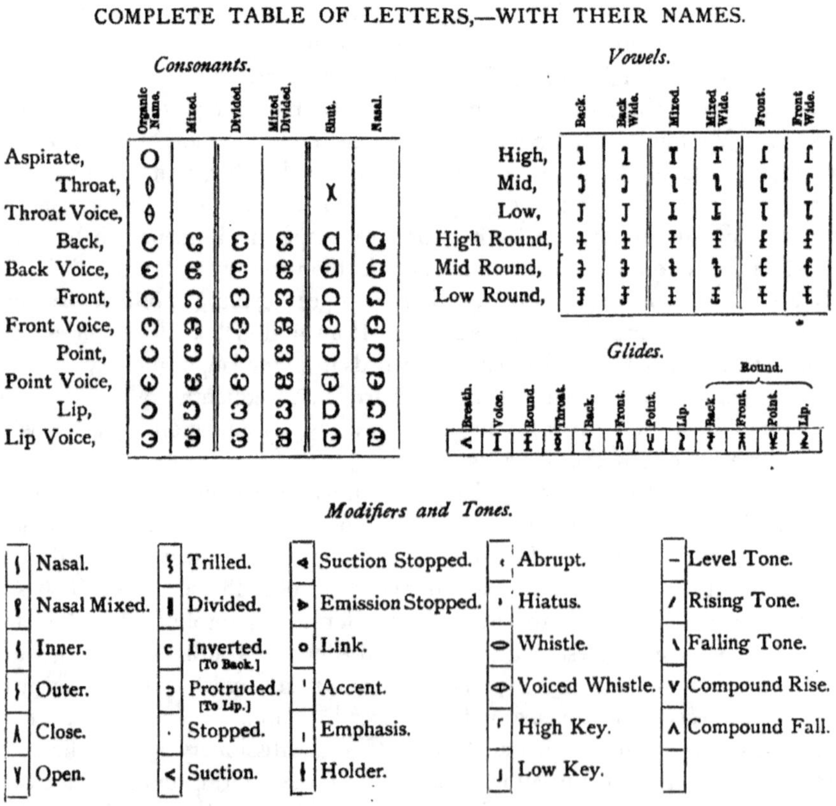

Figure 9.1 The letters of Alexander Melville Bell's (1867: 37) Visible Speech

The system of shorthand devised by Isaac Pitman (1813–1897) earlier in the century – which found use among journalists, secretaries and others up into the twentieth century for the rapid transcription of speech – had similar ambitions to scientific rigour in its representation of phonetic details (see Pitman 1840 [1837]). These systems were variously presented as initiatives for spelling reform – that is, as replacements for existing national orthographies – as well as means for teaching foreign languages, assisting deaf children in the acquisition of spoken language, and as systems of universal transcription.

The International Phonetic Association, which today is the main international learned society of phoneticians, was founded in Paris in 1886 by a group of language teachers who were principally interested in applying new phonetic methods to the teaching of modern languages. The society was initially called the 'Phonetic Teachers' Association', and its journal originally bore the title *The Phonetic Teacher*; a few years later the journal adopted the French title *Le Maître phonétique* (see Ashby and Tabain 2020; MacMahon 1986).

The founders of the Phonetic Teachers' Association were part of the so-called 'Reform Movement' in language teaching, which rallied around the 1882 manifesto of Wilhelm Viëtor (1850–1918), *Der Sprachunterricht muss umkehren!* (Language teaching must turn around!). Viëtor called for a radical change of direction in the teaching of modern languages, away from the rote memorisation of grammatical rules and vocabulary to the learning of languages through actual use. A central plank of Viëtor's proposal was a new emphasis on listening competence and correct pronunciation, to be helped along by adequate phonetic transcription.

The driving force behind the founding of the Phonetic Teachers' Association was the French phonetician Paul Passy (1859–1940), in co-operation with a number of like-minded colleagues, in particular the English phonetician Henry Sweet (1845–1912). In his 1877 *Handbook of Phonetics*, Sweet presented his 'Romic' transcription system. As the name suggests, Sweet's Romic was based on the Roman alphabet, a choice he made because the letters, whatever their theoretical faults, had proven their practical value over millennia of use (see Sweet 1877: 173). Romic followed many of the conventions established by existing systems based on Roman letters, and went on to directly inform the International Phonetic Alphabet later promulgated by the International Phonetic Association, which remains in use to this day, with many rounds of revision and reform.

Sweet offered his Romic alphabet in two forms: 'Narrow Romic' and 'Broad Romic'. Narrow Romic was capable of indicating all the minor distinctions of articulation that can be found in the world's languages, while Broad Romic was intended as a practical alternative for the transcription of a single language. Sweet emphasised the practical nature of Broad Romic, because of his hopes that it would find use in the reform of English spelling. His book bears the subtitle 'including a popular exposition of the principle of spelling reform', and contains a long appendix demonstrating how Romic could replace existing English orthography. In introducing Broad Romic, Sweet wrote:

> In treating the relations of sounds without going into minute details, and in giving passages of any length in phonetic writing, and especially in dealing with a limited

number of sounds, as in treating a single language, it is necessary to have an alphabet which indicates only those broader distinctions of sound which actually correspond to distinctions of meaning in language, and indicates them by letters which can easily be written and remembered. (Sweet 1877: 103)

Broad Romic therefore encapsulates a central idea of the classical phoneme concept, namely that the decisive factor in identifying phonemes is whether there is a phonetic contrast that serves to distinguish one word from another: 'those broader distinctions of sound which actually correspond to distinctions of meaning in language'. Passy adopted essentially the same principle in his own efforts at phonetic transcription. In his 1887 *Les sons du français, leur formation, leur combinaison, leur représentation* (The sounds of French: their formation, their combination, their representation), Passy wrote: '[W]e will distinguish two sounds when they serve or can serve to distinguish two words; we will merge them when their distinction would be useless from the point of view of meaning' (Passy 1887: 51).

Joachim Mugdan (1985: 146) has argued that this line of research into 'broad' phonetic transcription is what ultimately led to the formulation of the phoneme as the phonological unit – usually consisting of several phonetic variants – that can distinguish words. Mugdan locates the first attestation of this formulation in a 1912 paper by the Russian linguist Lev Shcherba (1880–1944), who wrote:

> [A] phoneme is the shortest general phonetic representation in a given language that is capable of associating with representation of meaning and of differentiating words and that can be emphasized in speech without distorting the phonetic structure of the word. (Shcherba 1912: 14, quoted in Mugdan 1985: 146)

Shcherba was a student of Baudouin de Courtenay from later in Baudouin de Courtenay's career, after he had become professor in St Petersburg, and as such the direct heir of Baudouin de Courtenay and Kruszewski's work on alternations. Shcherba was also in close contact with Passy. Mugdan contends that it is the convergence of the analysis of alternations and the accompanying terminology pioneered by Baudouin de Courtenay and Kruszewski with the theorisation of alphabetic principles in phonetic transcription systems that resulted in the modern notion of the phoneme. This notion would soon serve as the centrepiece of the structuralist conceptualisation and analysis of language, as we see in the next chapter.

9.3 Further reading

The most thorough investigation of the history of the phoneme concept is offered by Joachim Mugdan (1985, 2011, 2014) in a series of papers he published from the 1980s to the mid-2010s. The first of these is the most complete, his 1985 'The origin of the phoneme: Farewell to a myth' in the journal *Lingua Posnaniensis*.

A classical account of the contributions of Baudouin de Courtenay and Kruszewski to phonological theory can be found in Roman Jakobson's

(1971 [1960]) essay 'The Kazan' School of Polish linguistics and its place in the international development of phonology'. As we see in the next chapter, Jakobson was not only a historian of linguistics but also a key figure in the development and dissemination of structuralism. This dual role leads to a certain degree of myth-making in his historiography; his historiographic writings should therefore be approached with some caution. Mugdan's (2021) article on Baudouin de Courtenay in the *Oxford Bibliographies of Linguistics* offers the most up-to-date summary of scholarship on Baudouin de Courtenay and the Kazan School.

For a potted history of the International Phonetic Association, see Michael MacMahon's (1986) paper 'The International Phonetic Association: The first 100 years', in the *Journal of the International Phonetic Association*. For an exploration of the interaction between linguistic theory and colonial ideology in nineteenth-century Western scholars' extension of European alphabetic writing to languages around the world, see my 2019 paper 'Alternating sounds and the formal franchise in phonology', in the volume *Form and Formalism in Linguistics* (McElvenny 2019b).

10 Prague Circle structuralism

In this chapter, we arrive in the classical age of linguistic structuralism. 'Structuralism' is a term that played an outsized role in the twentieth-century humanities and social sciences, especially in the French-speaking world, where structuralist ideas came to serve as the general background to much work in such fields as anthropology, sociology and literary studies. While the various forms of structuralism that appeared up to the mid-twentieth century all had their own character, their generally acknowledged source lay in methodological and epistemological innovations emanating from linguistics.

The Russian linguist Roman Jakobson (1896–1982) is one of the central figures here, for his pioneering contributions to linguistic structuralism and also for the cross-pollination he effected between centres of learning in Europe and North America, and between different academic disciplines. Originally from Moscow, his peripatetic career included major stations in Prague, New York and Boston. His own work was not confined to linguistics, but included also literary studies, and he was in close contact with scholars working in anthropology and cybernetics.

It was Jakobson who first used the term 'structuralism' in print in a specifically linguistic sense. At the time, 'structuralism' already had some currency as a label for the theories of the Anglo-American psychologist Edward B. Titchener (1867–1927; see, e.g., Angell 1907), a student of Wilhelm Wundt (1832–1920), who we have met at several points in this book. But there are no direct connections between Titchener's psychology and Jakobson's linguistic structuralism. Rather, both Titchener's and Jakobson's work drew on common elements in the intellectual environment of the time. We might add that Titchener did not use the term 'structuralism' himself; he usually referred to his work as 'structural psychology' (e.g. Titchener 1898, 1909).

Jakobson developed his main structuralist ideas while working in Prague, where he was a core member of the Prague Linguistic Circle, and where he collaborated closely with fellow Russian linguist Nikolai Trubetzkoy (1890–1938). Trubetzkoy was professor of Slavic philology in Vienna and a key associate of the Prague Circle. The Prague Circle itself was a group of language scholars that formed around the Czech linguist Vilém Mathesius (1882–1945), professor of English philology at the Charles University in Prague.

The Prague Circle was an academic discussion group of a kind that was a feature of intellectual life in 1920s Central Europe. Another more famous 'circle' that we might want to compare it to is the Vienna Circle, which gave birth to logical positivism, one of the foundations of analytic philosophy (we meet the Vienna Circle properly in Section 16.3). The Vienna Circle, Prague Circle, and other similar circles of this era served as venues for academic debate, although each circle usually developed a party line, spelt out in a manifesto. These circles were also generally in contact with one another and exchanged ideas. In the following sections, we look at the character of the Prague Circle and its work, and see how its formulation of 'structuralism' shaped the further course of linguistics and humanities scholarship in the twentieth century.

10.1 Structuralism and phonology

The year in which the official position of the Prague Circle coalesced was 1928. In this year, the Circle members began preparing a series of 'Thèses' – essentially amounting to a manifesto – that were presented at the First International Conference of Slavists, held in Prague the following year, 1929 (see Durnovo et al. 1929). In connection with this public appearance of the Prague Circle, Roman Jakobson published an article in the popular press outlining the Circle's programme. It was in this article that he used 'structuralism' in a specifically linguistic sense for the first time. Jakobson wrote:

> Were we to comprise the leading idea of present-day science in its most various manifestations, we could hardly find a more appropriate designation than *structuralism*. Any set of phenomena examined by contemporary science is treated not as a mechanical agglomeration but as a structural whole, and the basic task is to reveal the inner, whether static or developmental, laws of this system. (Jakobson 2012 [1929]: 231, quoted from Jakobson 1971 [1929]: 711; Jakobson's italics)

The central preoccupation of structuralism, according to Jakobson, is therefore to capture and account for the 'structural whole' of languages, with the aim of revealing the 'inner [. . .] laws of this system'. The Prague Circle 'Thèses' (Durnovo et al. 1929) expand on this point to assert that the best way to capture the language system is to examine it in its synchronic aspect as a means of expression appropriate to a particular communicative end.

The methodological prototype embodying the conception of language and language study advocated in these programmatic texts was the approach to phonological research pioneered by Jakobson and his fellow Prague Circle member Nikolai Trubetzkoy. An incidental detail related by Jindřich Toman (1995: 144) in his history of the Prague Circle illustrates the key role Jakobson and Trubetzkoy's phonology played for the Circle: the hint for the password to the Circle's bank account, scrawled in their savings book, was 'The Main Area'; that is, the main area of the Circle's scholarly interests. The solution to this riddle was 'the discipline represented by N. S. T[rubetzkoy]'s name' – phonology.

The centrepiece of Jakobson and Trubetzkoy's phonology was phonemic analysis. As we saw in the previous chapter, the concept of the phoneme as the abstract unit that defines the phonological system of a language largely emerged in the school that formed around the Polish linguist Jan Baudouin de

Courtenay (1845–1929), who taught at various centres in the Russian Empire. While Jakobson and Trubetzkoy were never students of Baudouin de Courtenay, they were exposed to the tradition he established. Both Jakobson and Trubetzkoy came from Moscow, and had received the bulk of their education there before their emigration. Both left Russia in the early 1920s as the Bolsheviks secured their hold on power in the years following the October Revolution. Trubetzkoy's reasons for leaving the country were fairly clear: he was in fact Prince Trubetzkoy, a member of the high aristocracy, and therefore had great difficulty reconciling himself with the revolution. Jakobson, on the other hand, had a more ambivalent relationship to the revolution: he was initially enthusiastic about the renewal it promised but soon became disillusioned with the Bolsheviks.

Despite leaving Russia, both scholars remained within the conceptual world in which they had been raised, and indeed both remained committed to the idea of Russia. As the historian of linguistics Patrick Sériot (2014, 2023) has shown, Jakobson and Trubetzkoy were deeply invested in 'Eurasianism', the idea that the Russian Empire – and its successor, the Soviet Union – formed a natural cultural, linguistic and political unit. As Trubetzkoy put it: 'Eurasia represents an integral whole, both geographically and anthropologically. [. . .] By its very nature, Eurasia is historically destined to comprise a single state unity' (Trubetzkoy 1991 [1925]: 165). Jakobson and Trubetzkoy's Eurasianism found expression in their linguistic work in the notion of the *Sprachbund* or 'language union'. A supercharged diffusionist model, related to the wave theory that we saw in Section 7.2, Jakobson and Trubetzkoy's *Sprachbund* describes the situation in which a group of geographically contiguous languages converge typologically, even though they may have different genealogical origins. The languages of the Russian Empire, they argued, though belonging to diverse language families, have merged into a single organic type.

Jakobson and Trubetzkoy picked up the term and concept of phoneme as it had developed in Russian linguistics in the early twentieth century and took it in new directions. The classical definition of the phoneme as it was understood by Jakobson and Trubetzkoy can be found in Trubetzkoy's 1939 *Grundzüge der Phonologie* (*Principles of Phonology*), a book usually considered his magnum opus. Trubetzkoy wrote:

> Phonological units that, from the standard of a given language, cannot be analysed into still smaller successive distinctive units are phonemes. Accordingly the phoneme is the smallest distinctive unit of a given language. The signifier aspect of every word in the system of language can be analysed into phonemes, that is, it can be represented by a particular sequence of phonemes. (Trubetzkoy 1939: 34; English translation in Trubetzkoy 1969 [1939]: 35)

Here Trubetzkoy reiterates the key elements of the phoneme concept as defined by Lev Shcherba (1880–1944; Section 9.2): the phoneme is the smallest unit on the side of the signifier that serves to distinguish one word from another. Indeed, in a footnote Trubetzkoy cites Shcherba's definition of the phoneme.

But Trubetzkoy went a step further to consider the make-up of the phoneme itself. The phoneme, he added, is a bundle of phonologically distinct properties

(Trubetzkoy 1939: 35–6). There are phonetic differences in the sound system of each language that are significant and others that are not. For example, as we saw in the introduction to Chapter 9, aspiration on voiceless stops is a consistently patterned difference that occurs in the sound system of English, but this is not a difference that can distinguish one word from another. In English, it is only the presence or absence of voicing that serves to distinguish stops at the same place of articulation. Voicing is the distinctive feature, or 'phonologically relevant mark', as Trubetzkoy (ibid.) put it, that differentiates the English phoneme /p/ from the phoneme /b/.

Trubetzkoy's description of this difference as a 'phonologically relevant mark' reveals a further novelty of his conception of the phoneme. For Trubetzkoy, phonemes are not so much building blocks out of which words are made but rather 'distinctive marks' or significant elements into which the *Gestalt*, or whole shape, of the word can be analysed. He illustrated this approach with an analogy between the analysis of a word into phonemes and the analysis of a tune or melody into the musical tones out of which it is composed:

> Consequently one can say that each word can be *completely analysed* into phonemes, that is *consists of* phonemes in the same way as a tune composed in a major scale can be said to consist of the tones of that scale, although each tune will contain something that makes it a specific musical configuration. (Trubetzkoy 1939: 35; English translation in Trubetzkoy 1969 [1939]: 35; Trubetzkoy's italics)

The way in which phonemes are conceptualised not as components of words but as the products of analysis reveals much about the intellectual environment in which Trubetzkoy and Jakobson developed their phonological theory. Further telltale clues are the use of the term *Gestalt* and the analogy with a musical tune and its tones. In their conceptualisation of the phoneme, Trubetzkoy and Jakobson were deeply indebted to contemporary work in Gestalt psychology. We look at this influence, and the broader background to their structuralism, in the next section.

10.2 The sources of structuralism

Although Jakobson and his Prague Circle colleagues gave structuralism its name, they never claimed to have invented it. The great thinker to whom they attributed the insights animating their approach was Ferdinand de Saussure (1857–1913), specifically the Saussure of the *Cours de linguistique générale* (Saussure 1922 [1916]), which we examined in detail in Section 8.2. But Saussure was not the only source of inspiration for Jakobson and his colleagues. In fact, there are many ways in which Prague Circle doctrines differed from Saussure's, and even contradicted his ideas.

Even though Saussure is not mentioned by name in the Prague Circle's 1929 'Thèses', the text itself is constructed around the central theoretical pillars of the *Cours*: the dichotomies of synchrony and diachrony, *langue* and *parole*, and the notion of value. Two similar manifestos from the previous year, both authored principally by Jakobson, make explicit reference to Saussure: a paper on formalist literary analysis by Juri Tynianov (1894–1943) and Jakobson summons Saussure in support of the programme it outlines (Tynianov and Jakobson 1928), and the 'Proposition' presented to the First International Congress of Linguists by Jakobson, Trubetzkoy and their colleague Serge Karcevsky (1884–1955) sketches an approach to phonological research set out in Saussurean terms (Jakobson et al. 1971 [1928]).

It was in fact Karcevsky, one of the co-authors of this second text, who most likely introduced Jakobson to Saussure. Karcevsky had studied in Geneva from 1905 to 1917 and, although he was never enrolled in Saussure's course in general linguistics in its various iterations, he took other courses with Saussure and was most certainly aware of Saussure's ideas about general linguistics. On returning to Moscow in 1917, Karcevsky brought with him a copy of the published version of Saussure's *Cours*, which was keenly read within the Moscow Linguistic Circle, another of these early twentieth-century intellectual discussion groups, founded by Jakobson (see Joseph 2001: 1885).

Throughout his career, Jakobson continually cited the inspiration he claimed to have received from Saussure, even though there are other antecedents that would seem to have had a more direct influence on his ideas and methods. As we observed in the previous section, the concept of the phoneme that was central to his and Trubetzkoy's phonology owed much more to the work of Baudouin de Courtenay and his school. Indeed, there are respects in which Jakobson and Trubetzkoy's treatment of the phoneme is incompatible with Saussurean theory. From Section 8.2, we will recall Saussure's (1922 [1916]: 166) claim that 'in a language there are only differences *without positive terms*' (English translation in Saussure 1959 [1916]: 120). For Saussure, signifiers and signifieds are defined only by their differences from one another: the forms in which signifiers are realised and the things in the world that the signifieds refer to are completely irrelevant to the analysis of the linguistic system. But, as we saw in the previous section, Jakobson and Trubetzkoy did look at how the differences between phonemes are instantiated through 'distinctive features', such as place and manner of articulation.

Once they had turned their attention to the phonological substance of words, Jakobson and Trubetzkoy made the further discovery that not all distinctive features are created equal. In German, for example, voicing is a common feature that serves to distinguish many consonants, such as /d/ and /t/, two phonemes that differ from one another only in that the former is voiced and the latter voiceless. But the voicing contrast between these phonemes disappears – or is 'neutralised' – when they appear at the end of a word. The words *Rad* 'wheel' and *Rat* 'advice' are pronounced identically: [ʁaːt]. We know, however, that there is an underlying difference between the /d/ of *Rad* and the /t/ of *Rat* because when these phonemes are not at the end of the word, the contrast is retained: the plural form *Räder* is pronounced [ʁɛːdɐ], and the plural *Räte* [ʁɛːtə]. With this phenomenon in mind, Jakobson and Trubetzkoy argued that of the /d/ and /t/ in German, /d/ is the 'marked' form because it is distinguished by a feature that can be neutralised. Jakobson went on to investigate markedness from the perspectives of typology and language acquisition, and came to the conclusion that marked forms in a sense always represent an added burden for speakers. Marked sounds are, for example, less common cross-linguistically and tend to be learnt later by children (see Jakobson 1971 [1939]; Joseph et al. 2001: 19–26).

We will remember from the previous section that when Jakobson (1971 [1929]: 711) introduced 'structuralism' under this name, he identified its central task as being to capture the 'structural whole' of languages, which he contrasted to 'mechanical agglomerations'. The charge of treating languages as mechanical, atomistic phenomena was typically levelled against the Neogrammarians, who formed the dominant school of linguistic scholarship in the generation prior to Jakobson's (and who we met in Chapter 6). Although Jakobson (1971 [1929]) did not mention the Neogrammarians by name in this particular text, he was more explicit about his intended target in other texts written around this time (such as Jakobson et al. 1971 [1928]). Overcoming this alleged atomistic view was one of the achievements attributed to Saussure, even though, as we saw in Section 8.1, in his own lifetime Saussure's methodological breakthroughs, enabled by his conception of language as a system, were widely considered contributions to Neogrammarian scholarship.

It is important not to focus too closely on Saussure. The general principles of Prague Circle structuralism and the tenor of the arguments advanced in its favour are part of the broader intellectual climate of the time. Jakobson (1971 [1929]: 711) himself described structuralism as the 'leading idea of present-day science in its most various manifestations'. This was by no means an exaggeration, and Jakobson was not alone in this contention. We might cite the example of the German Neo-Kantian philosopher Ernst Cassirer (1874–1945), who later endorsed Jakobson's totalising claims for structuralism as embodying the guiding principles of contemporary science (see Cassirer 1945). The holism and system-oriented thinking that characterised Jakobson's structuralism, and the polemical contrast to atomistic and mechanical thinking were not a peculiarity of linguistic scholarship in this period, but could be found across the arts and sciences.

This holistic trend was especially pronounced in biology, medicine and psychology in the German-speaking world, where it was often – although not necessarily – bound up with a conservative, traditionalist world view. Due to the prestige of German science in this era, such positions enjoyed international currency. In their 2007 book *Objectivity*, the historians of science Lorraine Daston and Peter Galison discuss epistemological manifestations of such system-oriented ideas under the rubric of 'structural objectivity'. They highlight how researchers around the turn of the nineteenth to the twentieth century working on such disparate topics as the science of colour perception, the fundamentals of geometry and arithmetic, and the nature of physical space and time converged on the idea that we cannot know the world in its material substance, but rather that all we know are the relations between things in the world. Our perceptual capacities allow us to reach agreement on the relations between things in the world and this is what grants us objective knowledge.

Such ideas were widespread, but one of the most prominent strands of research that had a direct influence on Jakobson, Trubetzkoy and the Prague Circle more broadly was Gestalt psychology, which also emerged in the first decades of the twentieth century. There were various schools of Gestalt psychology, each with its own unique emphases, but uniting them all was the belief that human cognition is fundamentally holistic. The core area of Gestalt research was the psychology of perception. Gestalt psychologists carried out experiments designed to demonstrate how, when we encounter a phenomenon in the world, we first perceive the phenomenon as a whole and only then do we analyse it into parts. Gestalt psychologists generally contrasted their work to that of the philosopher and psychologist Wilhelm Wundt. Although Wundt acknowledged Gestalt processes, he still preferred to build up perception from atomistic sense data.

Throughout his writings, Jakobson cited the influence of Gestalt psychology on his own ideas. In the previous section, we saw Trubetzkoy (1939: 35) employ the terminology of Gestalt theory when he described phonemes as 'Gestalts'. The recurring comparison of the phonological systems of languages to musical melodies and keys, made by both Baudouin de Courtenay and Trubetzkoy – as we saw in the previous section and Section 9.1 – provides another textual link between structuralism and Gestalt theory. Christian von Ehrenfels (1859–1932), professor of philosophy in Prague from 1896 until 1929 and an inspiration to the first generation of Gestalt psychologists, famously highlighted in his 1890 essay 'Über Gestaltqualitäten' (On Gestalt qualities) the fact that a musical melody can be transposed into different keys and still be recognised as the same melody (Ehrenfels 1890: 262). A melody therefore does not consist in the exact notes that are played but in the relations between the notes. The recurring analogy of phonemes in a phonological system to tones in a melody or musical scale makes precisely the same point.

Avant-garde art in this period also took a turn that fed into structuralist thought. Jakobson was fond of pointing to the cubist movement in visual art, which typically involved abstract representations of the subject broken down into its elements, often shown simultaneously from different viewpoints. In the realm of language, Jakobson was closely associated with the literary movement of Russian Futurism and its genre of *zaum* – or 'transrational' poetry – which abandoned grammatical language and even words with a clear denotational meaning and instead embraced the creation of new word forms based on onomatopoeia and sound symbolism (see Waugh and Monville-Burston 2002: vi–xi).

The theoretical and methodological innovations of Prague School structuralism – and even the rhetoric with which they were put forward – accorded with the broader intellectual climate of the time. There was a general shift towards holistic and system-oriented thinking, which was usually presented in polemical opposition to the supposed atomism of previous generations. Emerging out of this milieu, structuralism gained in prominence and soon spread from its home in linguistics to many other humanities and social sciences.

10.3 The spread of structuralism

Jakobson was not only a driving force in the formation of structuralism within the Prague Circle, but was also responsible for spreading the ideas and methods it represented to different centres of linguistic scholarship and across disciplines. With the outbreak of World War II in 1939, Jakobson left Czechoslovakia, and ultimately Europe, departing for America in 1941. During this period of turmoil, he came into contact with numerous other scholars – many of whom were also displaced – and inspired them with the structuralist spirit.

Jakobson's first station on leaving Czechoslovakia was Denmark, a country that had declared itself neutral at the beginning of the war. In Denmark, Jakobson spent some months in close contact with the Copenhagen Linguistic Circle around Louis Hjelmslev (1899–1965). The Copenhagen Circle had been founded in 1931 on the model of the Prague Circle, and its members understood their work to be a variety of structuralism, kindred to that of the Prague Circle's. The Copenhagen Circle became known for the theory of 'glossematics', developed principally by Hjelmslev, in collaboration with Hans Jørgen Uldall (1907–1957). Highly abstract in nature, glossematics aimed to provide an axiomatised, formal account of language. Although the core principles of glossematics were already articulated in the 1930s, it was only after World War II that the theory found a broader reception (see further Rischel 2001; Thomas 2011: 201–6).

As Nazi Germany successively occupied Denmark and Norway, Jakobson sought refuge outside Europe, sailing for New York in 1941. In New York he became part of the vibrant scene of émigré intellectuals that had congregated in that city. He taught at the École Libre des Hautes Études, where he attracted large audiences for his lectures on linguistics and structural analysis. The École Libre was a francophone university in exile hosted by the New School for Social Research and funded principally by the Rockefeller Foundation, a private philanthropic foundation established by the Rockefeller family in the early twentieth century.

One attentive listener in Jakobson's lectures in New York was another exiled academic, the French anthropologist Claude Lévi-Strauss (1908–2009), who adapted the methods of Jakobson's linguistic structuralism to ethnography. In his doctoral thesis, which he defended in Paris in 1948 and published in 1949 as *Les structures élémentaires de la parenté* (*The Elementary Structures of Kinship*), Lévi-Strauss applied structural analysis to the classical ethnographic topic of kinship. In the following years, Lévi-Strauss extended his structuralism to annex all of anthropology, an effort that culminated in his 1958 *Anthropologie structurale* (*Structural Anthropology*). Lévi-Strauss's example was emulated by French scholars in psychology, literary studies and history to the point that structuralism of one kind or another became the theoretical foundation of the francophone humanities and social sciences, with an influence felt internationally (see Dosse 1997 [1991], 1997 [1992]).

After World War II, Jakobson stayed in the United States, eventually becoming a professor at Harvard University. In this capacity, he continued to develop and propagate his brand of structuralism in America. His ideas intermingled to a certain extent with existing American linguistic scholarship, represented by such figures as Franz Boas (1858–1942), Boas's student Edward Sapir (1884–1939), and Leonard Bloomfield (1887–1949). We meet Boas, Sapir and Bloomfield properly in Chapters 14, 15 and 16, where we discuss the movement of 'American structuralism'.

Jakobson remained active right up until his death in 1982 and taught many generations of linguists as well as scholars working in allied fields. One prominent protégé of Jakobson in these years – even if he was not directly a student of Jakobson's – is Noam Chomsky (b. 1928), who in the 1950s introduced generative grammar, which became the dominant school of linguistics internationally in the second half of the twentieth century (we briefly resume this thread of our story at the end of Section 16.4). Chomsky's institutional base was the linguistics department at the Massachusetts Institute of Technology (MIT), only a few kilometres from Harvard University. Chomsky shaped the MIT linguistics department into its modern form with his long-time collaborator Morris Halle (1923–2018), another student of Jakobson's.

10.4 Further reading

The best historiographic treatment of the Prague Linguistic Circle, combining the intellectual and cultural history of the period with the biographies of Circle members, is Jindřich Toman's (1995) *The Magic of a Common Language: Jakobson, Mathesius, Trubetzkoy, and the Prague Linguistic Circle*.

For a thorough outline of Roman Jakobson's contributions to linguistic and literary scholarship, see Linda Waugh and Monique Monville-Burston's introduction to the revised (2002) third edition of volume 1 of Jakobson's *Selected Writings: Phonological Studies*. For an account of the spread of structuralism from linguistics to other humanities and social sciences, see John Joseph's (2001) article 'The exportation of structuralist ideas from linguistics to other fields: An overview' in volume 2 of the handbook *History of the Language Sciences*. On the key role this exported structuralism took on in French academia in the mid-twentieth century, and its ultimate demise, see François Dosse's (1991, 1992) two-volume *Histoire du structuralisme*, which is available in English translation under the title *History of Structuralism* (1997a, 1997b).

The place of holism in German and broader European thought, which influenced the development of structuralism, is examined superbly in Anne Harrington's (1996) *Reenchanted Science: Holism in German Culture from Wilhelm II to Hitler*. The classic history of Gestalt psychology, another major influence on the development of structuralism, is Mitchell Ash's (1995) *Gestalt Psychology in German Culture, 1890–1967: Holism and the Quest for Objectivity*.

11 The beginnings of functionalism

In the next three chapters, we turn our attention to a side of language scholarship that has often been relegated to the margins of disciplinary linguistics: the study of meaning in language. We start in this chapter by tracing the beginnings of a family of approaches that are usually grouped under the heading of 'functionalism'. Functionalist approaches in linguistics came into full bloom in the 1920s, but to understand how classical functionalism took shape, we first have to go back to the heyday of the Neogrammarians at the end of the nineteenth century. The key figure whose work we explore in this chapter is Philipp Wegener (1848–1916).

From a sociological perspective, Wegener is a somewhat unusual figure in our story so far, in that he was not a professor but rather a teacher in a Gymnasium – that is, an academically oriented German secondary school – eventually moving up the ranks to become a headmaster. Although Wegener held a doctorate, he did not pursue a university-based career and made his scholarly contributions from the institutional periphery. Nevertheless, his ideas were taken up in mainstream Neogrammarian scholarship and continued to serve as a source of inspiration to following generations.

Wegener's main work was a short book, published in 1885, with the title *Untersuchungen über die Grundfragen des Sprachlebens* (Investigations into fundamental questions of the life of language). In this book, he presented a theory of the nature of language which to his contemporaries seemed radically novel. Contrary to received opinion of the time, Wegener contended that the purpose of language is not so much to reflect ideas in the mind or to transmit ideas to others, but that language is above all a form of action, a way of influencing people. In order to understand precisely what Wegener meant and why this seemed so radical, we have to first survey the context in which he put forward his views.

11.1 Philipp Wegener and language as action

We will recall from Chapter 5 that disciplinary linguistics in the mid-nineteenth century saw a seismic shift in how language was conceived, principally due to the polemical efforts of the American Sanskritist and general linguist William Dwight Whitney (1827–1894). In the 1860s and 70s, Whitney went on the warpath against what he saw as the metaphysical excesses of the leading linguists of the time. He rejected what he called the 'physical' theory of August Schleicher

(1821–1868), which treated language as a 'symptom' of brain function, as well as the 'psychological' theory of Heymann Steinthal (1823–1899), which, as part of *Völkerpsychologie*, saw each language as an expression of the collective mind of a people. Against such conceptions, Whitney advocated a view of language as an 'institution'. That is, each language is a human construct, a resource we share with other members of the speech community, which we take up and deploy in order to convey what we want to say. For Whitney, language is not primarily a window onto our biology or our minds, but just a cultural artefact, the accumulated co-operative work of the speech community.

Whitney's view resonated with the realist and pragmatic spirit of disciplinary linguistics towards the end of the nineteenth century. In Section 6.3, we saw that the Neogrammarians received Whitney's ideas positively, while at the same time acknowledging Steinthal's contributions to the field. They praised Steinthal for highlighting the interplay between psychology and language, although they were interested only in his psychology of individuals and not his talk of a shared mind of the people. This tension in Neogrammarian scholarship is perhaps most visible in Hermann Paul's *Principien der Sprachgeschichte* (Principles of language history), the so-called 'Neogrammarian Bible'. In the first edition of 1880, Paul devoted considerable space to refuting Lazarus and Steinthal's notion of a collective mind in *Völkerpsychologie*, but he also expressed appreciation for Steinthal's individual psychology, which he then proceeded to emulate.

The details of Steinthal's psychological theory fluctuated over the decades in which it was developed, but in general we can say that Steinthal treated a linguistic expression as the externalisation of internal mental representations in the speaker. This picture is most clearly drawn in his 1871 *Abriss der Sprachwissenschaft* (Sketch of linguistics). Like many theorists of psychology in this era, Steinthal adapted the *Vorstellungsmechanik* (literally 'mechanics of representation') pioneered by Johann Friedrich Herbart (1776–1841) in the early years of the nineteenth century. Herbart's mechanics imagined human minds as a kind of space filled with mental 'representations' that float around and 'associate' with one another to form more complex representations.

In Steinthal's version of the *Vorstellungsmechanik*, forms in language encode the internal representations in the mind, allowing us to send them to a listener, who can then decode them. There is, however, a complication to this story. As we saw in Section 3.5, Steinthal was a follower of Wilhelm von Humboldt (1767–1835) and, like Humboldt, he did not believe language to be merely a passive medium. Rather, he imagined a dialectic relationship between language and thought: in the process of articulating thoughts, the underlying representations interact with the linguistic forms, with the result that each shapes the other. The ways in which language and thought mutually influence one other are primary manifestations of the supposed collective mind of the people that is studied in *Völkerpsychologie*.

While Hermann Paul and his Neogrammarian colleagues distanced themselves from the idea of a collective mind in *Völkerpsychologie* – in Steinthal and Lazarus's and later Wundt's version – they very much embraced the *Vorstellungsmechanik* and the conception of language as a means for encoding and transmitting mental representations. Given the influential position of the Neogrammarians at this time, their conception became more or less the default view in mainstream linguistics. It was in this intellectual environment that Wegener, in 1885, presented his alternative conception of language.

Against the view that language is essentially a medium for conveying fully formed thoughts from speaker to listener, Wegener argued that language is fundamentally a type of action, a way for the speaker to grab and direct the attention of the listener. To illustrate this point, Wegener (1885: 12–15) described his observations of language acquisition by children. He pointed out that a child's first utterances are calls such as 'mama' and 'bottle': these are spontaneous directives to the caregiver to come to the child's assistance and resolve a present problem. The caregiver is sensitive to these calls and driven to respond by a general feeling of empathy. The most basic form of language is therefore the imperative bound to the immediate situation.

Over time, continued Wegener (1885: 15–19), the child will gradually develop a sense of displacement in their use of language. They will name objects that they wish to hold, such as their doll, thereby expressing a striving towards the future; or they may say 'bumped' or 'door' or 'rock' and thereby recount a past experience of falling over. The child will be able to modulate these minimal utterances with different tones of voice to make it clear whether they mean them as imperatives, expressions of desire, or the imparting of information.

But even as our language develops beyond the most basic cries for immediate attention and assistance, it always retains its imperative character. The only reason we talk, claimed Wegener (1885: 67), is to have some effect on the listener: 'The purpose of our speaking is always to influence the will or the knowledge of a person in such a way as seems worthwhile to the speaker.' This purpose is clear in commands, requests and demands, but it also holds, argued Wegener (ibid.: 65–7), in all other uses of language, even when we make statements and ask questions. When we make a statement, we want to make the listener aware of our point of view. Asking a question is in turn a kind of demand on the listener to provide information. Even light-hearted chatter has the goal of influencing the listener in order to cultivate good relations with them or to impress them. For Wegener, dialogue is the primary use of language: language is about the back and forth between interlocutors, as each influences the other. It is not primarily a matter of the monologic expression of representations.

In addition to highlighting the active nature of language, Wegener noted the importance of context to language use. Wegener (1885: 19–27) pointed out that the listener can only make sense of what the speaker says if both speaker and listener have access to a shared 'situation' or context. Once the shared context is secured, the speaker can comment on it, whether that is to provide new information about it, request some action from the listener in it, or similar. The 'situation' in which the speaker and listener find themselves is not only the immediate perceptual situation – that is, the time and place in which they are physically located – but also a common past that speaker and listener have through memories of shared experiences.

How the speaker and listener construe words is also dependent on their background, what Wegener calls their situations of consciousness and of culture.

These will be determined by their profession, interests, upbringing, and so on. Wegener (1885: 22–3) observes that most people, on hearing the sentence 'The boards have been freshly painted', will think of the weatherboards of a house. But if an actor says, 'The boards that mean the world', we will no doubt assume that they mean the floorboards of a stage. He also asks what ideas a French person would associate with the word 'Prussian' (ibid.: 25). At this time, in 1885, France and Prussia were still very much mortal enemies: just over a decade before, Prussia had humiliated France and established its hegemony in Central Europe through its victory in the Franco-Prussian War. Presumably the ideas that would come to the French person's mind when they heard the word 'Prussian' would be rather different from those in the average Prussian's mind.

As we will see in the next two chapters, these key features of Wegener's theory – language as action, and the analysis of the situation of speaking – were later picked up and elaborated by a number of scholars to become the foundations of functional theories of language.

11.2 Wegener's sources

While Wegener's theory of language as action may have seemed rather different from the dominant views in his immediate intellectual environment, it was not entirely new. We will remember from Section 3.2 that Enlightenment-era sensationist theories of the origin of language saw the beginnings of speech in the speaker's appeals to the listener and, in addition, imagined that the listener was compelled to respond to these appeals because of an innate empathy. Wegener's position would seem to represent a revival of these earlier ideas. It was only because of the overwhelming influence exerted by German language philosophy in the lineage of Herder, Humboldt, and like-minded thinkers that these earlier views became obscured in mainstream linguistics, making Wegener's ideas seem so novel.

There are also more recent antecedents of Wegener's ideas, from outside the German mainstream, but still from within the academic linguistics of the time. One of the clearest of these antecedents would have to be the work of the French linguist Michel Bréal (1832–1915), who we first encountered in Section 8.3. Bréal belonged to the same generation as William Dwight Whitney and, just as Whitney was the chief representative of comparative-historical linguistics in America, Bréal represented this new German science in France. Bréal had actually been born in Germany, in the border province of the Palatinate, which at that time was part of the Kingdom of Bavaria. He grew up in France, however, although he did study for two years in the late 1850s at the University of Berlin.

Like Whitney, Bréal was quite critical of some of the turns German linguistics had taken by the mid-nineteenth century, in particular in the materialist work of Schleicher. Also like Whitney, Bréal advocated for an alternative conception of language that looked at language primarily as an activity in which humans are engaged. Bréal was very much embedded in the mainstream linguistics of the time: in line with the rest of the field, his primary interest lay in studying historical language change, specifically changes in the meanings of words. He coined the term *sémantique* (semantics) to name this pursuit, a field whose ultimate aim, on his understanding, was to discover the putative laws governing meaning change. 'Semantics' has gone on to become the standard term – across linguistics, philosophy and allied disciplines – for those subfields concerned with the study of meaning.

The great synthesis of Bréal's work in this area is his 1897 monograph *Essai de sémantique* (Essay on semantics), although he had already presented key aspects of his theory in prior decades, in particular in lectures that he gave at the Collège de France, where he was professor. The first of these lectures, from 1866, was 'De la forme et de la fonction des mots' (On the form and function of words), and the second, from 1868, *Les Idées latentes du langage* (Latent ideas in language). Bréal's central point in these two lectures is that meaning does not inhere in words themselves, but rather that words are a stimulus to the listener to get them thinking along the same lines as the speaker. Our sentences do not so much contain meaning as evoke it. In order to engage in a successful exchange, people must share a certain degree of background knowledge about the world, their place in it, and the present context in which they are communicating. This shared background knowledge constitutes the 'latent ideas' that Bréal refers to in the title of his 1868 lecture. These ideas are associated with the words we use and are activated when we attempt to interpret a sentence.

The similarities of Bréal's account to Wegener's discussion of situations are obvious. In fact, one contemporary reviewer of Wegener's *Untersuchungen*, Frank Ziemer (1886), highlighted the similarities between Wegener's and Bréal's views, implicitly accusing Wegener of plagiarism. Wegener, for his part, claimed not to have known of Bréal and his work at all. It is, however, unlikely that Wegener was not aware of Bréal's work, given Bréal's prominence at the time. We know Wegener read other texts in which Bréal was cited, and so was exposed to his ideas, even if only at second hand (see Knobloch 1991: xxxv).

The Danish philologist Johan Nicolai Madvig (1806–1886) is another figure who frequently features in genealogies of nineteenth-century functionalist approaches to language (see Jespersen 1922: 84–5; Knobloch 1991: xvii, xxxii; Nerlich and Clarke 1996: 155–60). Already in the 1840s, Madvig had offered an account of language that emphasised its fundamental role as a means of communication and co-operation between interlocutors. But Madvig wrote in Danish, a language with little international currency. It was only in 1875, when he published his *Kleine philologische Schriften* (Short philological writings), a collection of his theoretical papers in German translation, that his ideas reached an international audience.

Madvig's book was read, reviewed and referred to by members of the Neogrammarian movement, and, although he never cited it himself, it is quite likely that Wegener was also familiar with the book. However, by the time Madvig's theoretical writings became widely known, pragmatic views had already received an extended exposition in the works of such scholars as Whitney and Bréal. Madvig cannot therefore be credited with effecting the pragmatic turn in linguistics of the mid-nineteenth century. Much as in the earlier case of his fellow Dane Rasmus Rask (1787–1832; see Section 2.4), assessing Madvig's contributions to linguistic theory is largely a matter of adjudicating a priority dispute.

There are several other possible antecedents of Wegener's notion of situation from outside disciplinary linguistics. The historian of linguistics Clemens Knobloch (1991: xxxii–xxxiii) points out that even Lazarus, Steinthal's collaborator in the development of *Völkerpsychologie*, spoke about the role of context in making sense of language. In his book *Geist und Sprache* (Mind and language), Lazarus (1884 [1856–67]) commented that there is often an 'incongruence' between mind and language: a particular word may evoke rather different representations in the minds of the speaker and listener. Only in the specific context of a given conversation will it be possible to discern the sense intended by the speaker. Furthermore, it will be easier for the speaker and listener to arrive at similar representations when they share elements of their background, taste, opinion, and so on.

More broadly, the difficulty of trying to recover and revive the circumstances and thinking of the author of an ancient text had always been a key problem in hermeneutics. Hermeneutics as a field was traditionally concerned with the task of Bible interpretation, making sense of the holy scriptures. During the course of the nineteenth century – with the rise of historicism in its various forms, which we discussed in Section 2.4 – hermeneutic ideas and methods were extended to the interpretation of historical sources and other antique documents of philological interest.

In the 1880s, hermeneutics received new emphasis in the work of the German philosopher Wilhelm Dilthey (1833–1911), who sought to make hermeneutic method, as he understood it, the basis of the *Geisteswissenschaften* (i.e. the humanities), as contrasted with the *Naturwissenschaften* (natural sciences). With the rising prestige of the natural sciences in this period, Dilthey and other like-minded philosophers felt the need to defend the humanities as a valid form of research. This struggle is in many respects a continuation of the mid-century debates surrounding materialism that we examined in Section 4.2, which similarly involved the encroachment of the natural sciences into the domain of spirit and culture.

Dilthey's position was to argue that the humanities have a special hermeneutic method that sets them apart from the natural sciences. While the aim of the natural scientist is to 'explain' (*erklären*) the phenomena of the natural world that they study, the humanities scholar seeks to 'understand' (*verstehen*) the inner experience of human consciousness. What exactly Dilthey meant by 'understand' is a matter of controversy, but at least this much is clear: Dilthey believed that to understand in this sense involves reconstructing the state of mind of the people we are studying, which we can only do with some knowledge of the physical and cultural world in which they live.

A similar contrast between *Verstehen* and *Erklären* as the principal methodological difference between the humanities and the natural sciences had already been set up by the German historian Johann Gustav Droysen (1808–1884) in the 1850s. A champion of historicism, Droysen pushed back against positivist historians who sought to discover 'laws' of history (see Beiser 2011: chaps 7 and 8). Dilthey's philosophical hermeneutics became a common point of reference in the philosophy of science from the 1880s onwards, and there is every reason to expect that Wegener would have been familiar with these debates. Wegener therefore drew on a number of proximal as well as more distant sources in formulating his ideas about language as action in a specific context.

11.3 Wegener and syntax

Although he advanced his conception of language as action in context as an alternative to mainstream views of the time, Wegener's proposals were not taken as an affront to accepted opinion, but were in fact well received among his contemporaries, in particular by the Neogrammarians. This keen reception is nowhere more visible than in later editions of Hermann Paul's *Principien der Sprachgeschichte*, the 'Neogrammarian Bible'.

If we look at successive editions of Paul's *Principien*, we see that Paul enthusiastically adopted many of Wegener's ideas. In the second edition, from 1886, one year after the appearance of Wegener's *Untersuchungen*, Paul introduced a distinction between what he called 'usual' (*usuell*) and 'occasional' (*okkasionell*) meaning (see chap. 4 of the 1886 and all subsequent editions). On Paul's understanding, 'usual' meaning is the whole range of representations that the speaker and listener associate with a particular word, while the 'occasional' meaning is a narrowed down set of representations tied to the specific situation of speaking. Paul incorporated these notions into his account of historical changes in word meaning, arguing that the usual meaning of a word can shift if the word is repeatedly deployed with a certain occasional meaning across different speech situations. The frequently occurring occasional meaning will gradually become entrenched, displacing the old usual meaning and creating a new one.

However, despite Paul's enthusiasm for Wegener's ideas, he seems to have felt that Wegener's work was only of marginal importance to linguistics proper. In a short review of Wegener's *Untersuchungen*, Paul (1885) commented that Wegener had much to say about the nature of communication, but that his writings had very little bearing on the actual business of linguistics, which should be about studying historical changes in linguistic forms (see Knobloch 1991: xxxii). This charge is not entirely fair: Wegener did undertake some linguistic analysis, in the area of syntax, proposing the two linguistic categories of 'logical subject' and 'logical predicate'.

Wegener's logical subject and predicate are derived from the traditional grammatical notions of subject and predicate, but they represent distinct categories. In a sentence, the logical and grammatical subject and predicate will often coincide, but not always – and they belong to different domains of analysis. The grammatical subject is the part of the sentence that is typically in the nominative case in those Indo-European languages that retain some level of case marking, and which triggers agreement on the main verb, while the grammatical predicate is made up of the main verb and its complements. The grammatical subject and predicate are therefore sentence elements defined in terms of formal properties.

The logical subject and predicate, on the other hand, are functional categories, defined in terms of the role they play in communication. On Wegener's (1885: 29–34) definition, the logical subject is the part of the sentence that anchors what is said in the current situation, while the logical predicate conveys the new contribution that the speaker wishes to make in this situation. For example, if we introduce someone by saying 'This is Herr Müller', the logical subject is 'this', a deictic expression that indicates who is meant in the present perceptual situation, while '. . . is Herr Müller' is the logical predicate; it conveys the new information that the speaker wishes to express: that the person being introduced is Herr Müller.

Wegener examined how these functional categories of logical subject and predicate are typically realised in German and other European languages. According to Wegener, the most basic linguistic means for marking the logical predicate is stress: the part of the sentence that is stressed will be interpreted as the logical predicate. If we say '*The Battle of Leipzig* was fought on the 18th of October' – where the italics represents the part of the sentence that would be stressed when spoken – the shared point of departure is the date 18th of October and the new information is that it was the Battle of Leipzig that was fought on this date, as opposed to some other battle. If, on the other hand, we say, 'The Battle of Leipzig was fought on the *18th of October*', the topic of the sentence is the Battle of Leipzig and the new information is the date on which it was fought, the 18th of October.

Wegener (1885: 31) pointed out that such modern European vernaculars as German, French and English have developed a range of grammatical constructions to explicitly mark the logical predicate, as a syntactic supplement to the basic means of stress and intonation. Among the examples he cites is what we would now call the cleft construction, as when in English we say, 'It was *his brother* who he came with', or 'It was *night* when he returned.'

The discussion of logical subject and predicate offered by Wegener built on an existing tradition of syntactic analysis in the nineteenth century. A number of scholars had already considered questions of how information is packaged in the sentence and proposed analyses that deconstructed the traditional grammatical distinction between subject and predicate. There are two predecessors in particular whose ideas would seem to have informed Wegener's formulations: the French linguist Henri Weil (1818–1909) and the German linguist Georg von der Gabelentz (1840–1893), the latter of whom we already met in Chapter 7.

In his 1844 study *De l'ordre des mots dans les langues anciennes comparées aux langues modernes* (On the order of words in the ancient languages compared with the modern languages), Weil laid the groundwork for much later syntactic analysis in the nineteenth century by observing the complex interactions between word order, grammatical subject and predicate, and the functional roles they play in the sentence. Gabelentz, in articles published in 1869 and 1871 in Steinthal's *Zeitschrift für Völkerpsychologie und Sprachwissenschaft* (on this journal, see Section 3.4), refined existing work of this kind to analyse sentences into what he called 'psychological' subject and predicate. While Gabelentz and Wegener differ in many details of their analyses, their respective notions of 'psychological' or 'logical' subject and predicate correspond quite closely in that they are both concerned with how sentences are structured in order to establish shared context and present new information.

The syntactic manifestations of information packaging in the sentence was another one of the new topics treated by Paul in the second edition of his *Prinzipien* and included in all subsequent editions, with prominent reference to Wegener, among other scholars (see Paul 1920 [1880]: chap. 6). The study of information structure, as it came to be known, was one of the main areas in which functional linguistics was elaborated in the following generations, in particular in the work of such figures as the Prague Circle founder Vilém Mathesius (1882–1945; see Mathesius 1975 [1961]: 79–85) and Michael Halliday (1925–2018; see Halliday 1985), a student of the London School that grew up around John Rupert Firth (1890–1960). We meet Firth and his approach to meaning in language in the next chapter.

11.4 Further reading

Clemens Knobloch's (1991) introduction to the reprinting of Philipp Wegener's *Untersuchungen über die Grundfragen des Sprachlebens* offers a succinct and insightful outline of Wegener's life and work in historical context. Brigitte Nerlich's (1990) *Change in Language: Whitney, Bréal, and Wegener* examines the pragmatic turn in linguistic scholarship in the second half of the nineteenth century, focusing in particular on the commonalities between William Dwight Whitney, Michel Bréal and Wegener. Chapter 9 of Brigitte Nerlich and David Clarke's (1996) *Language, Action, and Context: The Early History of Pragmatics in Europe and America, 1780–1930* treats Wegener and related German-speaking scholars of his time.

For an introduction to Wilhelm Dilthey's philosophical hermeneutics, see chapter 8 of Frederick Beiser's (2011) *The German Historicist Tradition*. The surrounding chapters cover other aspects of the debates on the foundations of the humanities that raged in this era. For a detailed exposition of notions of grammatical and 'logical'/'psychological' subject and predicate in the nineteenth and early twentieth centuries, see Els Elffers's *The Historiography of Grammatical Concepts: 19th and 20th-Century Changes in the Subject-Predicate Conception and the Problem of Their Historical Reconstruction* (Elffers-van Ketel 1991).

12 Meaning and British linguistics

While meaning may have been a relatively peripheral concern in the predominantly German field of comparative-historical linguistics, in the linguistic tradition that emerged in Britain in the early twentieth century, meaning did occupy a central place. In this chapter, we focus on two of the most influential figures in British linguistics of this era, John Rupert Firth (1890–1960) and Bronislaw Malinowski (1884–1942), and their varying notions of 'context of situation'.

Firth considered himself above all to be a linguist, but unlike the majority of his colleagues from the European Continent, his scholarship was motivated less by philological interests and more by the needs of such practical tasks as language learning and teaching. Malinowski, for his part, was not so much a linguist as an ethnographer. He was a pioneer of the 'participant observation' approach to ethnography, which demands that the ethnographer enter the society they are studying and describe it from the inside. To take on this role of honorary member of the community, the ethnographer must gain mastery of its language. It is these applied and ethnographic perspectives on language that set British linguistics apart from the comparative-historical schools on the Continent.

As we saw in Chapter 6, the Neogrammarians and their allies in Indo-European linguistics emphasised the importance of living, spoken languages in establishing the principles underlying the functioning of all human language. Their attitude inverted the traditional priorities of the field, which was built on the study of ancient texts and archaic inscriptions. But despite their avowed change in perspective, the primary sources on which most Neogrammarian scholarship was based continued to be written texts in dead Indo-European languages. By contrast, living languages – and languages often quite different in structure from the usual European model – were the starting point for many British linguists. In the following sections, we see how British linguists' efforts to grapple with diverse languages from around the world put questions of meaning, use and context at the very centre of their theorising.

12.1 John Rupert Firth and the 'study of meaning in its own terms'

The applied and ethnographic outlook of British linguistics is directly related to the institutional status of the field in Britain. In the nineteenth and early twentieth centuries, Britain was the largest colonial power in the world, and a major task for British linguists was documenting and teaching the languages spoken on their colonial frontiers. The entanglement of British linguistics with the affairs of the British Empire can be seen quite clearly on the example of John Rupert Firth, whose career depended on imperial institutions.

Firth began his career in 1914 as an officer of the Indian Education Service, a department of the British colonial government in India. During World War I, he joined the British Army and served in various regions of India and East Africa. His first major academic appointment, in 1919, immediately after the war, was as professor of English at the University of the Punjab in Lahore. Even after he returned to England in 1928, he was employed chiefly on the strength of his expertise in the languages of the colonised in India. For around a decade, he worked at University College London, before moving to the School of Oriental Studies – now the School of Oriental and African Studies – where he became professor in 1944. The School of Oriental and African Studies (SOAS) was founded with the explicit purpose of training British civil servants in the skills needed for colonial administration. Firth and his fellow linguists at SOAS provided training in the languages and cultures of the peoples his students would soon be sent out to govern.

But Firth himself was an ambivalent imperialist. He made his career within the structures of the British Empire, but he did not necessarily have a condescending attitude to the Empire's colonial subjects, their cultures and languages. He even spoke about 'de-Europeanising' himself, about broadening his linguistic and intellectual horizons through his contact with non-European cultures. He called India the 'home of phonetics' and acknowledged the inspiration he received from traditional Indian linguistic doctrines in developing his own ideas (see Rébori 2002: 175–83).

Firth's attitude perhaps derives in part from his own comparatively humble origins. Firth was from Yorkshire and had studied at the University of Leeds: he was not born into the intellectual and cultural establishment of Britain. In a sense, he also came from the periphery of the British Empire and had to acculturate himself to the language and norms of its elites. Nevertheless, it was the colonial project of the Empire that both gave Firth the opportunity to undertake his research and in many ways determined the direction of his interests. His background in bringing English language and culture to students in India, and later making Indian languages and cultures accessible to the British, drew his attention to the question of how we communicate, how we use languages to make meaning.

Before we embark on a detailed discussion of Firth's views, we should note that Firth never really set out a definitive version of his doctrines. Instead, he developed his ideas – often with a great deal of repetition – across numerous smaller papers and talks, the most significant of which were published in collected volumes (Firth 1957, and the posthumous Firth 1968). Firth did write two books in the 1930s, which were directed at a general, popular audience: *Speech* and *The Tongues of Men* (these books were reprinted posthumously in an omnibus volume as Firth 1964 [1930 and 1937]). These popular books offer up some of his ideas in a slightly livelier and more accessible form. The exposition of Firth's ideas given in this section is based on the two collected volumes of academic papers

(Firth 1957, 1968). For the sake of presenting a straightforward, coherent theory of language, we treat these volumes as single sources and do not delve into the differences and potential inconsistencies in the papers they contain.

According to Firth (1968: 145), 'The principal objective [of linguistics] is the study of meaning in its own terms', where Firth held a rather broad and somewhat idiosyncratic conception of 'meaning'. On Firth's understanding, every aspect of language – from sounds to the structure of words and sentences, to the way we interact in conversation – is imbued with meaning, and it is the task of the linguist to analyse these various facets of language in context. There is no single monolithic analysis that can be performed, rather 'descriptive linguistics is [...] a sort of hierarchy of techniques by means of which the meaning of linguistic events may be, as it were, dispersed in a spectrum of specialized statements' (ibid.: 183).

The proper object of study for the linguist, Firth averred, is the individual utterance in the context in which it is made, a view which represents a reversal of the Saussurean orthodoxy that had already become established by the 1920s, when Firth began writing. As we will recall from Section 8.2, Saussure is generally interpreted as having said that linguists should be concerned with *la langue*, the abstract system of each language, and not *la parole*, the application of *la langue* to make utterances. Firth (1957: 181), with explicit reference to this interpretation of Saussure, argued that it is only actual instances of language use that are real, while the abstract forms that linguists extract from utterances are mere figments of analysis.

To exemplify his contextual approach, Firth (1957: 26) examined the linguistic form /bɔːd/, for which he identified five different 'functions', each corresponding to a different level of analysis. The first of these, the 'phonetic function', is constituted by the sounds of the language in the context of other sounds: the way they can be strung together and replaced. Firth counted fifteen alternative vowel sounds that can potentially contrast with the /ɔː/ of /bɔːd/, producing such forms as /biːd/, /bɪd/, /bɛd/, /bæd/, /baːd/, /buːd/, and so on. Since Firth's discussion is concerned with spoken words, we reproduce most of the examples here in Firth's own phonetic transcription. Many of these phonetic forms could correspond to different words that may be distinguished orthographically. Readers whose own English pronunciation might diverge from that given in these examples must imagine the articulations of an ideal early twentieth-century Englishman – with or without a handlebar moustache – speaking in Received Pronunciation.

The second level is the 'lexical function', the way that the contrast between sounds serves to distinguish one word from another. The form /bɔːd/, for example, can be contrasted with /kɔːd/, /bɔːt/, or /pɔːt/, each of which would be interpreted as a different word in English. The next level is the 'morphological function': the contrast of the form with other forms that belong together in the same morphological paradigm. If we look again at the form /bɔːd/, Firth (1957: 25) observes that there are several different paradigms this form could belong to:

1. /bɔːd/, /bɔːdz/
2. /bɔːd/, /bɔːdz/, /bɔːdəd/, /bɔːdɪŋ/
3. /bɔː/, /bɔːz/, /bɔːd/, /bɔːɹɪŋ/

In the first paradigm, /bɔːd/ is a noun – orthographically 'board', or possibly 'bawd' – allowing for singular and plural inflection. In the second, it is a verb – 'board' – with different tense and agreement inflection. In the third paradigm, /bɔːd/ – 'bored' – is a past tense form of a different verb, which has the base form /bɔː/, 'bore'.

Superficially, the approach Firth sketches here looks very much like distributional analysis, which reached its highest degree of refinement in contemporary phonemic theory in America. We examine distributional analysis in detail in Section 16.4, but for the moment we may recall from Chapters 9 and 10 that phonemes are defined as the smallest phonological units of a language that create a contrast distinguishing one word from another. Phonemic theory states that it should be possible to describe the sound system of any language as an inventory of such contrasting phonemes, with supplementary rules accounting for regular variation in the way these phonemes are realised in actual speech.

But Firth was actually an opponent of phonemic theory: he felt that it was wrong to assume there is a single ultimate unit of analysis, such as the phoneme. Instead, the forms we see in languages are actually the product of various overlapping systems. Furthermore, he argued, the concept of the phoneme is not a discovery of pure science but merely the result of elevating the principles of alphabetical writing of the Western kind to a theoretical axiom (we saw related observations on this point in Section 9.2). Firth noted:

> We A B C people, as some Chinese have described us, are used to the process of splitting up words into letters, consonants and vowels, and into syllables, and we have attributed to them such several qualities as length, quantity, tone and stress. (Firth 1957: 122)

The Chinese language, observed Firth, provides an excellent example of the limits of traditional phonemic analysis. Phonemic theory's emphasis on 'letters', on dividing the sound stream up into segments, is a poor fit for the phonology of Chinese. In Chinese, 'tone' – the pitch contour of a syllable – can serve to distinguish one word from another, and is thus a primary phonological feature of the same degree of significance as any segmental phoneme. The traditional phonemic approach that treats the segment as the basic unit of analysis will have difficulty dealing with tone, since tone is a property of the entire syllable and cannot be reduced to the level of individual segments. Tone will have to be retrofitted into the phonological analysis as some sort of 'suprasegmental' feature.

In light of difficulties of this kind, Firth proposed his alternative approach of 'prosodic phonology', so called because it recognises 'prosodies' – phonological features that may belong to the syllable or otherwise extend across several segments – as first-order units of analysis. Firth's prosodic phonology is 'polysystemic': the analysis consists of several systems – those of segmental phonology, prosody, and so on – that interact to create the linguistic forms we see and hear, rather than being based on a single monolithic system that seeks to decompose the forms into fundamental units (on Firthian prosodic phonology, see further Anderson 2021 [1985]: 243–55).

If we now return to Firth's functional analysis, the fourth and fifth levels – which treat what Firth calls the 'syntactic' and 'semantic' functions – finally enter the realm of meaning in language as we would usually conceive of it. Firth's syntactic function is essentially the type of utterance that a form represents without specific situational information. For example, if we were to pronounce /bɔːd/ as /bɔːd/! (i.e. 'Bored!') – with a loud, level intonation – we can tell that the utterance is intended as an exclamation, whereas if we were to pronounce it as /bɔːd/? ('Bored?'), with a rising intonation, it would be a question.

The semantic function involves placing the utterance in a specific 'context of situation'. The example Firth (1957: 27) offers here is to imagine the responses that the utterance /bɔːd/? might give rise to in a conversation, such as 'no', 'not really', or 'go on'. Each pair of question and response conjures a specific 'context of situation', or a set of concrete circumstances under which the utterance is made. According to Firth, the factors we should consider in order to ascertain the context of situation include:

A. The relevant features of participants: persons, personalities.
   i. The verbal action of the participants.
   ii. The non-verbal action of the participants.
B. The relevant objects.
C. The effect of the verbal action.

(Firth 1957: 182)

That is, we need to look at who is involved in the situation (A), what they are saying (i), what they are doing (ii), what non-speaking inanimate objects are involved in the situation (B), and what the participants do or what happens to them as a result of what they say (C).

Firth (1957: 182) went on to observe that we can classify different contexts of situation and pick out the language that is typical of each one. This is essentially what is done in language textbooks, where a lesson might be based around a situation like travelling by train. The book will supply the relevant vocabulary, grammatical constructions, and dialogues exemplifying the standard conversational scripts that we follow in such a situation. Carving out a restricted language reflecting specific situations like this is the ideal path to linguistic analysis, believed Firth. Firth and his colleagues put these principles to work in the service of the British Air Ministry in World War II, when they analysed typical radio communications of Japanese fighter pilots to produce a crash course in Japanese for British intelligence officers. Graduates of the course were able to eavesdrop on Japanese radio communications and identify the signs of such situations as reconnaissance missions and imminent bombing raids.

Despite the concise list of factors quoted above, Firth did not treat the context of situation merely as a matter of the immediate physical environment in which a language is being used: the broader culture in which the language is embedded is also relevant. This cultural dimension was even more prominent in Malinowski's version of the context of situation, which we turn to in the next section.

12.2 Bronislaw Malinowski and the context of situation

The term 'context of situation' – which, as we saw in the previous section, played such an important role in Firth's functional theory of language – was originally coined by Bronislaw Malinowski. Malinowski's context of situation, as a key component of his ethnographically oriented linguistic analysis, was principally concerned with the cultural context in which a language is used.

Malinowski first articulated his notion of context of situation in response to fieldwork he undertook in the Trobriand Islands of New Guinea. By the time he set out for the South Pacific in June 1914, Malinowski was a postgraduate student at the London School of Economics, where he would later become a professor, making the School a major world centre of anthropological research. But Malinowski was originally from the Polish city of Kraków, which in this period was ruled by Austria. He was an ethnic Pole but an Austrian citizen and, when World War I broke out one month after his departure, he became an enemy alien in British-ruled territory. With the support of British colleagues, he avoided internment, and decided to stay in the Pacific during the course of the war. This extended sojourn gave him the opportunity to conduct long-term fieldwork in the region: he spent up to a year at a time in the Trobriand Islands, with interludes in other parts of New Guinea and Papua, and in Melbourne, Australia.

Malinowski was led to reflect on meaning in language by the difficulties he faced in bridging the cultural gulf between the Trobriand Islanders and himself as a European interloper. The first appearance of Malinowski's term 'context of situation' is in an essay called 'The problem of meaning in primitive languages', which he wrote as a 'supplement', or appendix, to the 1923 book *The Meaning of Meaning* by the English scholars Charles K. Ogden (1889–1957) and Ivor Armstrong Richards (1893–1979). As the title of this essay alerts us, Malinowski's account is bound up with all sorts of colonial prejudices about the differences between so-called 'civilised' and 'primitive' peoples. Without wanting to be apologists for Malinowski, we should note that his attitudes were at the more progressive end of the spectrum for his time. Although he continually invoked a contrast between the 'civilised' and the 'primitive', he never failed to point out the similarities between these two assumed poles, how much of the supposedly primitive remains part of the fabric of allegedly more civilised societies.

In his essay on 'The problem of meaning in primitive languages', Malinowski invites us to imagine ourselves in his place as a European trying to understand Kilivila, the language of the Trobriand Islanders:

> Imagine yourself suddenly transported on to a coral atoll in the Pacific, sitting in a circle of natives and listening to their conversation. Let us assume further that there is an ideal interpreter at hand, who, as far as possible, can convey the meaning of each utterance, word for word, so that the listener is in possession of all the linguistic data available. Would that make you understand the conversation or even a single utterance? Certainly not. (Malinowski 1956 [1923]: 300)

Even if we know the literal meaning of every word uttered by the Trobriand Islanders, argued Malinowski, we will still not understand what they are saying.

The European observer's difficulties in comprehending a Kilivila conversation illustrate perfectly the crucial role of context in understanding. On the one hand, the immediate physical situation is indispensable to understanding what is said because Kilivila – at that time – had no written form. A written text must be framed in such a way that it can be detached from the situation in which it is produced, while an utterance in an unwritten language will always be tied to a specific situation. But even more importantly, the great cultural difference between the European observer and the Trobriand Islanders means that the significance of much of what the Islanders say will simply escape the European. To demonstrate this point, Malinowski offered a sentence in Kilivila accompanied by a morpheme-by-morpheme interlinear gloss:

Tasakaulo   kaymatana   yakida;
We run   front-wood   ourselves;

tawoulo   ovanu;   tasivila   tagine
we paddle in place;   we turn   we see

soda;   isakaulo   ka'u'uya
companion ours;   he runs   rear-wood

oluvieki   similaveta   Pilolu
behind   their sea-arm   Pilolu
        (Malinowski 1956 [1923]: 300–1)

This utterance recounts an episode from an overseas trading expedition in which the teller of the anecdote raced ahead in his canoe, outpacing his companions in another canoe. The expressions 'front-wood' and 'rear-wood' refer to the canoes and their relative positions; they do so using culturally specific metaphors. To understand the significance of the reference to 'their sea-arm Pilolu' we similarly need to have knowledge of the local geography and the relation of the people to it. Above all, we need to know about the competitive character of Trobriand culture in order to appreciate the point of this anecdote: that the narrator is boasting of his exploits.

Malinowski's method for trying to make such wholly foreign texts accessible to his culturally European audience was to first provide a written transcription of the text accompanied by a literal interlinear gloss like that reproduced above. The glossed transcription was then followed by a detailed explanation in English of the content, context and significance of the text. Malinowski developed this technique into a fine art in his 1935 book *Coral Gardens and Their Magic*, the second volume of which is made up to large extent of texts presented in this fashion.

12.3 The background to Malinowski's functional model of language

The context of situation as it was developed by Malinowski and later adapted by Firth may remind us of the notion of 'situation of speaking' introduced by Philipp Wegener, which we examined in Section 11.1. Malinowski acknowledged the inspiration he received from Wegener, among other scholars, as did Firth (see Firth 1968: 139; Senft 2009).

The similarities between Malinowski and Wegener become even more apparent when we read Malinowski's account of the genesis and development of language: like Wegener, Malinowski contended that the most basic use of language is as a mode of action. He contrasted this to language as a 'condensed piece of reflection, a record of fact or thought' (Malinowski 1956 [1923]: 312), a use which is characteristic of modern science and literature, and which he believed is a later, derivative use of language.

To explicate his conception of language as a mode of action, Malinowski (1956 [1923]) provided a catalogue of the fundamental types of situation in which language is used. The first of these is 'language in action', where language is deployed to co-ordinate the activities of people in order to achieve some practical end. Here he offered the example of language used to co-ordinate the behaviour of participants in a fishing expedition. Next Malinowski mentioned the 'narrative situation'; the anecdote recounting the speaker's exploits on the trading expedition quoted in the previous section is a prime example of this category. Even this narrative use of language, argued Malinowski (ibid.: 313), is a kind of action: it is social action, intended to inspire feelings of 'pride or mortification, triumph or envy' in those present.

The purest form of social action through language is what Malinowski (1956 [1923]: 315) called the 'phatic communion'. The primary purpose of such linguistic activities as idle chatter and gossip, he observed, is simply to bring people together – the literal meaning of what is said is quite irrelevant. This use of language is found not only in so-called 'primitive' societies but also just as much in intercourse between Europeans, who will greet each other with such questions as 'How do you do?' and engage in aimless discussions about the weather. The content of these conversations is unimportant; these are merely conventional pleasantries that are exchanged in order to maintain social relations.

The parallels to Wegener continue in Malinowski's account of the acquisition of language by children. For a child, language is first and foremost a way of effecting action in the world: a cry of 'mama' summons the mother. When the child is hungry or uncomfortable, a suitable cry will cause the situation to be remedied (Malinowski 1956 [1923]: 319–20). This, according to Malinowski, is the first of three stages through which language develops. At this first stage, the utterance is nothing but a reflex-like reaction that correlates with a specific situation but does not involve any thought. At the second stage, however, an articulated or semi-articulated sound is actively produced to refer to a specific thing in the situation. It is only at the third stage that three fundamental differentiated uses of language emerge: speech in action, narrative speech, and the 'language of ritual magic'. Malinowski illustrated these stages of language development with the diagram reproduced in Figure 12.1.

Speech in action, as we saw above, is language used to co-ordinate an activity and actively handle things in the world. Narrative speech, on the other hand, is the situation where the things being talked about are not immediately present; the reference to them is mediated by an 'act of imagery'. The third and final use,

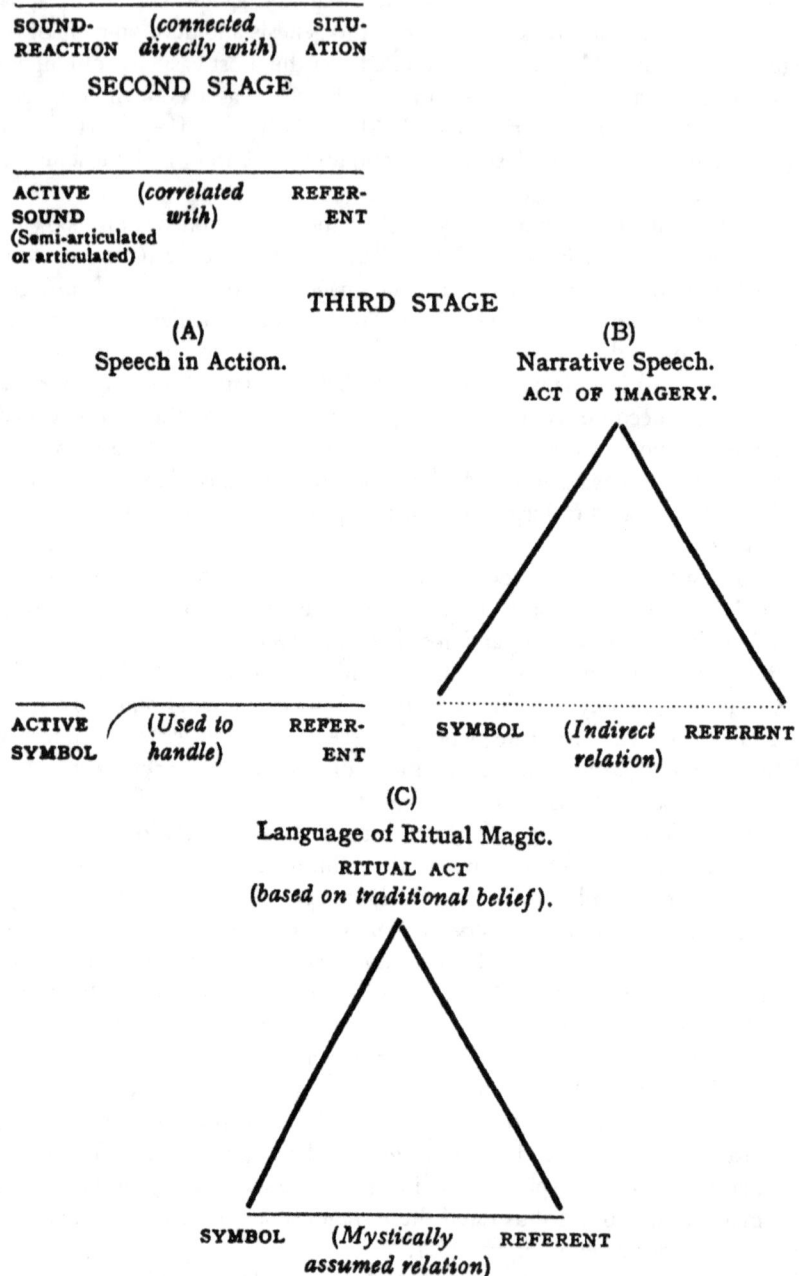

Figure 12.1 Malinowski's (1956 [1923]: 324) stages of language development

the language of ritual magic, arises in the situation where a ritual act is supported by a traditional belief that creates the link between what is said and its assumed effect in the world. Magical language, argued Malinowski (1956 [1923]: 322–5), is essentially adults' attempts to replicate the experience of their earliest childhood: magical spells seek to bring about change in the world in much the same way that the child uses language to summon its caregiver and secure relief from its problems.

As we can see in Figure 12.1, Malinowski represented narrative speech and the language of ritual magic as a triangle, at the bottom corners of which stand the 'symbol' and 'referent', and at the apex the way in which the symbol and referent are connected: either through an 'act of imagery' or a 'ritual act'. Malinowski chose this representation in order to integrate his theory with that presented in the body of Ogden and Richards's 1923 book *The Meaning of Meaning*, where his essay on 'The problem of meaning in primitive languages' appeared. One of the signature features of this book – for which it continues to be remembered today – is the so-called 'Triangle of Reference' or 'Semiotic Triangle', shown in Figure 12.2.

Ogden and Richards recognised two primary uses of language, 'referential' and 'emotive'. The referential use covers how language is employed to talk about things or states of affairs in the world, while the emotive uses include devices for

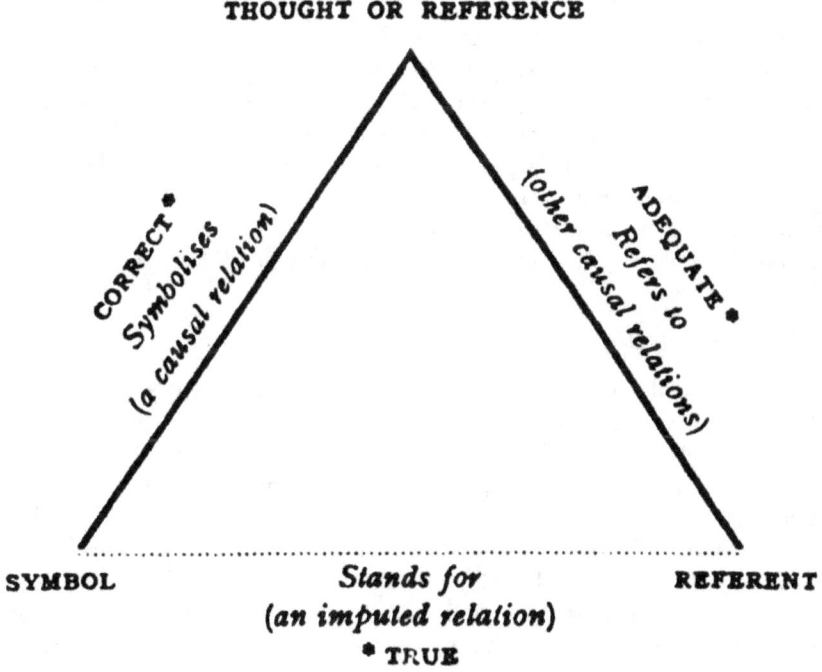

Figure 12.2 Ogden and Richards's (1956 [1923]: 11) 'Triangle of Reference' or 'Semiotic Triangle'

indicating attitudes towards the thing being spoken about or the listener, ways of appealing to the listener to try to sway their opinion, expressions designed to assert the certainty or authority of the speaker, and so on (see Ogden and Richards 1956 [1923]: 226–7). In separating out these two primary uses of language, Ogden and Richards sought to provide a normative account of how language should be used in science and philosophy: we should confine ourselves to the referential and avoid the emotive in order to cultivate rational, dispassionate discourse (see McElvenny 2018a: chap. 2). As we see in Section 15.3, Ogden and Richards's efforts to correct usage and eliminate abuses of language were part of a broader language reform movement in this era.

It is in the context of the referential function that Ogden and Richards presented the Triangle of Reference. Each of the three points of the triangle represents an element assumed to be involved in performing an act of reference – the 'symbol', 'referent' and 'thought or reference' – while the sides of the triangle show how each of these elements is connected to the others. At the base of the triangle, we see that in an act of reference a symbol 'stands for' a referent. We might naïvely assume that there is a direct connection between symbol and referent, but this connection is in fact merely 'imputed': in order to arrive at the referent, we must first go from the symbol to the 'thought or reference' in the minds of the speaker and listener, which then takes us to the referent. On this model, every act of reference involves some kind of mental representation.

Malinowski's diagrams in Figure 12.1 constitute both an adaptation and a critique of Ogden and Richards's model. The refined referential use illustrated by Ogden and Richards's triangle, argued Malinowski (1956 [1923]: 325), is strictly applicable only to the 'final stage of developed language'; that is, language as a 'condensed piece of reflection, a record of fact or thought', as we discussed above. By projecting Ogden and Richards's model back to the assumed earlier stages of development, Malinowski sought to show how the model has taken shape in the putative evolution of human language. But we must remember that Malinowski did not see non-referential uses of language as the sole preserve of allegedly 'primitive' peoples: he observed such uses also in 'civilised' European societies.

12.4 Further reading

There are several good articles that outline Firth's life and work. For an accessible exposition of his notions of meaning and context, see 'Firth on language and context', chapter 5 of John Joseph, Nigel Love and Talbot Taylor's (2001) *Landmarks in Linguistic Thought*, vol. 2. See also Patrick Honeybone's (2005) article 'J. R. Firth' in *Key Thinkers in Linguistics and the Philosophy of Language*. Victoria Rébori's (2002) article on 'The legacy of J. R. Firth' in *Historiographia Linguistica* examines some of the finer details of Firth's biography.

For a succinct summary of Malinowski's main contributions to ethnography and language study, see Gunter Senft's (2009) article 'Bronislaw Kasper Malinowski' in the volume *Culture and Language Use*. Michael Young's (2004) biography *Malinowski: Odyssey of an Anthropologist, 1884–1920* covers the first half of Malinowski's life, in which he undertook his first groundbreaking fieldwork in the Trobriand Islands and began to formulate the main ideas for which he would become known.

Chapter 11 of Brigitte Nerlich and David Clarke's (1996) *Language, Action, and Context: The Early History of Pragmatics in Europe and America, 1780–1930* examines several pragmatically oriented theories of language in Britain from the late nineteenth to the mid-twentieth century, including the work of Firth, Malinowski, and Ogden and Richards.

13 Functionalism in Central Europe and North America

In this chapter, our exploration of problems of meaning in the early twentieth century comes full circle. That is to say, we return to the Prague Circle – which we first met in Chapter 10 – by way of the Vienna psychologist Karl Bühler (1879–1963). We look at the interaction between Bühler and the Prague Circle, and see how they shaped one another's views on use and meaning in language.

Bühler came to the study of language through his efforts to lay down solid foundations for psychological research. In the early twentieth century, psychology was a field in flux. It was gaining its first firm institutional footholds but at the same time was riven by rival doctrines and schools. Throughout the nineteenth century, psychology had generally been considered a branch of philosophy: the leading psychologists of the time were for the most part professors of philosophy whose research consisted mainly of introspective reflection on thought processes. An independent discipline of psychology only began to emerge around the end of the century as the field took an empirical, experimental turn. In place of the earlier introspection, psychologists began formulating hypotheses to be tested in experiments conducted in elaborately equipped laboratories.

The first dedicated laboratory for experimental psychology was founded by Wilhelm Wundt (1832–1920) at the University of Leipzig in 1879. But Wundt's title remained Professor of Philosophy, and he did indeed consider himself to be first and foremost a philosopher. In the following decades, other psychological institutes sprang up around Germany and Europe, but at least in Germany these institutes usually remained under the aegis of philosophers. The University of Vienna came rather late to this game of modern experimental psychology. Although there had been several attempts to establish a psychological institute there, it was only in 1922 that this plan finally came to fruition, when Bühler – a German import, trained in Würzburg – took up a professorship at the university. The official designation of Bühler's position was still Professor of Philosophy, although with the additional specification 'with special attention to psychology and pedagogy' (see Benetka 1995: 18).

Observing the struggle for supremacy between competing psychological schools, Bühler diagnosed a 'crisis' in the field, as stated plainly in the title of his short 1927 book *Die Krise der Psychologie* (The crisis of psychology). In this book, Bühler surveyed the main theories current at the time and came to the conclusion that each focused on just one aspect of mental processes. What was needed was an ecumenical approach that would draw out the narrow themes addressed by each school and bring them together to create a more holistic view of the human mind. The domain in which these various perspectives on psychology can most profitably be brought together, argued Bühler, is the study of language. As we see in the following sections, it is this focus on language that brought Bühler into contact with contemporary linguistics.

13.1 Karl Bühler's *Sprachtheorie*

The culmination of Bühler's research into language was his 1934 book *Sprachtheorie (Theory of Language)*. The *Sprachtheorie* is an incredibly rich book that addresses a broad spectrum of topics, but in this section we will discuss only the first part of it, where Bühler set out a series of four axioms outlining what he believed to be the fundamental principles of human language.

In his first axiom, Bühler presented his so-called Organon model, which strove to offer a complete account of how signs function. As we discussed in Section 3.2, 'organon' means 'tool' or 'instrument' in Greek, and was long used as a collective title for Aristotle's writings on language and logic. Bühler (1934: 24), however, had a different antecedent in mind, namely the *Cratylus*, a dialogue of Plato (c. 429–347 BC) dealing with the philosophy of language. In this dialogue, the figure of Socrates describes 'names' – or words in language – as an *organon*, which we use to 'give information to one another, and distinguish things according to their natures' (Plato 1891 [1871]: 328). With this principle established, the dialogue moves on to its central topic: to what extent words as instruments are appropriate to their purpose (on the *Cratylus*, see Sedley 2020).

Bühler took Plato's description of words as instruments of communication and distilled from it three entities involved in the communicative situation: the 'sender' of a sign, the 'receiver' of the sign, and the thing or state of affairs in the world that the sign is about. The sign performs a different function in relation to each of these three entities. In relation to the sender, the sign's function is 'expression' (Bühler's German term is *Ausdruck*): the sign expresses the sender's inner thoughts or feelings. In relation to the receiver, its function is 'appeal' (*Appell*): the sign grabs the receiver's attention and directs their behaviour. Finally, in relation to things or states of affairs in the world, the sign's function is 'representation' (*Darstellung*): it represents or designates things and states of affairs. Bühler illustrated the components of this model and the relations between them in the diagram reproduced in Figure 13.1.

Each of the three functions reflects one of the three main aspects of human psychology that Bühler had earlier identified in his 1927 book *Die Krise der Psychologie*, and which he had accused existing schools of psychology of focusing on too narrowly (see Benetka 1995: 95–7). The expression of the inner states of the sender addresses the problem of phenomenal experience, which was the central concern of *Denkpsychologie* (the school in which Bühler himself had been trained at the University of Würzburg) as well as the closely related Gestalt psychology (which we encountered in Section 10.2). The appeal to the receiver, which directs the receiver's behaviour, answers to the interests of the behaviourists, who saw the study of externally observable behaviour as the key to a scientific psychology (we discuss

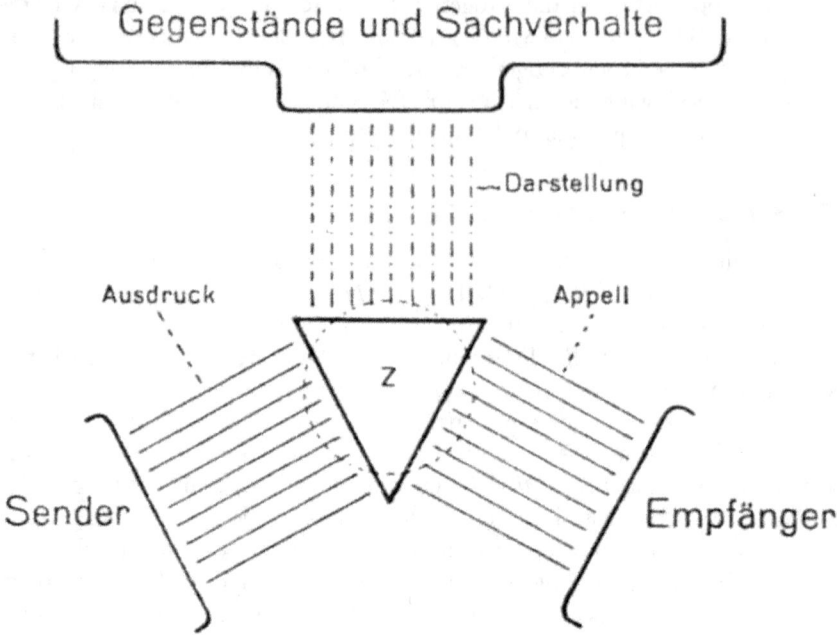

Figure 13.1 Karl Bühler's (1934: 28) Organon model

behaviourism in greater detail in Section 16.2). Finally, the representation of things and states of affairs in the world relates to the problem of how we co-ordinate reference through our shared culture, the quarry of humanistic psychology. Oriented towards hermeneutics (on hermeneutics, see Section 11.2), psychologists of the humanistic persuasion looked primarily at the relations between the minds of individuals and the cultural worlds in which they are embedded.

Even though Bühler tied his Organon model into his discussion of the problems of contemporary psychology, his semiotic thought is not necessarily anchored in psychology itself. Bühler's catalogue of functions – expression, appeal and representation – would seem to be much more closely aligned with the functional models emanating from linguistics and adjacent fields that we saw in Chapters 11 and 12. Bühler, who was extraordinarily well read in both contemporary and historical literature, cited many of the scholars we met in those chapters. In his *Sprachtheorie*, Bühler (1934) mentions Philipp Wegener on several occasions, as well as Alan Henderson Gardiner (1879–1963), a British Egyptologist in close contact with John Rupert Firth and Bronislaw Malinowski.

Gardiner developed a functional model of language very similar to Firth's and Malinowski's, which is set out definitively in his 1932 book *Theory of Speech and Language*. Interestingly, while Firth and Malinowski arrived at their functional theories through their study of living speech, Gardiner was driven to his theorising through his efforts to decipher Egyptian hieroglyphs, the remnants of a language not only no longer spoken but also no longer well understood.

The fact that Gardiner's insights came from his research into a dead language does not contradict the claim at the beginning of the previous chapter that it was British linguists' engagement with 'exotic' living languages – in contrast to Continental European scholars' focus on written texts – which led them to address questions of meaning in language. In line with the older philological tradition, Gardiner sought to understand the content of his texts, rather than treating them as sources of evidence for historical changes in linguistic form. While Firth and Malinowski took the perspective of outsiders thrown into a foreign cultural context, Gardiner found himself in the role of a researcher trying to interpret symbols created in a context that has disappeared through the passage of time and must be imaginatively reconstructed with the help of historical clues.

The deepest and most sustained interaction of Bühler's theory with mainstream linguistics emerges through his three other axioms, which are concerned with the formal properties of languages. Bühler's second axiom postulates that each language functions as a system of signs arranged according to the 'principle of abstractive relevance' (Bühler 1932: 44 et passim). This principle states that the units of a sign system are defined entirely by abstract qualities that are internally consistent within the system and which, crucially, are not determined by any material properties of the medium in which they are realised.

While Bühler's terminology may be new, the idea it names is not: it is the principle underlying phonemic theory, which we examined in Chapters 9 and 10. Phonemes are realised as certain actually articulated sounds, but the range of variation in sounds that can be considered the 'same' phoneme and the boundaries between phonemes are distinctions issuing from the structure of the sound system of each language alone. Bühler (1932: 44) acknowledged the inspiration he received from advances in modern phonology, in particular those made by the Prague Circle, in devising this axiom. In fact, he first expounded on this point using the example of the difference between phonetics and phonology in his 1931 paper 'Phonetik und Phonologie' (Phonetics and phonology), which was published in the Prague Circle's house journal.

Bühler goes beyond phonemic theory, however, in recognising two fundamentally different kinds of sign in language. Words or morphemes are not only signs but 'symbols'. That is to say, words and morphemes carry referential meaning: they refer to things and states of affairs in the world, and thereby serve the function of representation. Phonemes, on the other hand, are also signs, on Bühler's definition, but they are not symbols. They only serve to distinguish one word from another and do not themselves carry referential meaning.

This distinction between linguistic forms capable of carrying referential meaning and those that mark only contrasts internal to the linguistic system is today usually treated under the rubrics of 'double articulation' or the 'duality of patterning'. The first of these terms comes from the post-World War II work of the French linguist André Martinet (1908–1999; see Martinet 1980 [1960]: 13–15), while the second was coined by the American linguist Charles Hockett (1916–2000; see Hockett 1958: 574–5). The two terms are embedded in different theoretical contexts and therefore have slightly different orientations, but what they have in common is that they seek to capture the idea that there are two tiers of linguistic signs: those that merely signal differences within the linguistic system and those that are 'meaningful' in the sense that they contribute to the referential or propositional content of an expression.

Bühler's third axiom answers to Ferdinand de Saussure's (1857–1913) distinction between *la langue* and *la parole*, which we discussed in Section 8.2, and the related distinction of Wilhelm von Humboldt (1767–1835) between *ergon* and *energeia*, which we saw in Section 3.3. These two oppositions are essentially concerned with the difference between a concrete instance of language use – Saussure's *parole* and Humboldt's *ergon* – and the abstract potentiality of language, Saussure's *langue* and Humboldt's *energeia*. Starting from these oppositions, Bühler elaborated his own four-fold scheme with the parts: *Sprechhandlung* (speech action) and *Sprachwerk* (language work), plus *Sprechakt* (speech act) and *Sprachgebilde* (language structure). Although these terms have been rendered in English on occasion – not least of all in the 2011 English edition of Bühler's *Sprachtheorie* – no English translation has become established. For this reason, and since these are technical terms within Bühler's framework, divorced from ordinary usage, we use Bühler's original German terms in the exposition below.

Sprechhandlung and *Sprechakt* look at language from the perspective of an activity, how people actually use language in practice, while *Sprachwerk* and *Sprachgebilde* look at language structures. Each of these pairs in then divided up into different 'levels of formalisation', as Bühler (1934: 49–50) put it. The *Sprechhandlung* and *Sprachwerk* are concerned with specific instances of language use: the *Sprechhandlung* is a specific utterance and the *Sprachwerk* the linguistic content of the utterance or, as we might say today, the 'text'. *Sprechakt* and *Sprachgebilde*, by contrast, abstract away from the specific instance to reach a higher level of generalisation.

We can illustrate Bühler's distinction between *Sprachwerk* and *Sprachgebilde* on the example of a grammatical construction in English, such as the so-called split infinitive (a construction that in traditional prescriptive grammar is often considered an 'error'). A famous instance of the split infinitive that might come to mind is Captain Jean-Luc Picard's rousing statement of his ship's mission: 'To boldly go where no one has gone before.' If we talk about this specific statement then we are at the level of *Sprachwerk*. But if we talk about split infinitives as a structural feature of English, then we are at the abstract level of *Sprachgebilde*.

Bühler (1934: 50) pointed out that this same contrast in level of abstraction can be observed in numbers. We might talk about a pair of eyes or a pair of socks as specific instances of the numerical quantity of a pair. This would be the equivalent of *Sprachwerk*. But for the abstract concept of pair – which would be equivalent to *Sprachgebilde* – the actual items that form the pair are irrelevant. *Sprechhandlung* and *Sprechakt* similarly involve different levels of abstraction. The *Sprechhandlung* is a specific utterance in context, while the *Sprechakt* involves analysing the utterance according to the more general semantic and pragmatic categories that it manifests.

Bühler's (1932: 69–78) fourth and final axiom set up a taxonomy of linguistic elements that can carry referential meaning. He recognised two classes, the first of which is made up of words or morphemes and the second of sentences. Words or morphemes are analytic in nature: they allow us to divide the world up into things, processes, and other conceptual components. Sentences, on the other hand, are synthetic: when we put words together into sentences, we reconstruct the world from the components we have identified and the relations between them.

Once again Bühler compared this aspect of language to numbers. Our decimal number system consists of ten numerals – from 0 to 9 – which are like words or morphemes. These numerals can be combined through the syntactic means of place value to name an infinite range of numbers. The final syntactically composed number is akin to a sentence in language. Bühler (1934: 75–6) commented that linguists had long recognised this distinction between the two classes of referential signs, even if it sometimes appeared in 'strange disguise'. Here he mentioned Schleicher's notions of conceptual and relational elements in language, which we examined in detail – along with related ideas – in Chapters 3 and 4.

We must note that the distinction Bühler made in the fourth axiom is different from that in the second axiom. The second axiom divides significant elements in language up into those that can carry referential meaning and those that merely signal differences within the linguistic system – this is the issue of 'double articulation' or the 'duality of patterning', as we would now call it. The fourth axiom, by contrast, is concerned with different kinds of meaning-bearing elements.

13.2 Bühler and the Prague Circle

The axioms of language research presented in Bühler's 1934 *Sprachtheorie* – which we examined in the previous section – show that he was both a keen reader of contemporary linguistic scholarship, especially the new structuralism of the Prague Circle, and eager to contribute to its further development. Bühler's contributions were in turn accepted by the Prague Circle linguists. The influence of Bühler's ideas is, for example, prominent in Nikolai Trubetzkoy's 1939 *Grundzüge der Phonologie*, his chief work on phonological theory, which we discussed at length in Section 10.1. Trubetzkoy (1939: 40) not only acknowledged Bühler's 'principle of abstractive relevance' as the fundamental concept underlying phonology and linguistic signs more generally, but also adapted the three functions of Bühler's Organon model to his phonology (ibid.: 17–18).

Trubetzkoy (1939: 18) argued that the representational function of the Organon model is obviously relevant to phonology because the signifier side of words necessarily consists of phonological units. We may object, however, to this extension of Bühler's theory, since it would seem to ignore the distinction in Bühler's second axiom between signs that bear referential meaning and those that do not. The phonological units that serve to mark one signifier off from another are precisely the non-referential, system-internal signs that inspired Bühler to make this distinction in the first place.

Perhaps less controversially, Trubetzkoy held that the functions of expression and appeal also manifest themselves in phonology. But these two functions fall into the domain of a special subfield of phonology that Trubetzkoy called 'phonostylistics' (*Lautstilistik*; Trubetzkoy 1939: 28–9). According to Trubetzkoy, the expressive function manifests itself in phonology predominantly in the way that pronunciation reflects the identity of the speaker. He offers such examples as the variations in vowel and consonant articulation and intonation that we might consider to belong to regional or class accents, or that speakers might use to project a certain image of themselves, such as talking in a very feminine or manly way (ibid.: 19–24).

This kind of variation, Trubetzkoy (1939: 18) pointed out, belongs to the study of phonology because it is conventional. There are innumerable differences in the speech of individuals that reveal their personal characteristics – we can tell, for instance, whether someone is large or small from the sound of their voice – but these differences are determined by the physical properties of the speaker's body and are not conventional parts of the language system. Features of accent, on the other hand, are entirely conventional.

Trubetzkoy (ibid.: 20–1) compared this aspect of phonology to the study of costumes in folklore. A tailor must know whether a person is large or small in order to make a costume for that person, but for folklorists these distinctions are not important. The folklorist is interested only in the designs and decorations dictated by custom that show the gender, social class, occupational group, and so on, of the wearer. The kind of phonological distinctions Trubetzkoy saw as relevant to the expressive function are more or less those that would be studied today in variationist sociolinguistics.

Conventionally determined phonological forms can also be used to trigger certain feelings in the listener, argued Trubetzkoy (1938: 24–7), thereby serving the function of appeal. As an example, he pointed out how in German there is a conventional process of lengthening of consonants and vowels in a word, typically used to inspire a sense of delight in the listener, as when a speaker says 'Schschöön!' A similar lengthening process can be used in English to produce more or less the same effect: 'Beauutiful!'

While this specific process of lengthening is clearly conventional and therefore belongs to phonology, the emotional effect on the listener can vary depending on the intonation contour with which it is paired. A subtle change in intonation could turn delight into irony, for example. But such intonational patterns, observed Trubetzkoy, seem to come about through a natural outpouring of emotion and so do not belong to the conventional system of phonology. Consequently, the boundaries of the appeal function in phonology are not clearcut and deserve further research.

In Trubetzkoy's 1939 *Grundzüge*, his magnum opus on phonology, we see how the principles outlined in Bühler's *Sprachtheorie* were incorporated into the very heart of Prague Circle structuralism. But an even more extensive and innovative adaptation of Bühler's theory came from Trubetzkoy's long-time Prague Circle collaborator, Roman Jakobson. As we see in the next section, Jakobson took up Bühler's theory in earnest after his emigration to the United States, and combined it with ideas circulating in his new American home.

13.3 Roman Jakobson and cybernetics

Like Trubetzkoy, Roman Jakobson (1896–1982) had already adopted elements of Bühler's language theory into his writings in the 1930s, during the time he was associated with the Prague Circle. But Jakobson's engagement with Bühler's work only came into full bloom after World War II, when Jakobson had firmly integrated himself into his new intellectual environment in America (on Jakobson's peripatetic career, see Section 10.3). Mixing Bühler's ideas with the latest technical trends in America, Jakobson developed his own functional model of language.

The definitive formulation of Jakobson's functional model appeared in his 1960 essay 'Linguistics and poetics', which began life as a presentation at a 1958 conference on stylistics. In this essay, Jakobson explored the relationship between disciplinary linguistics and poetics, the study of the literary devices characteristically used in poetry. He concluded that linguistics and poetics are two complementary fields, each of which needs the other in order to paint a full picture of language. In order to show how these fields are intertwined, Jakobson undertook an investigation into the various functions that language serves.

Jakobson's starting point was the three functions posited by Bühler, those of representation, expression and appeal, although Jakobson renamed these the 'referential', 'emotive' and 'conative' functions. Despite this change in terminology, Jakobson's conception of these three functions is more or less the same as Bühler's. As we saw in Section 13.1, these three functions deal with the relationships between a symbol and the three entities involved in a communicative situation: the 'sender' of a symbol (expression), its 'receiver' (appeal), and the thing or state of affairs in the world that the symbol is about (representation).

In addition to these three entities in the communicative situation, argued Jakobson, we must also consider the medium of communication itself, which has three aspects: the 'message', or the content of what is said; the 'contact', or the channel through which the sender maintains their connection to the receiver; and the 'code', essentially the language being used to communicate (Jakobson 1981 [1960]: 21). Each of these three aspects of the medium of communication is associated with an additional function. The function associated with the 'contact' or channel of communication is the 'phatic' function, a term Jakobson took from Malinowski (and which we examined in Section 12.3). The 'code' is associated with what Jakobson calls the 'metalingual' function. This is the function invoked whenever we discuss the words that we use to communicate, such as when we say, 'I don't follow you – what do you mean?' or 'Do you know what I mean?', and so on (ibid.: 25).

Finally, the 'poetic' function – the core concern of poetics, whose relationship to linguistics is the topic of Jakobson's essay – is employed whenever we focus on the message, or the content of what is said. This function, according to Jakobson (1981 [1960]: 25–6), involves looking at the formal properties of specific instances of language. As an example, Jakobson conjured an anecdote about a 'girl' who uses the epithet 'the horrible Harry' to talk about someone she does not like. When asked why '*horrible* Harry' and not 'dreadful', 'terrible', 'frightful', or similar, she replies simply that 'horrible' fits better. An analysis under the poetic function would reveal the importance of the auditory echo of 'horrible' and 'Harry' to her choice of words.

A functional model of language consisting solely of a 'poetic' function contrasted to a single broad function of 'communication' can already be found in the 1929 'Thèses' of the Prague Circle (Durnovo et al. 1929: 14), the Circle's manifesto, which we discussed in Section 10.1. But the model Jakobson published in 1960 had undergone significant evolution and elaboration since his Prague Circle days. One of the main influences that shaped the evolution of Jakobson's ideas was work in the new field of information theory, which grew out of American telecommunications research during World War II, and which Jakobson came in contact with after his arrival in the United States.

The inaugural publication on information theory is classically considered to be the 1948 paper 'A mathematical theory of communication' by Claude Shannon (1916–2001), an engineer at Bell Telephone Laboratories, the research and development arm of the American Telegraph and Telephone Company (AT&T), which at the time operated the United States telephone network as a private monopoly. Shannon's problem was to quantify the information sent over telephone and radio connections as a foundation for a formalised, mathematical study of communication. The goal was to measure the amount of information contained in a message in order to calculate both the bandwidth required to transmit the message as well as the level of interference that could be tolerated in a channel before the message would degrade.

Information theory reached the broader public with the 1949 book *The Mathematical Theory of Communication*, which reproduced Shannon's essay from the year before with an introduction by his colleague Warren Weaver (1894–1978) explaining Shannon's theory in terms more accessible to a lay audience. Jakobson most probably became acquainted with information theory through this book, and through his personal contact with Weaver: Weaver was an important functionary at the Rockefeller Foundation, with which Jakobson was also closely associated, as both consultant and funding recipient (see Section 10.3).

Information theory was closely entwined with 'cybernetics', another new field to have emerged from the technological innovations spurred on by World War II. At an abstract level, cybernetics was the science of self-regulating systems, a fact highlighted in the name of the field, a neologism derived from the Greek word *kubernetes*, meaning 'steersman' (see Wiener 1948: 19). Cybernetics had its origins in the work of the American mathematician Norbert Wiener (1894–1964) in World War II to improve the design of servomechanisms for aiming anti-aircraft guns. These were electromechanical devices which, when fed with information about the speed and heading of an aircraft in the sky, could calculate its anticipated position and aim the gun in time for the human operator to pull the trigger. Wiener articulated a theory describing the functioning of these devices, stated at such a level of generality that it was applicable to the design of robots and computers of all kinds.

But Wiener also believed that his theory could be used to explain systems in both the natural world and human society: these more expansive ideas were presented in his 1948 book *Cybernetics: Or Control and Communication in the Animal and the Machine*. Scholars and scientists across such fields as biology, ecology, anthropology and psychology became keen converts to the cybernetic gospel. They accepted the contention that all complex systems – from human society to the human mind, to living organisms and ecosystems – could be treated as specific cases of the self-regulating mechanisms studied by cybernetics. Cybernetics was seen not only as a way to provide new scientific accounts of the workings of society and the mind, but also as a source of potential solutions to political and social ills, which could be engineered away through the proper application of cybernetic principles.

As the media theorist and historian of science Bernard Dionysius Geoghegan points out in his 2011 paper 'From information theory to French theory' (expanded upon in his 2023 book *Code*), not only Jakobson but also the French anthropologist Claude Lévi-Strauss – who we met in Section 10.3 – looked to cybernetics as a master science supplying the principles on which other, more specialised sciences could be constituted. Jakobson and Lévi-Strauss sought to reframe linguistics and anthropology in cybernetic terms as a way of putting their respective fields on a modern, scientifically rigorous footing.

In his efforts to align linguistics with cybernetics and information theory, Jakobson assimilated the classical Saussurean notions of *la langue* and *la parole* – which we met in Section 8.2 – to the information theoretic concepts of 'code' and 'message', which Claude Shannon had given a precise, mathematical definition in his 1948 paper (see Van de Walle 2008). Interestingly, Jakobson seemed to embrace information theory with its notions of 'code', 'message', 'sender' and 'receiver' as a way of returning the act of communication to centre stage in linguistics. Linguists, felt Jakobson (1981 [1960]: 21), had fallen into the habit of fetishising the forms of languages without considering what those forms are actually used for, what they actually mean.

As we see in Chapter 16, it is true that American linguistics of the mid-twentieth century – the environment in which Jakobson put forward his functional model – had retreated to a large extent from the problems of meaning and communication (see also McElvenny 2018a: 156–9). While meaning had merely been peripheral to much of late nineteenth-century linguistics, in the American linguistics of the post-World War II Bloomfieldian school it was actively banished from scientific consideration.

But it is strange that Jakobson would try to make information theory into the saviour of meaning. Information theory assumes that there is always a single, definite message that is transmitted from sender to receiver using a fixed code. The sender and the receiver, and the context in which the message is exchanged, may have an influence on how the message is encoded and decoded, and noise may interfere with the message, but there is always a single message that is in principle recoverable. The story of senders, receivers, messages and codes told in information theory does not allow for any active process of interpretation.

If the various hermeneutically oriented approaches we have encountered in this book have shown us anything, it is that meaning does not inhere in symbols; rather, symbols must be imbued with meaning. For their own part, Shannon and Weaver insisted in their 1949 book that information theory was not concerned with meaning at all. However, in his introduction to the book, Weaver (in Shannon and Weaver 1949: 24–8) did allow for the tantalising possibility that information theory might at the very least lay the necessary groundwork for the future study of meaning.

Bühler was also favourably disposed towards cybernetics. Like Jakobson and Lévi-Strauss, Bühler found himself in American exile as a result of World War II. In the 1930s, in lockstep with Germany, Austria came under the sway of fascism, which made Bühler's position in Vienna extremely uncomfortable. Matters came to a head in 1938, when the home-grown 'Austrofascist' dictatorship was overrun and absorbed by Nazi Germany. After being harassed and arrested by the Gestapo, Bühler left Central Europe, eventually landing in the United States. By this time already over sixty years old, he never really gained a foothold in America, and ended his career as a psychologist in private practice in Los Angeles, occasionally teaching at the University of Southern California.

But Bühler did continue to write in exile, making several attempts to adapt his ideas to the American context (see McElvenny and Knobloch 2023). In his final book, the 1960 *Das Gestaltprinzip im Leben des Menschen und der Tiere* (The Gestalt principle in the life of man and animals), Bühler revisited his semiotic theories in relation to both human and animal communication, with explicit reference to cybernetics (cf. Ungeheuer 2004 [1967]).

The fate of Jakobson and Bühler is emblematic of the further development of science and scholarship in the twentieth century. After World War II, the centre of gravity of scientific research moved from Europe to America, and new American doctrines – infused with ideas and methods brought by the European exiles – determined the future direction of most scientific fields, including linguistics. Although linguistics continued to be practised in Europe after World War II, European linguists increasingly looked to America for inspiration. We turn to the American scene in the following chapters.

13.4 Further reading

The best secondary literature on Karl Bühler is in German. Here we can recommend above all the 2018 book *Karl Bühlers* Krise der Psychologie: *Positionen, Bezüge und Kontroversen im Wien der 1920er/30er Jahre*, edited by Janette Friedrich, and the 1984 two-volume *Bühler-Studien*, edited by Achim Eschbach. Gerhard Benetka's (1995) *Psychologie in Wien: Sozial- und Theoriegeschichte des Wiener Psychologischen Instituts 1922–1938* offers a comprehensive history of the Vienna Psychological Institute led by Bühler. In English, Werner Abraham and Achim Eschbach's introductory essays in the 2011 *Theory of Language: The Representational Function of Language*, an English translation of Bühler's *Sprachtheorie* (Bühler 2011 [1934]), provides a succinct outline of Bühler's scholarly contributions. Part I of the 1982 *Karl Bühler: Semiotic Foundations of Language Theory*, by Robert Innis, similarly treats the central topics in Bühler's semiotic thought. Section 9.7 of Brigitte Nerlich and David Clarke's (1996) *Language, Action, and Context: The Early History of Pragmatics in Europe and America, 1780–1930* examines Bühler's functional model of language in historical context.

Information theory and cybernetics have received a great deal of historiographic attention. An excellent history of information theory in the genre of popular science is James Gleick's (2011) *The Information*. Cybernetics and computing in the context of World War II and the Cold War are the subject of Paul

Edwards's (1997) *The Closed World: Computers and the Politics of Discourse in Cold War America*. Steve Heims's (1991) *The Cybernetics Group* is a study of the postwar 'Macy Conferences', where cybernetic theory was elaborated and applied to many different problems. Bernard Dionysius Geoghegan's (2023) *Code* presents a radically revised history of cybernetics, which casts anthropology, psychology and other human sciences as sources rather than mere recipients of cybernetic ideas, and which traces the connections of cybernetics to postmodernist 'French theory'.

14 The beginnings of American structuralism

In the final three chapters of this book, we cross the Atlantic to trace the development of linguistics in America from the end of the nineteenth into the first half of the twentieth century. The approaches to linguistics that emerged in America in this period are generally known as 'American structuralism', a retrospective label introduced by the linguistic anthropologists and historians of the field Dell Hymes and John Fought. Hymes and Fought (1981 [1975]) identified four 'principal figures' who laid the foundations for American structuralism: Franz Boas (1858–1942), Edward Sapir (1884–1939), Benjamin Lee Whorf (1897–1941), and Leonard Bloomfield (1887–1949). In this chapter, we focus on the first of these figures, Franz Boas, and his school. We turn to the other three in the following chapters.

In the patriarchy-affirming mode of much intellectual history, Boas is often referred to as the 'founding father' of American anthropology. But Boas was in fact a German import: he was born and raised in the Prussian province of Westphalia, and received his entire education in Germany. It was in the United States, however, that Boas made his academic career, and it was his work and the work of his students that brought about a paradigm shift in American anthropology. The study of language played a key role in the Boasian revolution: linguistics was one of the 'four fields' of anthropology as it was conceived by Boas – alongside cultural anthropology, the ethnographic description and comparison of cultures; archaeology, the investigation of material remains; and physical anthropology, the measuring of human bodies and cataloguing of their diversity.

It is fair to say that it was with Boas and his students that a peculiarly American tradition of linguistics first started to develop. Linguistics had of course been practised in America before Boas's arrival; we will recall in particular the work of William Dwight Whitney (1827–1894), who we met in Chapter 5. As we observed in that chapter, Whitney's American background gave him a unique perspective on the study of language, but his gaze was still directed towards Europe: his main scholarly models and interlocutors were all on that continent. Paradoxically, it is only with the advent of Boas, a European by birth and education, that a characteristically American anthropology and linguistics began to take shape.

It is no coincidence that this new American linguistics was tied to anthropology. In Chapter 12, we saw how British linguistics was also intertwined with ethnography, much more so than in other European countries. There we observed how the British Empire provided institutional structures that furthered the study of the languages and cultures of peoples around the world who had been colonised by the British. British linguistics benefitted from the imperatives of imperial communication and control. In similar fashion, the settler colonial state that is the United States provided resources for research into the languages and cultures of the Indigenous inhabitants of the lands on which it was built.

Boasian linguistics, as part of a broader anthropological project, was concerned principally with the documentation, description and classification of Indigenous languages, primarily in North America, but also in other parts of the world. In the following sections, we will examine the nature of the Boasian school of anthropology, the attitudes and beliefs that animated it, and the specific contributions of Boas to the development of linguistic theory.

14.1 Franz Boas and the Boasians

Franz Boas not only made foundational contributions to anthropological theory in America, but was also instrumental in turning the field into a recognised academic discipline. When Boas settled in America in 1887, there was only one professor of anthropology in the entire country – a certain Daniel Garrison Brinton (1837–1899), who we meet properly in Section 14.3 – and no established academic pathway to train as an anthropologist.

The main institution supporting anthropological research in America of the late nineteenth and early twentieth centuries was the Bureau of Ethnology, an independent research unit funded by the US government and affiliated with the Smithsonian Institution. The Bureau had been founded in 1879 by John Wesley Powell (1834–1902), a geologist, explorer and solider – that is, an all-round adventurer-scholar. The primary duty of the Bureau was to supervise the ethnographic records and collections of the US government, although it also undertook extensive original ethnographic and linguistic survey work under Powell's direction. Much of Boas's early research in the United States was funded by the Bureau.

While new professorships in anthropology were established at several American universities in the last decade of the nineteenth century, the first viable graduate programme was that set up by Boas at Columbia University in New York in 1899. Boas's programme helped to professionalise the field and produced a number of scholars who not only had an incomparable impact on the further development of anthropology but also became prominent public intellectuals. First among those who specialised in linguistics is Edward Sapir, the second of Hymes and Fought's 'principal figures' in American structuralism. In the next two chapters, we examine in detail some of Sapir's major contributions to linguistics.

Among Boasian ethnographers, we must mention the names of Ruth Benedict (1887–1948) and, above all, Margaret Mead (1901–1978). Benedict is a prime example of the anthropologist as public intellectual, a role well illustrated by her 1946 book *The Chrysanthemum and the Sword*, an ethnography of Japan written during World War II. The express purpose of Benedict's book was to describe the patterns of Japanese society in order to show how Japan could be reconstructed after the war to create a co-operative partner for America in the future.

Benedict was also co-supervisor, along with Boas, of Margaret Mead's doctorate. Mead's first book, the 1928 *Coming of Age in Samoa*, was an immediate bestseller. The controversial – and sensational – claim of her book was that Samoan teenagers enjoyed much freer love lives than their 'Western' counterparts. As a result, argued Mead, Samoan teenagers did not suffer from the repressed sexuality and associated neuroses that plague youth in the West. This book launched Mead's lifelong career as a social commentator, in which she deployed insights she claimed to have won through her field research into supposedly 'primitive' cultures to diagnose and suggest remedies for social ills in America.

A novelty of Boas's school was that it included scholars who came from the communities that were studied. Boas welcomed those who could act in the roles of both anthropologist and informant. An important figure in this connection is Ella Cara Deloria (1889–1971), who came from a Dakota background. Deloria completed several research projects under Boas's direction, such as the 1932 *Dakota Texts*, a collection of Dakota tales recorded by Deloria, and the 1941 *Dakota Grammar*, co-authored by Boas and Deloria. Another famous member of the Boasian circle was Zora Neale Hurston (1891–1960), who was African American. Her 1935 book *Mules and Men* is a collection of folklore from the African American communities in which she grew up, retold in literary form.

From our present-day perspective, one of the most striking features of Boas's school is that it was not made up solely of upper middle-class – or even aristocratic – white males, who represent the vast majority of scholars we have met so far in this book. In this connection, we might observe that Boas, Sapir and several of Boas's other students were from Jewish families, which in both Germany and America was a minority background, subject to overt and covert discrimination. For the first time, we are beginning to see the academic space open up to new groups of people. This opening up is partly a function of the era, the new twentieth century, and in particular the roaring twenties of that century. But even in this environment, Boas's circle was considered particularly progressive, both in terms of its composition and in the views it entertained.

14.2 Boasian anthropology

Franz Boas's approach to anthropology was shaped by his German background and was in many respects out of step with assumptions that prevailed in America at the time. Most American anthropologists of the era held an evolutionary conception of human society and culture: they believed that every people passes through a series of predetermined stages in an ascent from primitive life to civilisation. Boas, by contrast, had absorbed a more relativistic conception of cultural diversity through his education in Germany. It was this view that he propagated and developed further in America.

The touchstone of evolutionary thought in nineteenth-century American anthropology was the work of Lewis Henry Morgan (1818–1881), a lawyer, politician and gentleman anthropologist. In his 1877 book *Ancient Society*, Morgan outlined a deterministic scheme of social evolution with the primary stages of 'savagery', 'barbarism' and finally 'civilisation'. The only group of people to have reached the highest levels of civilisation, according to Morgan, are contemporary Europeans. The Indigenous inhabitants of America, on the other hand, have never passed beyond the stages of savagery and barbarism. In Morgan's scheme, the chief determinant of a people's evolutionary stage is technology, and each of the stages is supposed to correlate with different social arrangements, architectural styles, and even structures of language.

Boas had been inducted into a rather different tradition in Germany, largely under the influence of Adolf Bastian (1826–1905), director of the Berlin Museum für Völkerkunde (Museum of Ethnology). While completing his habilitation – a postdoctoral qualification required in Germany to become a professor – Boas worked as a scientific assistant to Bastian in the museum. Bastian was known above all as an advocate of the 'psychic unity of mankind', the principle that all humans, no matter what their ancestry or where they live, share in a single common humanity.

Bastian argued that the mental world of every people consists at base of the same 'elementary thoughts' (*Elementargedanken*), but that these elementary thoughts are arranged in different ways to produce the 'ethnic thoughts' (*Völkergedanken*) of specific peoples. The anthropologist's task, according to Bastian, is to record as much as possible of the diversity of human cultures, of the different 'ethnic thoughts', in order to build up a picture of the unity of humanity. Bastian was highly critical of such contemporaries as Morgan and his followers who sought to discover universal laws governing the development of human culture. It may one day be possible to find such universal laws, conceded Bastian, but all present anthropological theories lack a sufficient empirical basis, and are at the very least premature (on Bastian's views, see Bunzl 1996: 46–52).

The tension between trying to discover universal laws and studying the historical development of particular individuals is a recurring theme in the human sciences of the nineteenth century, which we have come across a number of times in our story so far (see especially Chapters 2–4). As Matti Bunzl demonstrated in his 1996 essay 'Franz Boas and the Humboldtian tradition', the positions occupied by Bastian and Boas can be located in a tradition of German scholarship that emerged in the wake of the brothers Wilhelm and Alexander von Humboldt.

In Chapter 3, we examined the wide-ranging contributions of Wilhelm von Humboldt (1767–1835) to the study of language and history, as well as some of the work he inspired, most notably the *Völkerpsychologie* of Heymann Steinthal (1823–1899) and Moritz Lazarus (1824–1903). Alexander von Humboldt (1769–1859) we have not yet met: Alexander's fame rested for the most part on his exploring expeditions to the Americas from 1799 to 1804. On these expeditions, Alexander focused on investigating the natural environment, but he also made detailed records of the societies, cultures and languages of the peoples he encountered. In their writings, both Wilhelm and Alexander emphasised the importance of amassing data on the character and history of individuals – whether individual languages, cultures or natural species – before positing general laws governing their life and development. This effort to uncover the universal through comprehensive study of individuals in their particular historical circumstances is an aspect of Humboldtian scholarship that was emphasised in many subsequent interpretations, especially those current in Germany.

One of the clearest demonstrations of the clash between Boas's Humboldtian inclinations and the evolutionary predilections of his American colleagues is the debate on the arrangement of museum collections which Boas instigated soon after his arrival in America. Boas was an advocate of organising museum exhibits around Bastian's principle of 'geographical provinces'. On this principle, all artefacts stemming from a single people should be presented together in one display in order to provide a complete picture of that people's material culture. Individual displays should then be organised by geographical region, with peoples who live in the same part of the world placed alongside one another. This is the scheme according to which the exhibits in the Berlin Museum für Völkerkunde were arranged: Bastian's aim was to quite literally showcase the individuality of each ethnic group in its geographical context.

By contrast, Otis T. Mason (1838–1908), the curator of the ethnographic collections of the Smithsonian Institution in Washington DC, arranged his exhibits to reflect presumed stages of evolutionary development. Artefacts were first divided up according to the purpose they were intended to serve: hunting implements in one display, food storage in another, and so on. Within these primary functional categories, Mason then ordered items in sequence of the putative evolutionary stage they represented. Objects from diverse cultures from all corners of the world were therefore arrayed alongside one another, out of their original cultural context.

In 1887, Boas decried Mason's approach to the arrangement of the Smithsonian collections in a letter to the generalist scientific journal *Science*. There Boas argued that:

> We have to study each ethnological specimen individually in its history and in its medium, and this is the important meaning of the 'geographical province' which is so frequently emphasized by A. Bastian. By regarding a single implement outside of its surroundings, outside of other phenomena affecting that people and its productions, we cannot understand its meaning. (Boas 1887a: 485)

Boas's critique was not favourably received by the American anthropological establishment. Mason (1887) replied in a subsequent issue of *Science* to reject Boas's arguments. He was joined by John Wesley Powell, the head of the Bureau of Ethnology, who wrote his own closely argued reply. Powell's (1887) main contention was that there can be no single correct systematisation of museum exhibits, since every ethnographic theory is only provisional and cannot claim absolute scientific validity. But the arrangement by geographical province advocated by Boas, Powell added, had several serious faults. First of all, Boas's approach is simply unworkable in practice: dedicating a display to each people would lead to sprawling museum galleries, confusing to the visitor and containing many duplicate items. Quite apart from these practical problems, the concept of an individual people and culture central to Boas's system fails to recognise the fluidity of ethnic identity: the composition of ethnic groups varies over time, and even at a single point in time groups may have fuzzy boundaries, shading into one another. This fluidity of ethnic identity is particularly characteristic of the Americas, averred Powell, and has been exacerbated by the disruption caused by European colonisation.

Somewhat surprisingly, given the arguments we have seen so far in this section, Powell (1887: 614) concluded his response to Boas with the observation that 'the unity of mankind is the greatest induction of anthropology'. The implication of Powell's statement is that Mason's arrangement of the Smithsonian collections was preferable, since it attempted to tell a coherent story about the commonalities between different human groups, by fitting them into a single evolutionary scheme. The approach proposed by Boas, on the other hand, offered no big picture – it would merely present an unordered selection of materials with no overarching narrative. In any case, Boas's classification by ethnic group had obvious scientific faults in that it did not accommodate the fluidity of ethnic identity.

In a rejoinder to Powell, Boas (1887b: 614) insisted that his approach would 'exhibit the individual phenomenon', while Mason's system makes 'classifications that are not founded on the phenomenon, but in the mind of the student'. Furthermore, he pointed out that his approach had already been implemented in other museums – such as the Berlin Museum für Völkerkunde – and so had demonstrated its practicability.

Just a few years after this exchange in the pages of *Science*, Boas had the opportunity to put his ideas into practice. Frederic W. Putnam (1839–1915), curator of the Peabody Museum of Archaeology and Ethnology at Harvard University, invited Boas to assist him in the curation of an ethnological exhibition for the 1893 World's Fair in Chicago. But there was a second ethnological exhibition at the Chicago World's Fair, organised by Washington anthropologists, among them Mason and Powell. Visitors to the Fair therefore had the opportunity to see duelling approaches to the arrangement of ethnographic collections, Bastian and Boas's arrangement by geographical province and the evolutionary system of Mason.

The individualising approach of Boas's ethnography and archaeology also guided his linguistics. In the next section, we see a similar confrontation between Boas and the Americanist establishment play out in the study of American languages.

14.3 Alternating sounds

While still embroiled in the debate over the arrangement of museum collections – which we examined in the previous section – Boas launched a second attack against his American colleagues, this time on the linguistic front. Once again, Boas pitted his individualising Humboldtian views against the evolutionism of American anthropologists. The opening salvo in Boas's attack was his 1889 article 'On alternating sounds'.

The 'alternating sounds' of Boas's title refer to the seemingly unpredictable variations in pronunciation that were claimed to be characteristic of many American languages. Speakers of American languages, it was said, will randomly change the sounds in their words. But when challenged on these changes, they will insist that their pronunciation is always the same. To give just one example, it was reported that in the Mexican language Chiapanec a speaker will at one time pronounce the word for 'devil' as *Tixambi* and at another as *Sisaimbui*, or pronounce the word for 'hell' variously as *Nakupaju* and *Nakapoti* (see Brinton 1890 [1888]: 398).

These Chiapenec examples are quoted from an 1888 address to the American Philosophical Society in Philadelphia by Daniel Garrison Brinton, professor of American linguistics and archaeology at the University of Pennsylvania (who we first encountered in Section 14.1). Brinton's topic at the meeting was 'The language of Palæolithic Man'. The subsequent printed paper, published 1890, bore the title 'The earliest form of human speech, as revealed by American tongues'. As is immediately apparent from these titles, Brinton used this occasion to advance the view that American languages represent an earlier stage of human evolution. One striking property of 'primitive' languages, Brinton (1890 [1888]: 397) argued, is that their sounds 'are singularly vague and fluctuating'.

In ascribing chaotic phonetic variation to American languages and treating this as a manifestation of their 'primitiveness', Brinton was invoking a common trope of the time. In Section 7.1, we saw a similar view expressed in relation to Old World languages: Georg von der Gabelentz (1840–1893) asserted that Basque and Berber, as languages 'at a lower cultural level', allow much greater variation in pronunciation than those in the Indo-European family and as such cannot be made subject to absolute sound laws.

Responding to views of this kind, Boas argued in his 1889 article that the phonetic variation supposedly attested in American languages was not an inherent property of 'primitive' languages at all, but solely the result of perceptual error on the part of the language researcher. All languages, European and American alike, make use of a fixed and finite repertoire of the total range of sounds that can be produced by the human articulatory organs. When an observer encounters a sound in a foreign language that is not present in their native repertoire, they will perceive it as a similar sound that is in their repertoire. The mapping of foreign to native sound may vary from occasion to occasion, creating the illusion of alternating sounds (Boas 1889: 52).

Boas was no doubt right to impugn the perception of his colleagues when they accused American languages of phonetic fluctuation, but the potential for cross-linguistic phonological interference was already well recognised in the literature of the time (see McElvenny 2019b). John Wesley Powell, for example, in the 1880 second edition of his *Introduction to the Study of Indian Languages*, warned of 'synthetic sounds' in American languages. These are sounds whose articulation is intermediate between familiar sounds found in English. 'Such a synthetic sound', wrote Powell (1880 [1877]: 12), 'will be heard by the student now as one, now as another sound, even from the same speaker.' The synthetic sound remains constant; it is the observer's perception of it that changes. But the wording of Powell's account placed the blame for this difficulty on the languages themselves: synthetic sounds have an 'indefinite character' and are 'not differentiated as they are in English' (ibid.). Boas's breakthrough was to centre languages and relativise the authority of European observers. The supposed signs of primitiveness in American languages were revealed to be nothing more than the misperceptions of linguists.

But Boas's position should not be confused with epistemic humility. He did believe in the possibility of correctly capturing the precise sound articulated. While previous transcribers of American languages may have been afflicted with a phonological filter, the goal of the Boasian linguist must be to eliminate this interference altogether. Even after phonemic analysis became established in linguistic scholarship in Europe and America in the 1920s – as we see in Chapters 10 and 16 – Boas maintained a preference for fine-grained phonetic transcription. It was not enough for the observer to simply acculturate themselves to the phonemes of a foreign language; they had to step outside the relativistic confines of the phonemic system and record the pure phonetic datum as accurately as possible (see Anderson 2021 [1985]: 271–6).

Despite his later resistance to phonemic analysis, Boas's account of the individual phonetic repertoire of each language evinces an awareness of phonological theory as it was developing in the 1880s (a story we traced in Chapter 9). But his conception of each language as an individual that must be understood on its own terms owes most to his Humboldtian background. The links to Humboldtian scholarship are clearly visible in the chief monument of Boasian linguistics, the *Handbook of American Indian Languages*, a compendium surveying the languages of North America, published in four volumes from 1911 to 1941. Each volume contains sketch grammars of American languages – written to Boas's specifications by Boas himself and his students – accompanied by sample texts. The first volume of the *Handbook* contains a long introduction by Boas setting out the goals and approach of the work. Towards the end of the introduction, Boas emphasises his individualising attitude to language description:

> No attempt has been made to compare the forms of the Indian grammars with the grammars of English, Latin, or even among themselves; but in each case the psychological groupings which are given depend entirely upon the inner form of each language. In other words, the grammar has been treated as though an intelligent Indian was going to develop the forms of his own thoughts by an analysis of his own form of speech. (Boas 1911: 81)

Boas's invocation of 'inner form' in this passage aligns him squarely with Humboldtian scholarship: as we saw in Section 3.5, the term 'inner form' was first used by Humboldt, and subsequently filled out and popularised by Steinthal. In this tradition, the 'inner form' of a language is the set of underlying structural principles that imbues the language with its individual character.

But Humboldt's writings could be read in very different ways. In his day, Daniel Garrison Brinton was in fact considered the most authoritative interpreter of Humboldt in America, and Brinton saw in Humboldt a fellow proponent of deterministic cultural and linguistic evolution. In Section 4.3, we saw that Humboldt did indeed toy with such views, and was cited by August Schleicher (1821–1868) in support of Schleicher's own deterministic developmental theory of 'morphology'. This tension between evolutionary and individualising interpretations of Humboldt reappears in Section 15.2, where we look at Boasian attitudes to linguistic relativity.

Just as he had done in ethnography and archaeology, Boas tackled the evolutionary prejudices that dominated research into American languages. In line with a reading of Humboldt popular in Germany, Boas insisted that each language is an individual that must be studied on its own terms. The assumed deficits of American languages were shown to be failures on the part of linguists to appreciate the individual nature of those languages. In the following chapters, we see how this relativising impulse – elaborated in different directions – would become a central thrust of American structuralism.

14.4 Further reading

As the generally recognised founder of modern American anthropology, Franz Boas is the subject of numerous secondary studies, some better than others, and not all of which can be recommended. The classic historical treatment of the early years of the Boasian school is Regna Darnell's (1998) book *And Along Came Boas: Continuity and Revolution in Americanist Anthropology*. On the connections between Boasian and Humboldtian scholarship, see Matti Bunzl's (1996) 'Franz Boas and the Humboldtian tradition: From *Volksgeist* and *Nationalcharakter* to an anthropological concept of culture' in the volume Volksgeist *as Method and Ethic: Essays on Boasian Ethnography and the German Anthropological Tradition*.

For discussion of the details of Boasian linguistics in historical context, see Michael Mackert's articles in *Historiographia Linguistica*, 'The roots of Franz Boas' view of linguistic categories as a window to the human mind' (1993) and 'Franz Boas' theory of phonetics' (1994). My own paper 'Alternating sounds and the formal franchise in phonology' (McElvenny 2019b) in the volume *Form and Formalism in Linguistics* critically examines Boas's positions on the question of phonological variation in 'primitive' languages. Margaret Thomas's (2023) chapter 'Boas' "purely analytical approach" to language classification in the backdrop to American structuralism' in *The Limits of Structuralism: Forgotten Texts in the History of Modern Linguistics* shows how Boas's individualising attitude to ethnography and linguistics manifested itself in his approach to the classification of American languages.

15 Linguistic relativity

A notion classically associated with the anthropological end of American structuralism – of which we saw the beginnings in the previous chapter – is that of 'linguistic relativity', often referred to under the name of the 'Sapir–Whorf hypothesis'. Described briefly, this is the idea that the language we speak influences the way we think and how see the world. Inherently fascinating, the topic of linguistic relativity is a perennial favourite in popular expositions of linguistic science, and is constantly revisited in academic language research. While there are numerous versions of linguistic relativity – ranging from 'strong' views that claim language determines thought and perception to 'weak' views that imagine a more subtle connection – any relativistic doctrine tends to be rather polarising: linguists are typically either keen adherents of relativism or vehement opponents.

The common binominal designation 'Sapir–Whorf hypothesis' incorporates the names of Edward Sapir (1884–1939) and Benjamin Lee Whorf (1897–1941). As we discussed in Section 14.1, Sapir was one of the most prominent pupils of Franz Boas (1858–1942), and contributed perhaps more than anyone else to the further development of the linguistic side of Boasian anthropology. While not always in agreement with Boas's methods and conclusions, Sapir continued and expanded – with innovations of his own – the research into the Indigenous languages of the Americas that had been put on a modern scientific footing by Boas. Through his teaching at the University of Chicago from 1925 to 1931 and Yale University from 1931 until shortly before his death in 1939, Sapir supervised a number of students who would carry the Boasian torch into the next generation.

Whorf was one of Sapir's graduate students at Yale. As we will see in the following sections, Whorf already had an interest in the possible links between language, thought and perception before he came to work with Sapir. Indeed, it was largely these interests that drove him to pursue the study of linguistics: Whorf sought a more solid foundation for his amateur explorations of language. But, in a sense, Whorf remained forever an amateur. Although he presented his work at academic conferences, published in academic journals, held research grants, and even taught for a time at Yale, Whorf resisted calls from his colleagues to become a full-time academic. Instead, he continued in his career as a technical inspector for a fire insurance company, on the grounds that this position allowed him to maintain the lifestyle to which he was accustomed and afforded him greater freedom in following his intellectual interests. Whorf's semi-outsider status perhaps aided in his becoming a figurehead of linguistic relativity – the most widely read presentations of his relativistic ideas were in articles he wrote for a general audience.

Although questions of linguistic relativity are today indelibly linked with Sapir and Whorf through the label 'Sapir–Whorf hypothesis', we must note that neither Sapir nor Whorf ever actually formulated anything that could be described as a 'hypothesis', in the sense of a definite proposition that can be tested empirically. Moreover, Sapir and Whorf's views were not identical, or even internally consistent. In this chapter, we examine what Sapir and Whorf actually wrote and how this was later branded as a 'hypothesis'. We then explore how their ideas were just one expression of a common sentiment in the intellectual environment of the first half of the twentieth century.

15.1 The Sapir–Whorf hypothesis

The first attestation of the term 'Sapir–Whorf hypothesis' in print would seem to be in the 1954 paper 'The Sapir–Whorf hypothesis' by Harry Hoijer (1904–1976), who had been a student of Sapir's at Chicago. Hoijer's paper had been written for an interdisciplinary conference he convened the previous year to consider 'the problem of meaning and the relationship of language to other aspects of culture' (Hoijer 1954a: vii). Most contributions to the conference revolved around Whorf's pronouncements on this problem, interpreted in various ways.

The term 'Sapir–Whorf hypothesis' therefore entered usage over a decade after the death of both its namesakes, amid confusion over what exactly this hypothesis consisted in, and in controversial discussion of its validity and implications. For his part, Hoijer (1954b: 92) located the first statement of this putative Sapir–Whorf hypothesis in an article by Sapir on 'The status of linguistics as a science'. Much as in the case of William Jones's 'philologer passage' (see Section 2.1), it has become standard practice in discussions of linguistic relativity to reproduce this quotation from Sapir. Let us maintain this tradition:

> Language is a guide to 'social reality'. [. . .] Human beings do not live in the objective world alone, nor alone in the world of social activity as ordinarily understood, but are very much at the mercy of the particular language which has become the medium of expression for their society. It is quite an illusion to imagine that one adjusts to reality essentially without the use of language and that language is merely an incidental means of solving specific problems of communication or reflection. The fact of the matter is that the 'real world' is to a large extent unconsciously built up on the language habits of the group. No two languages are ever sufficiently similar to be considered as representing the same social reality. The worlds in which different societies live are distinct worlds, not merely the same world with different labels attached. [. . .] We see and hear and otherwise experience largely as we do because the language habits of our community predispose certain choices of interpretation. (Sapir 1929 [1928]: 209–10)

From the evidence of this passage, Sapir would seem to have endorsed a strong version of linguistic relativity: reality is a social construction made through the medium of language, and languages differ to the point that the realities they create are incommensurable. As we see in the following sections, however, Sapir offered a more restrained account in other writings.

Sapir's boldness in the passage quoted above no doubt derived from the aims of the article in which it appeared. 'The status of linguistics as a science' began life as an address in 1928 to a joint meeting of the Linguistic Society of America, the American Anthropological Association, and the sections of the American Association for the Advancement of Science concerned with anthropology and language. Sapir's take-home point in this address was that linguistics had a key role to play in analysing the workings of the social realities created by language and, as such, should serve as a methodological model for other social sciences. American linguists at this time were engaged in a concerted effort to raise the professional and institutional profile of their field: the Linguistic Society of America had been founded only four years before, with the goal of cultivating the 'professional consciousness' of linguists (Bloomfield 1925). Sapir's address was part of this broader effort: it was essentially an advertisement for the discipline of linguistics – and advertising is a genre not usually marked by nuance and modesty.

Whorf espoused similar views on the relationship between language, habitual thought and reality in a number of articles, directed at both academic and general audiences. The most significant of Whorf's articles were reprinted, alongside several previously unpublished manuscripts, in the posthumous collected volume *Language, Thought, and Reality*, edited with an introduction by one of Whorf's most devoted disciples, the American psychologist John B. Carroll (1916–2003).

One of the clearest single statements of Whorf's position can be found in his 1940 article 'Science and linguistics', originally a contribution to the *MIT Technology Review*, the alumni magazine of Whorf's undergraduate alma mater, the Massachusetts Institute of Technology. Whorf (1956 [1940]: 207–9) opened his article by criticising what he called 'natural logic', the idea that 'correct, rational or intelligent *thinking*' (Whorf's italics) is a mental process that operates separately from language. On this view, language is merely a means for expressing thoughts already formulated according to universal laws of reason. While the resulting expression might be dressed up in the garb of a particular language, underneath there remains a naked, unadorned proposition, which is the same for everyone. Contrary to this view, Whorf insisted that every language is inextricably involved in the formulation of thoughts and, as such, every language brings with it its own metaphysics:

> The categories and types that we isolate from the world of phenomena we do not find there because they stare every observer in the face; on the contrary, the world is presented in a kaleidoscopic flux of impressions which has to be organized by our minds – and this means largely by the linguistic systems in our minds. (Whorf 1956 [1940]: 213)

The allegedly pure representations of modern mathematics and logic are merely distillations of the characteristic thought patterns laid down in the grammars of 'Standard Average European' languages, to use a term that Whorf (1956 [1941]a: 138) introduced in another paper. Modern science, mathematics and logic were invented by 'Westerners' speaking European languages, and these languages guide their speakers to think in certain ways. Blind to this process, Western scientists assumed that they were uncovering the laws of pure reason, when they were simply describing the peculiar structure of their native languages. The apparent universal nature of modern science, argued Whorf (1956 [1940]: 214), is an illusion, arising from the exportation of Western modes of thought to other parts of the world.

The fundamental differences in thought and perception occasioned by language become clearer when we compare languages built on very different grammatical plans. Whorf illustrated this point with examples from Hopi, a Uto-Aztecan language spoken in the South-Western corner of North America. Hopi, claimed Whorf (1956 [1940]: 216–18), conceptualises time in a radically different way from the Standard Average European languages. The tense systems of European languages divide time into a past, present and future, which leads Europeans to think of time as an inexorable flow that can be measured in quantified units. Hopi verbs, on Whorf's analysis (see also Whorf 1956 [1950]), do not indicate time in the European sense, but instead distinguish between a manifested event, an expected event, and the statement of a general law about events. For the Hopi speaker, there is no universal flow of time, but rather just events that have been experienced by the speaker and those that are expected or hoped for.

On Whorf's estimation, the abstract measurable time that ticks away in the background of Western physics is a product of the interpretation of the world imposed by Standard Average European languages. A physics formulated by Hopi speakers would not recognise time in this sense; it would be constructed on a different basis. Whorf (1956 [1940]: 217) suggested that this alternative basis might be the notion of 'intensity'. Hopi speakers do not talk of 'speed' or 'rapidity', which as concepts defined as spatial displacement over time are dependent on the Western notion of flowing time. Instead, the Hopi speak of the 'intensity' of a motion. This concept of 'intensity' could be generalised to cover all phenomena:

> We may have to introduce a new term I, intensity. Every thing and event will have an I, whether we regard the thing or event as moving or just enduring and being. Perhaps the I of an electric charge will turn out to be its voltage, or potential. (Whorf 1956 [1940]: 217)

Elsewhere, Whorf (e.g. 1956 [1936]: 55–6) implied that the perceptual habits fostered by the Hopi language might even grant its speakers a deeper understanding of some natural phenomena than can be achieved through the concepts of modern physics.

Whorf (1956 [1940]: 214) dubbed the creation of such fundamentally different perspectives on the world through language the 'linguistic relativity principle', a term – as we saw in the opening of this chapter – that remains current today as a synonym of the 'Sapir–Whorf hypothesis'. Whorf was no doubt led to this turn of phrase by Albert Einstein's (1879–1955) theory of relativity, which revolutionised modern physics in the first half of the twentieth century. A central innovation of

Einstein's special relativity was to collapse the space and time of classical physics into the single four-dimensional mathematical manifold of 'spacetime', a reconceptualisation of fundamental Western categories of experience similar to those Whorf imagined in his alternative Hopi physics (see Whorf 1956 [1950]: 58).

It is in the linguistic relativity principle that Whorf sees the ultimate justification for linguistic research. Like Sapir's (1929 [1928]) address on 'The status of linguistics as a science', Whorf's 1940 article is essentially an advertisement for linguistics. The linguist is concerned with the diversity of views embodied in the languages of the world. By investigating this diversity and exploring the range of variation, the linguist can help to reveal the multitude of alternate realities:

> We cut nature up, organize it into concepts, and ascribe significances as we do, largely because we are parties to an agreement to organize it in this way – an agreement that holds throughout our speech community and is codified in the patterns of our language. [...] This fact is very significant for modern science, for it means that no individual is free to describe nature with absolute impartiality but is constrained to certain modes of interpretation even while he thinks himself most free. The person most nearly free in such respects would be a linguist familiar with very many widely different linguistic systems. As yet no linguist is an any such position. (Whorf 1956 [1940]: 213–14)

Sapir and Whorf's respective pronouncements on linguistic relativity were therefore embedded in arguments for the utility of Boasian-style linguistics, which concentrated on the description of 'exotic' languages. However, as we see in the next section, Boasian linguistics actually chafed against many existing views on the possible connections between language, thought and perception.

15.2 Boasian linguistics and relativity

The idea that language and thought are somehow interlinked was by no means original to Sapir and Whorf. As we saw in Chapters 3 and 4, in the tradition of language scholarship that emerged in the wake of Wilhelm von Humboldt (1767–1835) it was usually believed that there is a dialectic relationship between the structure of a language and the typical thought patterns of its speakers: in a continual back and forth, a people's thinking guides the evolution of linguistic forms and linguistic forms in turn shape the evolution of their thought. The ultimate aim of most nineteenth-century language typology was to catalogue the supposed correspondences between the characteristic features of a language and the assumed mental disposition of its speakers.

Franz Boas's anthropological project – as we saw in Section 14.2 – could trace a direct lineage to Humboldt and his followers. Boas was a strong advocate of the historical particularism that characterised many leading interpretations of Humboldt in Germany: Boas held that each language and culture was unique and had to be understood on its own terms. In Section 14.3, we saw this principle applied to the investigation of American languages. In describing the sound systems and grammar of American languages, Boas sought the Humboldtian 'inner form of each language'. His grammars were to be written 'as though an intelligent Indian was going to develop the forms of his own thoughts by an analysis of his own form of speech' (Boas 1911: 81).

Sapir inherited these views from Boas, but he also had independent links to the German philological tradition. Sapir's undergraduate major was in German, and his master's thesis (Sapir 1907) was on the 1772 *Abhandlung über den Ursprung der Sprache* (*Treatise on the Origin of Language*) of Johann Gottfried von Herder (1744–1803). As we observed in Section 3.2, Herder's text is widely considered a waypoint on the road to the linguistic ideas later developed by Humboldt and his successors.

In recounting the background to the Sapir–Whorf hypothesis, it has become customary to highlight this Humboldtian heritage (see Joseph 2002: 71; cf. Koerner 2002). However, both Boas and Sapir were very critical of some of the ways in which Humboldt was interpreted. In particular, they rejected the widespread evolutionary assumption that there is a hierarchy of successive levels of development in the grammatical structure of languages. The structures of some languages, it was believed, had developed further than others, making them superior vehicles for refined thought. As we saw in Section 4.3, the most extreme exponent of this view in mainstream linguistics of the nineteenth century was perhaps August Schleicher (1821–1868), who appealed to Humboldt's writings, among other sources, in support of his theory of 'morphology'. While not all scholars were as explicit as Schleicher, postulating schemes of language evolution in which grammatical and mental processes were tied together was a common undertaking in this era, and most scholars engaged in this project cited Humboldt as their inspiration. Among American scholars, Daniel Garrison Brinton (1837–1899) was the chief representative of this interpretation of Humboldt, as we discussed in Section 14.3.

In his introduction to the 1911 first volume of the *Handbook of American Indian Languages*, Boas (1911: 64–7) acknowledged the possibility of links between language and habitual patterns of thought, although he denied that these links are in any way an index of the mental abilities of speakers. He repeated several well-worn examples of alleged deficits in American languages, such as the claim that American languages lack abstract terms or that they have no facility for expressing higher numerical quantities. These limitations do exist, wrote Boas, but not because the structure of these languages constrains the thinking of their speakers or because the speakers are mentally incapable of grasping such concepts. Rather, these peoples simply have no need to talk in abstract terms or count to higher numbers and so have never had occasion to produce such forms in their languages. If this need arose, their languages would soon adapt.

Boas similarly sought to sever the essentialising connections set up in earlier scholarship between a people's language and their alleged cultural and 'racial' traits. Even though, as we have seen in previous chapters, this was a vast topic, admitting of many nuances, the overriding assumption in most nineteenth-century scholarship was that there must be necessary links between language, lifestyle and biological heritage. Boas observed, however, that the repeated failure to find any solid links of this kind proved these nineteenth-century projects to be futile (see Boas 1911: 7).

Sapir perpetuated these Boasian positions in his own work. In his 1921 book *Language*, an introduction to linguistics intended for both beginning students in the field and the general public, Sapir dedicated an entire chapter to the problem of 'Language, race, and culture' (the title of chapter 10). Here Sapir (1921: 232–3) supported the idea that '[l]anguage and our thought-grooves are inextricably interwoven, are, in a sense, one and the same', but he argued that there are no 'significant racial differences' in thought across the human species. It is therefore impossible to align 'race' and language with one another. He denied also that there is any 'causal relation' between culture and language – one does not drive the evolution of the other. Since there are no causal connections between language, 'race' and culture, linguistic structure – 'morphology', as Sapir wrote – cannot be a sign of the level of cultural development:

> [A]ll attempts to connect particular types of linguistic morphology with certain correlated stages of cultural development are vain. Rightly understood, such correlations are rubbish. [...] When it comes to linguistic form, Plato walks with the Macedonian swineherd, Confucius with the head-hunting savage of Assam. (Sapir 1921: 233–4)

But Sapir was still interested in the Humboldtian project of investigating the structural diversity of the world's languages, even if he rejected the common aim of tying structure to the supposed mental and cultural development of speakers. Chapters 4 to 6 of Sapir's *Language* survey various grammatical 'processes' and 'concepts' attested in the languages of the world, and offer a fine-grained analysis of how these features can cluster to produce a characteristic 'type or plan or structural "genius"' (Sapir 1921: 127) of a language. But Sapir's types do not fit into any overarching deterministic scheme of language evolution. Neither do they pinpoint some immutable essence underlying individual languages: over time, languages frequently drift from one type to another (ibid.: 154–6).

Even though Boas and Sapir were both in many ways inheritors of the Humboldtian tradition, their writings evince scepticism regarding key ideas in Humboldtian scholarship, especially with respect to supposed links between language and thought – that is, linguistic relativity. Both Boas and Sapir rejected the ultimate aim of many nineteenth-century Humboldtians to find connections between linguistic forms and cultural and 'racial' traits, which were often embedded in deterministic schemes of language evolution. As we see in the next section, Sapir's – and, for that matter, Whorf's – relativistic views had much more in common with other ideas in their contemporary intellectual milieu.

15.3 Analytic philosophy and mysticism

The tensions we saw in the previous section suggest that the traditional narrative casting the Sapir–Whorf hypothesis as a latter-day outgrowth of nineteenth-century Humboldtian scholarship is in need of qualification. In his 1996 paper 'The immediate sources of the "Sapir–Whorf hypothesis"' (reprinted in expanded form as chapter 4 of Joseph 2002), the historian of linguistics John Joseph argued that Sapir and Whorf owe a much greater debt to ideas in their direct intellectual environment of the early twentieth century.

Examining Sapir's writings of the early 1920s, Joseph (2002: 75) identified a change in Sapir's relativistic rhetoric coinciding with his first reading of the 1923 book *The Meaning of Meaning* by Charles K. Ogden (1889–1957) and Ivor Armstrong Richards (1893–1979). We already encountered this book in Section 12.3, in our exploration of the linguistic views of the Anglo-Polish anthropologist Bronislaw Malinowski (1884–1942): one of Malinowski's most significant essays on language, 'The problem of meaning in primitive languages', was published as a 'supplement' to this book. Sapir (1923) wrote a glowing review of *The Meaning of Meaning*, and was soon echoing its themes and referring to it favourably in other publications.

Ogden and Richards's book was just one expression of a widespread moral panic around the use and abuse of language in philosophical and political discourse which began to grip intellectuals towards the end of the nineteenth century. The young twentieth century only exacerbated the panic as public discourse was distorted by new forms of propaganda, disseminated by such new technologies as radio and film, which accompanied and facilitated such catastrophic upheavals as World War I and the political polarisation that saw the rise of totalitarian governments across Europe. The perceived crisis of language and meaning, and the desire to overcome it are the burning problems that motivated *The Meaning of Meaning*.

The source of the trouble, argued Ogden and Richards, is that we let our language dictate our thought. We assume that our usual turns of phrase are simple reflections of the truth, when in fact they twist and conceal it. We focus so narrowly on words that we never ask what they really mean, and how they mean:

> [W]ords come between us and objects in countless subtle ways, if we do not realize the nature of their power. In logic, as we have seen, they lead to the creation of bogus entities, the universals, properties and so forth [. . .] By concentrating attention on themselves, words encourage the futile study of forms that has done so much to discredit Grammar; by the excitement which they provoke through their emotive force, discussion is for the most part rendered sterile; by the various types of Verbomania and Graphomania, the satisfaction of naming is realized, and the sense of personal power factitiously enhanced. (Ogden and Richards 1956 [1923]: 45)

The sentiment articulated by Ogden and Richards lay at the heart of most academic critiques of language at this time. This is the same period that saw the beginnings of analytic philosophy – which would go on to become one of the major strands of English-speaking philosophy in the twentieth century – in the work of such figures as Bertrand Russell (1872–1970) and Ludwig Wittgenstein (1889–1951) at the University of Cambridge, where Ogden and Richards were also based. Russell and Wittgenstein were similarly convinced of the pernicious influence of unexamined language on thought. Each in their own way, they sought to improve reasoning by rooting out the confusions and fallacies in European philosophy engendered by blind subservience to the thought patterns embodied in Indo-European languages. In a series of public lectures Russell delivered in London in 1918, he commented:

> The influence of language on philosophy has, I believe, been profound and almost unrecognized. If we are not to be misled by this influence, it is necessary to become conscious of it, and to ask ourselves deliberately how far it is legitimate. The subject-predicate logic, with the substance-attribute metaphysic, are a case in point. It is doubtful whether either would have been invented by a people speaking a non-Aryan [i.e. non-Indo-European] language; certainly they do not seem to have arisen in China, except in connection with Buddhism, which brought an Indian philosophy with it. (Russell 1918–19: 38)

Sapir and Whorf embraced this sentiment in many of their pronouncements on linguistic relativity. In his 1924 article 'The grammarian and his language' – like the later 'The status of linguistics as a science' (see Section 15.1), an advertisement for disciplinary linguistics, but aimed at a general audience – Sapir repeated, with direct reference to Ogden and Richards, the warning that we must not allow our language to mislead us:

> To a far greater extent than the philosopher has realized, he is likely to become the dupe of his speech-forms, which is equivalent to saying that the mould of his thought, which is typically a linguistic mould, is apt to be projected into his conception of the world. Thus innocent linguistic categories may take on the formidable appearance of cosmic absolutes. (Sapir 1949 [1924]: 157)

Linguistics can save us from this danger, argued Sapir, by allowing us to fathom the range of diversity in conceptions of the world:

> Perhaps the best way to get behind our thought processes and to eliminate from them all the accidents and irrelevances due to their linguistic garb is to plunge into the study of exotic modes of expression. At any rate, I know of no better way to kill spurious 'entities'. (Sapir 1949 [1924]: 157)

We will recall from Section 15.1 that Whorf (1956 [1940]: 213–14) later made a similar point in the presentation of his own version of linguistic relativity: 'The person most nearly free in such respects [describing nature impartially] would be a linguist familiar with very many widely different linguistic systems.'

While Sapir and Whorf presented knowledge of linguistic diversity as a way out of the philosopher's predicament, the early analytic philosophers generally held much less relativistic views. For Russell and the early Wittgenstein, there were not many equally valid descriptions of the world offered by each language, but just one correct description, which all existing languages obscure in different ways. Russell devised new logical notations intended to more accurately reflect what he took to be the true underlying structure of propositions. Ogden and Richards were engaged in the same project in *The Meaning of Meaning* (see McElvenny 2014). Building on the functional model of language they set out in that book – which we examined in Section 12.3 – Ogden and Richards outlined a method of 'definition' to unpack and paraphrase the meaning of words. Through this process of definition, we can achieve clarity about the 'thoughts or references' that our words evoke and thereby break the spell of language over our thought.

Such initiatives for language reform were not a purely academic phenomenon. Ogden and Richards's book was enthusiastically received by a broad readership, and was in fact just one title in a burgeoning genre of guides to applied semiotics. Books in this genre typically began by proposing a model of how words and other signs are used to make meaning and then proceeded to offer techniques for identifying and avoiding the misleading, manipulative or abusive use of words in propaganda, philosophical debates, and so on.

Perhaps the most famous project in this vein – at the vulgarising end of the spectrum – was the 'General Semantics' of Alfred Korzybski (1879–1950). In his 1933 book *Science and Sanity*, Korzybski proposed the therapeutic device of diacritic marks that can be applied to texts in order to clarify the meaning of words. An ecumenical guide to applied semiotics of this era – drawing on *The Meaning of Meaning* and *Science and Sanity*, among other works – is the 1938 *The Tyranny of Words* by the American author Stuart Chase (1888–1985). Chase also wrote the foreword to *Language, Thought, and Reality*, the 1956 collected volume of Whorf's writings.

Philosophical critiques of language merged with the other great language engineering effort of this period, the international language movement. Gathering momentum in the 1880s and reaching a peak just before World War II, the international language movement was a gaggle of competing projects that all strove to fashion a single language for international communication. The chief motivation for these projects was to break down the barriers between peoples and promote mutual understanding in this age of nationalism and war. But allied to this goal was the hope that an international language would also be a more suitable medium for rational thought and modern scientific research. In their structure, most international languages proposed in this era followed the example set by Esperanto, which represented a sort of consciously constructed creole, with a grammar and vocabulary derived from a mixture of the principal European languages, regularised for both ease of learning and 'logical' consistency (see McElvenny 2018a: 58–77).

While Russell and Wittgenstein were both critical of the international language movement, among their colleagues there were many philosophers and logicians who not only subscribed to the movement's goals, but actively participated in the construction and further development of language projects. Ogden proposed his own international language, 'Basic English', a refined and simplified version of Standard English (see Ogden 1933 [1930]). Ogden's Basic was essentially an application of the method of definition from *The Meaning of Meaning*. The chief contrivance of Basic was its core vocabulary of 850 English words, 'scientifically selected' for their reliability in reference. Small in size and therefore supposedly easy to learn, this core vocabulary offered a restricted repertoire of terms that speakers could use to paraphrase anything they wished to say in a more precise and logically sound form (see McElvenny 2015).

Sapir, too, was drawn into the international language movement, as the head of linguistic research at the International Auxiliary Language Association (IALA), an American private research foundation dedicated to the international language problem. Under the auspices of IALA, Sapir and his students produced studies comparing the cross-linguistic expression of various grammatical categories, research intended to determine the optimal forms for a future international language. Through the course of this work, Sapir never surrendered his relativism to the absolutism of the philosophers. In a 1929 report to IALA, Sapir argued that the aim should not be to find the perfect logical form for the international language. Rather, the international language would be a product of 'Occidental culture' and, as such, should simply strive to exploit the structural features already shared by most European languages:

> [S]o far as the logical structure of a language is concerned, we are perhaps not at the end of our researches [...W]e, who are fashioning Occidental culture[,] have been using certain useful linguistic tools. These tools vary from place to place, but by and large are remarkably similar [...W]hy not use the common bond of experience which is implicit in the use of all these tools in a simplified and regularized form? (Sapir 1929: 17–18)

Whorf, who was never directly involved in the international language movement, maintained a similar scepticism regarding the pretensions of the language constructors. In his 1941 article 'Languages and logic', another of his popular expositions of linguistic relativity for the *MIT Technology Review*, Whorf (1956 [1941]b: 244) commented that, in Ogden's Basic English, 'an eviscerated British English, with its concealed premises working harder than ever, is to be fobbed off on an unsuspecting world as the substance of pure Reason itself'. Despite the philosophers' exertions, no single language can capture pure reason and provide an unbiased view of the world. Only by accumulating the alternative perspectives contained in different languages can we approach the truth: 'The only correctives [to a provisional analysis of reality] lie in all those other tongues which by aeons of independent evolution have arrived at different, but equally logical, provisional analyses' (ibid.).

We should note that Whorf's resolute commitment to relativity was not exclusively intellectual in character, but was interwoven with his religious convictions. From a young age, Whorf had been deeply involved with theosophy, an esoteric religious movement with universalist aspirations that rests heavily on an appropriation of elements of Hinduism and Buddhism refracted through the lens of Western mysticism. Several of Whorf's articles on linguistic relativity were specifically written for a theosophical audience, and Whorf frequently implied that his ideas about the influence of language on thought and perception were part and parcel of theosophical teaching. In his posthumous 1942 article 'Language, mind, and reality', published in the journal *The Theosophist*, Whorf (1956 [1942]: 252) wrote: 'This doctrine [of linguistic relativity] is new to Western science', but 'it is known, or something like it is known, to the philosophies of India and to modern Theosophy'.

From the evidence presented in this chapter, it would seem that Sapir and Whorf's respective relativistic views were an amalgam of philological tradition, modern philosophy, and mysticism, deployed as a justification for research into linguistic diversity on the Boasian model. Their talk of 'thought-grooves', 'social reality', and the 'kaleidoscopic flux of impressions which has to be organized by our minds' is captivating, and has ensured enduring interest in their work on linguistic relativity. But this rhapsodic praise of linguistic and mental diversity was not necessarily to the taste of all linguists in this period. In the next chapter, we meet a somewhat more austere vision of linguistics as a science in the work of Leonard Bloomfield.

15.4 Further reading

An approachable and more or less scientifically sound introduction to linguistic relativity, which treats present-day research as well as its historical background, is Guy Deutscher's 2010 *Through the Language Glass: Why the World Looks Different in Other Languages*. Sapir and Whorf's own publications dealing with linguistic relativity remain very readable. The main papers, most of them cited in the text of this chapter, are collected, for Whorf, in the volume *Language, Thought, and Reality: Selected Writings of Benjamin Lee Whorf* (Carroll 1956), and for Sapir in the *Selected Writings of Edward Sapir in Language, Culture and Personality* (Mandelbaum 1949).

For specific discussion of the historical context of the 'Sapir–Whorf hypothesis', see John Joseph's essay on 'The sources of the Sapir–Whorf hypothesis' in his 2002 book *From Whitney to Chomsky: Essays on the History of American Linguistics*, and Konrad Koerner's 2002 paper 'On the sources of the Sapir-Whorf hypothesis' in the volume *Toward a History of American Linguistics*. Detailed reconstruction and exposition of Whorf's ideas can be found in Penny Lee's 1996 book *The Whorf Theory Complex: A Critical Reconstruction*, which draws on both published and archival sources. Regna Darnell, in chapter 19 of her 1990 biography *Edward Sapir: Linguist, Anthropologist, Humanist*, examines the relationship between Sapir and Whorf. John B. Carroll's introduction to the 1956 *Language, Thought, and Reality* contains a succinct biography of Whorf.

On the fate of Humboldtian language typology from the end of the nineteenth to the beginning of the twentieth century, see my paper 'Gabelentz' typology: Humboldtian linguistics on the threshold of structuralism' in the volume *The Limits of Structuralism: Forgotten Texts in the History of Modern Linguistics* (McElvenny 2023c). For discussion of philosophical critique of language and the international language movement in the early twentieth century, with a focus on Ogden's Basic English, see chapter 3 of my book *Language and Meaning in the Age of Modernism: C. K. Ogden and His Contemporaries* (McElvenny 2018a). Ken Hirschkop's (2019) *Linguistic Turns, 1890–1950: Writing on Language as Social Theory* – in particular chapter 6 – addresses many of the same topics.

16 The culmination of American structuralism

We end our story in this chapter by examining the main developments in American linguistics between the two World Wars. The history of American linguistics in this period is of worldwide significance, since it set the stage for the further development of the field internationally after World War II. The postwar period was an era of American political and economic hegemony, which entailed increasing dominance in the academic and intellectual spheres.

The leading theorists who determined the direction of American linguistics in the interwar period were Edward Sapir (1884–1939) and Leonard Bloomfield (1887–1949). As we will recall from Chapter 14, they are two of Hymes and Fought's (1981 [1975]) 'principal figures' of American structuralism. Franz Boas (1858–1942) had already made the synchronic description of 'exotic' languages – that is, languages not built on the 'Standard Average European' model (see Section 15.1) – a central focus of American linguistics. Sapir and Bloomfield's chief contribution was to elaborate the techniques necessary for this task and, each in their own way, to put this undertaking on a solid scientific footing.

In their methods, both Sapir and Bloomfield drifted towards formalist approaches to the study of language. That is to say, they sought to describe linguistic forms – the sounds, structures and processes in languages – as self-contained systems, and put to one side considerations of what those forms might mean or how they might be used. Bloomfield was the more consequential of the two in his commitment to formalism. He also expended more energy in trying to integrate linguistics into the broader American scientific scene.

Perhaps because of the crisp, clearly defined solutions Bloomfield seemed to offer, his writings were treated by many younger linguists as a kind of constitution of American structuralism that codified the basic principles of the movement. The methods he pioneered, and rationalisations he gave for those methods, were emulated and extended by scholars of the next generation. In the following sections, we first explore Sapir and Bloomfield's formalist turn, and how Bloomfield sought to ally his work with the latest trends in psychology and the philosophy of science. We then observe the extension and radicalisation of formalism in the next generation, and the denouement of American structuralism after World War II.

16.1 Edward Sapir, Leonard Bloomfield and formalism

In their writings, both Edward Sapir and Leonard Bloomfield emphasised that the linguist can – and indeed should – study the formal patterns found in each language without reference to their meaning, use or any other external factors. This formalist attitude embraced by Sapir and Bloomfield was in many ways a continuation of existing tendencies in linguistic scholarship, sharpened by the latest advances in the field.

In his 1921 book *Language*, an introduction to linguistics as he conceived it, Sapir (1921: 9–10) commented that he did not wish to treat language as a 'concrete mechanism', as it would be studied by the physiologist or the psychologist. Rather, he sought to undertake 'an inquiry into the function and form of the arbitrary systems of symbolism that we term languages'. That is, Sapir imagined languages to be abstract entities that can be investigated without consideration of how they are actually manifested in the brains and bodies of speakers.

Furthermore, Sapir held that the formal side of the arbitrary system constituted by each language operates to a large extent independently of the functions it is called on to perform. In the arrangement of its sounds, observed Sapir (1921: 63), 'every language has an inner phonetic system of definite pattern'. Although he did not use the term 'phoneme' in *Language*, this 'inner phonetic system' to which he referred was nothing other than the phonology of a language as understood in phonemic theory (we traced the origin and development of phonemic theory in Chapters 9 and 10).

In addition to its 'inner phonetic system', every language also has 'a definite feeling for patterning on the level of grammatical formation'. Sapir (1921: 63) continued: 'Both of these submerged and powerfully controlling impulses to definite form operate as such, regardless of the need for expressing particular concepts or of giving consistent external shape to particular groups of concepts.' Sapir therefore saw languages not only as abstract systems, but also recognised that their formal structures, in both phonology and grammar, are shaped by their own inherent principles.

In a review of Sapir's *Language*, Bloomfield (1922) praised Sapir for proclaiming language to be the autonomous province of the linguist, a self-sufficient object of study separate from the concerns of the physiologist or psychologist. But at the same time, he lamented Sapir's lapses in not following through on this promise: several chapters of Sapir's book discuss the 'conceptual' aspects of grammar, and others even address questions of how linguistic form may be connected to culture and 'race'. We will recall from Section 15.2, however, that even though Sapir broached such topics, he was very cautious in his conclusions, and rejected essentialising and deterministic accounts of links between linguistic structures and patterns of thought and culture.

In his own programmatic statements on linguistics, Bloomfield strove even more strenuously for the separation of form and function. One of the clearest expressions of this attitude is Bloomfield's 1926 paper 'A set of postulates for a science of language', an attempt to offer a succinct set of axioms defining the fundamental principles and methods of linguistics as a science. In his 'Postulates',

Bloomfield (1926: 155) defined a language as the 'totality of utterances that can be made in a speech-community'. Studying a language therefore amounts to capturing the total range of utterances that can be made in that language. Every linguistic form has a meaning and every meaning corresponds to a form, but the 'utterance is made up wholly of forms'. That is to say, the object of investigation proper to the linguist is the forms that make up utterances, of which the language is in turn comprised.

The basic unit of form in Bloomfield's scheme was the 'morpheme': it is a 'recurrent (meaningful) form which in turn cannot be analyzed into smaller recurrent (meaningful) forms' (Bloomfield 1926: 155). 'Morpheme' was an existing linguistic term: as we will recall from Section 9.1, the term had been introduced by Jan Baudouin de Courtenay (1845–1929) in the 1880s as part of the study of alternations which gave rise to modern phonemic theory. Baudouin de Courtenay's morpheme was similarly the minimal meaning-bearing part of a word. One level lower, Bloomfield's morphemes are made up of phonemes, the 'distinctive sounds' which serve to distinguish one morpheme from another but which bear no meanings themselves. This distinction between meaning-bearing morphemes and meaningless phonemes is the same as that later captured by the notion of 'double articulation' or the 'duality of patterning', which we introduced in Section 13.1.

On Bloomfield's analysis, linguists can therefore decompose linguistic forms to a point where meaning is absent, but they have no methods to reduce meaning to a level where forms play no role. For this reason, argued Bloomfield, it makes sense for linguists to pursue an approach to the study of language that takes form as the starting point (Bloomfield 1926: 157).

The general contours of Sapir and Bloomfield's formalism should be fairly familiar to us by this point. Neogrammarian historical-comparative linguistics of the late nineteenth century had already taken a formalist turn in its methods and rhetoric. As we saw in Section 7.3, it was the Neogrammarians' obsession with treating linguistic forms – with their various alternations and diachronic transmutations – as autonomous objects of study that constituted the 'positivism' in linguistics decried by Karl Vossler (1872–1949). Neogrammarian 'positivism' was formalist in the sense in which we use the term here: although the Neogrammarians gestured towards physiological forces as the driver of sound change and psychological processes as producing counteracting analogies, these causal factors were thought to lie outside linguistics proper. The task of the Neogrammarian linguist was simply to observe the changes in forms and devise rules describing them.

Both Sapir and Bloomfield began their university studies in Germanic philology and were inducted into Indo-European linguistics, which in their student days was dominated by Neogrammarian doctrine, with its formalist bent. After completing his master's degree in German, Sapir moved into Boasian linguistic anthropology as a doctoral student (see Section 15.2). However, Sapir always maintained an interest in historical-comparative research, and applied its methods to the American context. Indeed, Sapir's continued allegiance to historical-comparative research became a point of friction between him and Boas. In the absence of ancient written records, Boas believed historical reconstructions in American languages to be irredeemably speculative: he felt that in many cases it was impossible to determine whether lexical and morphological similarities between American languages were due to common historical origin or more recent borrowing. Sapir, for his part, felt that Boas simply lacked the relevant linguistic training and did not understand the methods (see Darnell 1998: chap. 12).

Bloomfield was more deeply rooted in Indo-European tradition than Sapir and stayed longer in the fold. Bloomfield had a family connection to historical linguistics: his uncle was Maurice Bloomfield (1855–1928), a noted Sanskritist and Indo-Europeanist who had been a student of William Dwight Whitney (who we met in Chapter 5). Leonard Bloomfield wrote his doctoral dissertation (Bloomfield 1909–10) on a topic in Germanic historical linguistics, and his first university appointments were as a German language instructor and professor of comparative philology. It was only after he was ensconced in a professorial chair that Bloomfield turned his attention to the synchronic description of non-Indo-European languages, in particular the Austronesian language Tagalog and American Indigenous languages.

Bloomfield also had a personal connection to the Neogrammarians. In order to be promoted from language instructor to assistant professor at the University of Illinois, he had to prove he had studied with the greats of his field in Germany. In the academic year 1913–14 – just before the outbreak of World War I – Bloomfield travelled to Germany to receive instruction from the ageing founders of the Neogrammarian movement. Bloomfield is perhaps the last leading American linguist who was obliged to make such a pilgrimage in aid of career advancement. In subsequent generations, a homegrown American education was sufficient for most to make a career in linguistics, and after World War II an American PhD soon became the gold standard in research qualifications, attracting students from around the world who could expect to go on to illustrious careers in America and internationally.

In a letter from 1919, Bloomfield cited Pāṇini and the Indo-Europeanist Jacob Wackernagel (1853–1938) as his chief masters in linguistic method (see Hockett 1987: 41). Pāṇini was the ancient Sanskrit grammarian whose abstract analyses inspired much work in nineteenth-century European linguistics (see Sections 2.3 and 8.3). Wackernagel could perhaps best be described as a peripheral member of the Neogrammarian movement: although he trained with Neogrammarians and was sympathetic to their views, he avoided involvement in their theoretical debates about exceptionless sound laws and preferred to engage directly with data. The lesson Bloomfield (1919, in Hockett 1987: 41) claimed to have learnt from Pāṇini and Wackernagel was to have '[n]o preconceptions; find out which sound-variations are distinctive (as to meaning), and then analyze morphology and syntax by putting together everything that is alike.'

The earliest stirrings of structuralism only served to accentuate the formalist attitude to language, and Sapir and Bloomfield were caught up in the structuralist wave as it swept across the Atlantic from Europe. The 1916 *Cours de linguistique générale* of Ferdinand de Saussure (1857–1913), often cited as the founding document of structuralism (as we discussed in Chapter 8), wove formalism into the very fabric of the theory. A key motivation for Saussure in putting forward the notion of *la langue* was to fashion a distinct object of study for linguistics that demarcated it from psychology and other sciences, such as anthropology, traditional normative grammar, philology, and so on.

As we observed in Section 8.2, Saussure's *langue* is the abstract synchronic system that constitutes each language, considered independently of its use in *la parole*. While language undeniably has a mental and social basis, the abstraction of *la langue* allows the linguist to study language on its own terms, without becoming entangled in these heterogeneous factors. Saussure (1922 [1916]: 25) commented: '[A]mong so many dualities, language [*la langue*] alone seems to lend itself to independent definition and provide a fulcrum that satisfies the mind' (English translation in Saussure 1959 [1916]: 16). We saw at the beginning of this section that Sapir's formalism in *Language* was directed towards a similar demarcation of linguistics from other sciences. In his review of Sapir's *Language*, Bloomfield (1922: 142) cited Saussure's *Cours* on this point as 'giving a theoretic foundation to the newer trend of linguistic study'.

But Sapir and Bloomfield's respective turns to formalism were more than just a continuation of existing disciplinary trends. As the historian of linguistics Jean-Michel Fortis argued in his 2019 paper 'On Sapir's notion of form/pattern and its aesthetic background', Sapir's understanding of linguistic form owed much to aesthetic theory as adumbrated by Benedetto Croce (1866–1952) and contemporary art theorists. Croce – we will recall from Section 7.3 – was an Italian philosopher and interpreter of Wilhelm von Humboldt (1767–1835), who Karl Vossler cited as an influence on his 'idealism' in linguistics. Sapir (1921: iii, 237, 239) mentions Croce explicitly in both the preface and final chapter – on 'Language and Literature' – of *Language*.

Sapir's debt to scholarship in aesthetics is visible in the way he conceived of patterns in language as being created by an 'innate striving for formal elaboration and expression', as Sapir (1949 [1924]: 156) put it in his 1924 essay 'The grammarian and his language'. According to Sapir, language structure is not the accidental result of accumulated usage, but rather the deliberate product of a drive for formal arrangement. In his paper, Fortis demonstrated that this notion of a form-drive has deep roots in German art theory.

In contrast to Sapir's humanistic approach to linguistic form, Bloomfield took a hard-nosed scientistic stance. In the following sections, we locate the main influence on Bloomfield's attitudes in the psychological school of behaviourism. The opposition between Sapir's abiding humanism and Bloomfield's scientism is perhaps summed up most succinctly in an observation by the anthropologist C. F. 'Carl' Voegelin (1906–1986), who had known both Sapir and Bloomfield personally. Sapir, Voegelin said, 'spoke deprecatingly of Bloomfield's sophomoric psychology', while Bloomfield 'referred to Sapir as a "medicine man"' (Voegelin in Hockett 1970: 539–40).

16.2 Bloomfield and behaviourism

The scientific outlook embodied in the mature work of Leonard Bloomfield was shaped above all by the psychological doctrines of 'behaviourism'. Bloomfield not only framed his theories in behaviourist terms, but also took his cue from behaviourists in formulating justifications for linguistic research.

Behaviourism arose in the period of foundational conflict that accompanied the institutionalisation of psychology as an academic discipline around the turn of the nineteenth to the twentieth century. We briefly surveyed the chief competing schools of this period in Section 13.1. The trademark of behaviourism, setting it apart from other schools, was an uncompromising empiricism. Even though experimental approaches had become increasingly prevalent in psychology towards the end of the nineteenth century, introspection, where the researcher reflects on their own thoughts, remained a core research method in many psychological schools, often used in conjunction with experimentation. The behaviourists, however, rejected any talk of what might be going on – invisibly – inside people's heads. The psychologist, argued the behaviourists, can only appeal to the observable external manifestations of mental activity, namely behaviour.

Introducing the term 'behaviourism' in his 1913 manifesto 'Psychology as the behaviorist views it', the American psychologist John B. Watson (1878–1958) summarised the approach with the following words:

> Psychology as the behaviorist views it is a purely objective branch of natural science. Its theoretical goal is the prediction and control of behavior. Introspection forms no essential part of its methods, nor is the scientific value of its data dependent on the readiness with which they lend themselves to interpretation in terms of consciousness. The behaviorist, in his effort to get a unitary scheme of animal response, recognizes no dividing line between man and brute. The behavior of man, with all its refinement and complexity, forms only a part of the behaviorist's total scheme of investigation. (Watson 1913: 158)

On Watson's account, the behaviourist must abandon any consideration of conscious human thought and instead simply investigate the manifest behaviour of their experimental subjects. Furthermore, there is no difference in kind between human and animal psychology: human behaviour differs from that of animals like dogs and rats only in that it is made up of more complex sequences of reactions to stimuli.

To demonstrate a causal connection between a specific stimulus and a response, behaviourists typically devised experiments to 'condition' or train their subjects, whether animal or human, to react in a certain way to a particular stimulus. A notorious example is the 'Little Albert' experiment conducted by Watson and his then-graduate student Rosalie Rayner (1898–1935). Watson and Rayner trained a baby known pseudonymously as 'Albert B.' to have a fear reaction to cute, furry things. Over several experimental sessions, Little Albert was presented with a rat, which he reached out to touch. But as soon as Albert touched the rat, a metal bar was struck behind his head to produce a loud, scary noise that upset him. After several weeks in which this conditioning procedure was repeated, it was found that Albert would immediately respond with fear to the sight of the rat, without any sound being made. Albert extended this fear response to other furry creatures and objects, such as a rabbit, a dog, a fur coat, cotton wool, and a Santa Claus mask with beard. He did not react negatively to other, non-furry stimuli, however, such as toy blocks (the published report of the experiment is Watson and Rayner 1920).

The process of conditioning not only served the purpose of proving connections between stimulus–reaction pairs, but was also an instrument of regulating behaviour. As we can read in the quotation from Watson above, a key goal of behaviourism was to 'control' behaviour. This goal was part of the ethos of the social sciences in this era, especially in the United States. American society in the late nineteenth and early twentieth centuries was undergoing massive changes, with increasing industrialisation, urbanisation and immigration. In order to master the challenges presented by these changes, professional elites in America embarked on programmes of rational social reform, in a movement that is generally referred to as 'progressivism'. Proponents of progressivism believed that, given the right opportunities and guidance, every man, woman and child could acquire the necessary skills and moral virtues required to be a productive, upstanding member of society.

Social scientists – not least among them psychologists – eagerly aligned themselves with progressivist aspirations. Conditioning was marketed as a technique for efficiently raising children, correcting deviancy, or simply improving the behaviour of the average citizen. In a 1926 article in *Harper's Magazine*, a journal with a general middle-class readership, Watson (1926: 728) envisaged a future where behaviourism 'may be able to help the home, the school, the church, society to bring up a socialized but individual human product'.

Bloomfield's conversion to behaviourism was a result of his contact with Albert Paul Weiss (1879–1931), a leading behaviourist and a colleague of Bloomfield's at the Ohio State University. Bloomfield's behaviourism was already on show in his 1926 'Postulates for a science of language', a text we introduced in the previous section. There Bloomfield (1926: 155) defined meaning in language as 'a recurrent stimulus-reaction feature which corresponds to a form', casting his account in behaviourist terms. Bloomfield's 'Postulates' were in fact inspired by Weiss's 1925 paper 'One set of postulates for a behavioristic psychology' (first delivered orally in 1924). Weiss aimed in his paper to outline axioms underlying behaviourist psychology, just as Bloomfield sought to do for linguistics in his 1926 paper.

The comprehensiveness of Bloomfield's conversion to behaviourism is most striking when we compare the two introductory books on linguistics that he wrote in the course of his career. The first of these, the 1914 *Introduction to the Study of Language*, more or less emulated Neogrammarian approaches to psychology: Bloomfield (1914: iv, 316) gestured towards the writings of Wilhelm Wundt (1832–1920; for discussion of the Neogrammarians' attitude to Wundt, see Section 6.3). Bloomfield's second introductory book, however, the 1933 *Language*, is thoroughly behaviourist. In illustrating the nature of language, for example, Bloomfield sketched the following hypothetical scene:

> Suppose Jack and Jill are walking down a lane. Jill is hungry. She sees an apple in a tree. She makes a noise with her larynx, tongue, and lips. Jack vaults the fence, climbs the tree, takes the apple, brings it to Jill, and places it in her hand. Jill eats the apple. (Bloomfield 1933: 22)

Jill's 'state of hunger and the sight or smell of the food are the *stimulus*', continued Bloomfield (1933: 24). If Jill had been alone then her '*reaction*' may have been to move towards the food. But in the presence of Jack, Jill's reaction was to produce noises – to use language – which in turn served as a stimulus to Jack, causing him to actualise the reaction of securing the food. Bloomfield concluded:

> [Jack] performed the actions that were beyond Jill's strength, and in the end Jill got the apple. *Language enables one person to make a reaction (R) when another person has the stimulus (S). [. . .] The division of labor, and, with it, the whole working of human society, is due to language.* (1933: 24; Bloomfield's italics)

Bloomfield's scenario not only reveals an intriguing 1930s conception of gender roles, but also assimilates language to behaviourist sequences of stimulus and reaction. On this account, language is simply a means for extending these sequences and distributing them across individuals.

We might also observe that Bloomfield's physiological description of Jill's speech as 'mak[ing] a noise with her larynx, tongue, and lips' is reminiscent of the materialist or monist terms in which August Schleicher (1821–1868) conceived of language, which we saw in Section 4.2. These parallels are no coincidence: the behaviourists were in many ways the heirs to scientific materialism and Comtean positivism (which we encountered in Section 7.3) in their banishment of the mind and soul, and worship of the natural sciences (on behaviourism, materialism and Comtean positivism, see further Leahy 2018 [1987]: chap. 11).

Bloomfield's adherence to behaviourism extended to adopting behaviourist fantasies of controlling people to create rational agents in a well-ordered society. In a 1929 address on 'Linguistics as a science' – partly intended as a response to Sapir's 'The status of linguistics as a science' of the year before (see Section 15.1) – Bloomfield touted linguistics as the willing servant of the progressivist agenda. While Sapir saw a key role for linguistics in revealing the myriad possible perspectives on the world, Bloomfield saw it as a tool for manipulating human behaviour:

> I believe that in the near future – in the next few generations, let us say – linguistics will be one of the main sectors of scientific advance, and that in this sector science will win through to the understanding and control of human conduct.
>
> In the domains of physics and biology science has for some time been working with success and has given us great power. In the domain of anthropology – that is, in the study of man's super-biological activities – science has been unsuccessful. [. . .]
>
> The truth of this contrast and its tragic import appear plainly in the fact that our achievements in non-human science do us little good, because we cannot understand or control their human consequences. We make powerful engines, but we have no way of deciding who is to use them, and we have seen them used for our destruction. We can prevent suffering and widen the scope of life, but the fruition of

these our powers is disturbed by such means as the hazards of gambling. (Bloomfield 1930 [1929]: 553–4)

16.3 Bloomfield and logical positivism

The positivistic attitude animating Bloomfield's behaviourism – which we explored in the previous section – was widespread in the early twentieth century and found expression in the doctrines of many different schools. The most prominent articulation of this attitude as an explicit philosophy of science was made in the 'logical positivism' – also known as 'logical empiricism' – of the Vienna Circle. In the 1930s, Bloomfield came into contact with leading members of the Vienna Circle and found in their ideas confirmation and reinforcement of many of the positions to which he had already been led by behaviourism.

The Vienna Circle was an academic discussion group, most active in Vienna in the late 1920s and early 1930s, dedicated to the task of securing the epistemological foundations of modern science. Through this work, the Circle became one of the central locations at which early analytic philosophy was incubated – alongside the Cambridge of Bertrand Russell (1872–1970) and Ludwig Wittgenstein (1889–1951), which we visited in Section 15.3.

The most vocal members of the Vienna Circle did not view their philosophy as a purely academic project, but sought to 'fashion tools of thought for the everyday', as they put it in their 1929 manifesto (Verein Ernst Mach 2006 [1929]: 10–11). They presented a public image of the Circle as a socially engaged collective devoted to combating 'metaphysics' by furthering the 'scientific world conception' (*wissenschaftliche Weltauffassung*). In the parlance of the Circle, the 'scientific world conception' referred to the understanding of the world imparted to us by modern science, while 'metaphysics' was a label – practically reduced to a slur – for all traditional philosophy. The Vienna Circle was therefore invested in making an intellectual intervention for the improvement of society on rational lines, an aspiration we have seen expressed repeatedly in this period (in particular in the previous section and Section 15.3).

The signature doctrine of the Vienna Circle in the 1930s was 'physicalism', a position that coalesced in a debate between the Circle members Otto Neurath (1882–1945) and Rudolf Carnap (1891–1970). The classical exposition of the theory is Carnap's 1931 paper 'Die physikalische Sprache als Universalsprache der Wissenschaft' (The physical language as the universal language of science), which was published in English translation in 1934 as the short book *The Unity of Science*. At the heart of physicalism is the notion of the 'physical language'. This is the language of the scientific discipline of physics, the key feature of which is that it talks about things in the world in a way that is both mathematically precise and independent of the perceptions of any individual.

Any statement in the physical language can be verified – that is, tested for its truth – by translating it into a 'protocol language', a language that describes the experiences of an individual observer. There are as many of these protocol languages as there are observers. Furthermore, a statement in the 'sub-language' of any genuine science – chemistry, biology, psychology, sociology, and so on – can be translated into the physical language. It is this possibility of translation that guarantees both the scientific validity of these sub-languages and the 'unity of science', the underlying coherence of these patchwork disciplines in capturing one common reality.

'Metaphysical' statements, by contrast, cannot be translated into the physical language and are therefore nonsense from a scientific perspective. In another paper, his 1931 'Überwindung der Metaphysik durch logische Analyse der Sprache' (The elimination of metaphysics through logical analysis of language), Carnap gave the example of the 'metaphysical' proposition 'Das Nichts selbst nichtet' (The nothing itself nothings), a phrase made famous by the contemporary German philosopher Martin Heidegger (1889–1976). It is impossible to translate this phrase into 'logically correct language'. As such, the phrase is 'meaningless [. . .] in [the] strictest sense' (Carnap 1959 [1931]: 61); it contains merely an expression of a *Lebensgefühl* (attitude to life).

Bloomfield embraced the physicalism of the Vienna Circle, although he claimed to see in it nothing more than a confirmation of his existing behaviourism. In his 1935 Presidential Address to the Linguistic Society of America, 'Language or ideas?', Bloomfield stated that Carnap and Neurath had arrived at much the same insights as Albert Paul Weiss and other behaviourists: the only scientific way to talk about the world, including human thought, is in physical terms. A linguistics informed by behaviourism, argued Bloomfield, has a key role to play in the elaboration and testing of physicalism, since the linguist can show how woolly unscientific terms like 'ideas' can be reformulated in a rigorous physicalist jargon:

> Non-linguists (unless they happen to be physicalists) constantly forget that a speaker is making noise, and credit him, instead, with the possession of palpable 'ideas'. It remains for linguists to show, in detail, that the speaker has no 'ideas', and that the noise is sufficient – for the speaker's words act with a trigger-effect upon the nervous systems of his speech-fellows. Linguists, then, will have to read the description of the universe, as men have written it, and wherever they come upon the mention of an 'idea' (or any synonym such as 'concept', 'notion', or the like), they will have to replace this mention by terms relating to language. (Bloomfield 1936 [1935]: 93)

Shortly after this address was delivered, Bloomfield and Carnap became colleagues at the University of Chicago. As was the fate of so many European scholars and intellectuals in this period, most of the leading members of the Vienna Circle – including Carnap and Neurath – were driven out of Central Europe by the rise of fascism. While on a lecture tour of the United States in 1935, Carnap decided not to return to Europe, and took up a position in Chicago in 1936.

In the following years, Bloomfield collaborated directly with Carnap and Neurath, on the *International Encyclopedia of Unified Science*. Spearheaded by Neurath, the *Encyclopedia* was an attempt to realise the project of the unity of science by bringing together scientists from disparate disciplines to outline the scope and tools of their respective fields, and to show how these fitted into the total ensemble of the sciences. Bloomfield contributed an article to the 1938 first volume of the *Encyclopedia* on 'Linguistic aspects of science', in which he laid out his now familiar behaviourist account of language, with its two sides of form and function. Here he pointed out the centrality of language to the modern sciences: scientific statements must always be made in a language, even if it might be the highly restricted and specialised languages of mathematics and logic.

Bloomfield eagerly embedded his linguistics in the philosophical frameworks provided by behaviourism and logical positivism, not only adopting their theoretical positions, but also aligning the role and purpose of linguistics with their rhetoric. These frameworks provided support for the formalist model Bloomfield had developed, in line with existing tendencies in the field of linguistics (as we saw in Section 16.1), which recognised two sides to language: linguistic forms and their meanings. Meaning was a matter of stimulus–reaction sequences, a problem to be examined with the methods of behaviourist psychology. Linguistic form, which could be reduced to a level where meaning was no longer relevant, was the special subject of linguistics, the compartmentalised discipline that contributed to the total unity of science.

Bloomfield's views became something akin to a dogma in the linguistics of this period. However, as we see in the following section, many linguists in the next generation felt that even Bloomfield was not sufficiently devout.

16.4 Distributionalism

In Section 16.1, we observed how Edward Sapir and Leonard Bloomfield, the two leading figures in American linguistics of the interwar years, converged on the position that every language exhibits formal structures which operate independently of any external factors. This formal layer of language is the exclusive domain of the linguist, one of whose core tasks is to isolate and describe these forms. Sapir and Bloomfield laid the theoretical and technical groundwork for this task, but its elaboration was the work of the next generation. The principles of linguistic analysis this generation set down are generally known as distributionalism.

In its ideal formulations, distributionalism is an inductive approach that involves scanning a corpus of linguistic data in order to discover the recurring formal patterns in a language. This approach represents the methods practised and taught by Sapir and, in particular, Bloomfield distilled to their essence. In his obituary of Bloomfield, the American linguist Bernard Bloch (1907–1965) commented that Bloomfield's 'approach and his method have come to be almost matters of orthodoxy to many students', an achievement Bloch attributed above all to the impact of Bloomfield's 1933 book *Language* (Bloch 1949: 91).

The principles of distributionalism were progressively articulated in papers and books produced in the 1930s and 40s. One the earliest of these publications was the 1934 paper 'The phonemic principle' by Morris Swadesh (1909–1967), which was intended to synthesise existing discussions of phonemic analysis and provide a complete account in one place. Swadesh (1934: 117, note 1) stated that he was 'most directly indebted to Professor Sapir, as my teacher, for my understanding of the phonemic principle', but cited also Bloomfield's *Language* as a source, alongside papers published in the *Travaux du cercle linguistique de Prague*, the house journal of the Prague Linguistic Circle (which we met in Chapter 10).

One of the major contributions of Swadesh's 1934 paper was to introduce the term 'complementary distribution', a name for one of the key insights informing the notion of the phoneme, and a central concept of distributionalism. We have already become acquainted with complementary distribution without using the term: it is the principle that the variant realisations of a phoneme – the 'allophones' of a phoneme – will never appear in the same phonological environment and will therefore never contrast with one another to distinguish words. To return to our illustration from the beginning of Chapter 9, aspirated and unaspirated voiceless stops in English never appear in the same environment. If we were to analyse a corpus of English speech data, we would find, for example, that the aspirated [pʰ] in 'park' will never appear after /s/ at the beginning of a word; this is the environment of the unaspirated variant [p], as in 'spark'. These two allophones, [pʰ] and [p], are in complementary distribution.

The further development of distributionalism is largely a story of extending the techniques of phonemic analysis to other parts of grammatical description. A milestone along this route is the 1942 paper 'Morpheme alternants in linguistic analysis' by Zellig Harris (1909–1992). Harris's (1942: 169) explicit aim in this paper was to put forward 'a technique for determining the morphemes of a language, as rigorous as the method used now for finding its phonemes'. To this end, he made morphemes into units structurally parallel to phonemes: just as a phoneme is made up of allophones in complementary distribution, '[a] morpheme unit is [. . .] a group of one or more alternants which have the same meaning and complementary distribution' (ibid.: 171).

The striving for greater formal rigour led some members of the younger generation to voice mild criticism of their masters. In the 1948 paper 'A set of postulates for phonemic analysis' – whose title and structure were explicitly modelled on Bloomfield's 1926 paper 'A set of postulates for a science of language' – Bernard Bloch (1948: 6) expressed dissatisfaction with Bloomfield's continued appeal to meaning in his phonemic analyses: 'Bloomfield invokes meaning as a fundamental criterion and arrives at his definition of the phoneme without stating in detail the intermediate assumptions that lead to it.' Bloch, by contrast, sought to 'avoid all semantic and psychological criteria', even though meaning can be 'a useful shortcut in the investigation of phonemic structure' (ibid.: 5).

American linguistics, increasingly dominated by the nascent doctrine of distributionalism, received unprecedented institutional support in World War II. American soldiers were being sent to the furthest reaches of the globe, where they needed to be able to communicate with the local inhabitants, both as allies and as enemies. Investment in foreign language training became a priority for the US government. The Intensive Language Program, organised by the American Council of Learned Societies and later integrated into the US Army Specialized Training Program, was just one initiative that provided an opportunity for linguists to apply their skills to the task of foreign language training. Under the auspices of the Intensive Language Program, Bloomfield wrote the 1942 *Outline Guide for the Practical Study of Foreign Languages*, essentially a manual on field linguistics. The book guides the reader through the elicitation and analysis of a language with a native speaker informant. The 1942 *Outline of Linguistic Analysis*, by Bernard Bloch and George Trager (1906–1992), was a companion volume focusing on the technical details of linguistic analysis. The Intensive Language Program also produced numerous textbooks on specific foreign languages. Bloomfield contributed books on Dutch and Russian.

Support for language research during the war was so sumptuous that the American linguist Charles Hockett (1916–2000) later commented he felt like a 'war millionaire' (Hockett 1980: 99), like a profiteer whose business had benefitted unreasonably from the misery of the war. While other young people risked their lives fighting on the front or were obliged to labour in factories, Hockett and his colleagues were able to devote themselves to their scientific passions in safety and comfort.

Now the dominant doctrine in an ascendent discipline, distributionalism received its grand formulation a few years after the war, in Zellig Harris's 1951 book *Methods in Structural Linguistics*. The exclusive focus on formal distribution as the basis of linguistic analysis is set out plainly in the opening pages:

> It is of course possible to study various relations among parts or features of speech, e.g. similarities (or other relations) in sound or in meaning, or genetic relations in the history of the language. The main research of descriptive linguistics, and the only relation which will be accepted as relevant in the present survey, is the distribution or arrangement within the flow of speech of some parts or features relatively to others. (Harris 1951: 5)

The manuscript of Harris's 1951 *Methods* was proofread by one of his gifted students, a young Noam Chomsky (b. 1928). Famously, in the 1950s Chomsky rebelled against the strictures of the uncompromisingly empiricist methods that had become the default doctrines of American linguistics. In his own theory of 'generative grammar', Chomsky reopened fundamental questions on the nature of language and its study, and thereby helped to instigate the 'cognitive revolution' of the late 1950s. With repercussions felt across the human sciences, the cognitive revolution hailed a retreat from behaviourist dogma and turned scholars' attention once again to the workings of the human mind. But this is the story of the postwar era.

16.5 Further reading

Dell Hymes and John Fought's (1981 [1975]) *American Structuralism* remains the classic account of the developments in American linguistics sketched in this chapter. For an exposition of the history of distributionalism that goes into great technical detail, see Fought's (2001) article 'The "Bloomfieldian School" and descriptive linguistics', in volume 2 of the handbook *History of the Language Sciences*. Sapir (1921) and Bloomfield's (1933) introductory books on linguistics, which both bear the title *Language*, remain accessible to the present-day reader and provide excellent outlines of their respective views.

For studies of the transition from distributionalism to Chomsky's generative grammar, see Peter Matthews's (1993) *Grammatical Theory in the United States from Bloomfield to Chomsky* and Frederick Newmeyer's (2022) *American Linguistics in Transition: From Post-Bloomfieldian Structuralism to Generative Grammar*. Matthews's book emphasises the continuities between these two approaches, and is rather critical of the revolutionary rhetoric surrounding Chomsky and his school. Newmeyer's book is much more sympathetic to the Chomskyan camp.

An introduction to the history of behaviourism can be found in chapter 11 of Thomas Leahey's (2018 [1987]) *History of Psychology: From Antiquity to Modernity*. A good introductory guide to the Vienna Circle and logical positivism is Friedrich Stadler's (2015 [2011]) *The Vienna Circle: Studies in the Origins, Development, and Influence of Logical Empiricism*. Henry Hiż and Pierre Swiggers's (1990) article 'Bloomfield, the logical positivist' in *Semiotica* examines Bloomfield's connections to the logical positivism of the Vienna Circle.

17 Conclusion

Our story began in the final decades of the eighteenth century and concluded around the middle of the twentieth century. In this period spanning some 170 years, the world did not stand still: the intellectual and institutional environment in which such figures as Sir William Jones (1746–1794) and Friedrich Schlegel (1772–1829) made the first stirrings of historical-comparative linguistics (see Sections 2.1 and 2.2) was not the same as that in which Roman Jakobson (1896–1982) wedded his structuralism to cybernetics (Section 13.3) or Zellig Harris (1909–1992) presented his synthesis of the distributionalist paradigm (Section 16.4). Nevertheless, we have sought to show in this book that there is a certain coherence to linguistic scholarship in this period. It is this coherence that allows us to speak of 'modern linguistics'.

The chief sociological fact uniting modern linguistics as a field is its institutionalisation as an academic discipline. For the most part, the main contributors to linguistic research were salaried professors at universities. Several key scholars in our story – including Wilhelm von Humboldt (1767–1835; Sections 3.2 and 3.3), Heymann Steinthal (1823–1899; Sections 3.4, 3.5 and 4.4), Philipp Wegener (1848–1916; Chapter 11) and Benjamin Lee Whorf (1897–1941; Chapter 15) – never achieved the status of professor (or never even sought this status) but they were all, each in their own way, associated with universities. In this connection, Humboldt deserves special mention as the very architect of the modern research university (Section 2.3).

The coherence of the field extends beyond its sociological context, and comprises also the content and approach of linguistic scholarship in this era. But coherence does not entail uniformity: our story has been one of recurring controversies centring around the conceptualisation of language. Linguists have continually disagreed on what exactly language is and where its limits lie. A key move in demarcating linguistics as its own field, separate from philology, was to treat linguistic form as an object that can be sequestered and studied independently of how language is used. Under this conception, the role of languages as means of communication or vehicles of literature faded into the background as theoretical structures and patterns of their grammars and sound systems – their forms – were brought into focus.

Franz Bopp (1791–1867) embarked on this form-focused course in elaborating the methods of comparative grammar (Section 2.3). August Schleicher (1821–1868) took these principles to an extreme in declaring languages to be autonomous organisms, literally with a life of their own (Sections 4.1 and 4.2). While retreating from the metaphysical implications of Schleicher's position, the Neogrammarians doubled down on the underlying commitment to formal autonomy in positing exceptionless laws of sound change (Sections 6.1 and 6.2). Ushering in the structuralist era, Ferdinand de Saussure (1857–1913) eschewed all metaphysical question and simply made the abstract *langue* a fundamental postulate of linguistic scholarship (Section 8.2). Following this trend, the American structuralists – Edward Sapir (1884–1939), Leonard Bloomfield (1887–1949), and even more so their students – developed increasingly austere analytic methods concentrating on the distribution of forms (Sections 16.1 and 16.4).

There was, however, always an ambivalence about this fetishisation of form. Although Jacob Grimm (1785–1863) teased out the laws governing sound change in the Germanic languages, he saw these not as the immanent laws of independent entities, but as the movements of the *Volksgeist* animating this group of languages (Section 2.4). For Humboldt, the 'character' of a language, revealed through its literature, was far more important than its 'structure', represented by its grammatical forms (Section 3.3). This fact was often forgotten by his form-obsessed followers. Steinthal, one of the most prominent Humboldt interpreters of the nineteenth century, emphasised the formal aspects of Humboldt's writings, building a system of language classification around the Humboldtian notion of 'inner linguistic form'. But the importance of inner form for Steinthal ultimately derived from his belief that it encapsulated the *Volksgeist* of a language community (Section 3.5). Even Schleicher, who cited Humboldt as an inspiration for his own work, did not deny the promise of inner form, although he made its investigation a task for future research (Section 4.4).

In the midst of these conflicts over linguistic form, many linguists continued to consider how languages are actually used in practice and chided their colleagues for disdaining this topic. In the mid-nineteenth century, William Dwight Whitney (1827–1894) emphasised the nature of language as a 'human institution', in opposition to Schleicher's 'physical' and Humboldt and Steinthal's 'psychological' theories (Sections 5.1 and 5.2). The Neogrammarians paid lip-service to Whitney's conception of language, even if it had little influence on their day-to-day work (Section 6.3).

Research into meaning, use and the psychological implications of language remained a mainstay of linguistic scholarship up into the twentieth century – in the work of such figures as Philipp Wegener (1848–1916; Chapter 11), John Rupert Firth (1890–1960) and Bronislaw Malinowski (1884–1942; Chapter 12), and Karl Bühler (1879–1963) and Roman Jakobson (1896–1982; Chapter 13) – although such questions were often considered peripheral or auxiliary to linguistics proper. Even the American structuralists, as they laid the groundwork for strict formal methods of analysis, continued to write about the possible connections between language, thought and culture. Sapir and Whorf provide the most striking examples (Chapter 15), but Bloomfield also addressed questions of meaning (Chapter 16) and was criticised for it by his more radical disciples.

The discipline of linguistics did not develop in splendid isolation, but through constant interplay and exchange with neighbouring fields. How linguists sought to position themselves in the academic space – who they saw as their allies and rivals – helped to shape their conceptualisations of language. In the nineteenth century, models drawn from biology frequently buttressed the ambitions of those who would talk of autonomous linguistic form: Schlegel's coinage of comparative grammar, which received methodological elaboration at the hands of Bopp, was inspired by contemporary advances in comparative anatomy (Sections 2.2 and 3.1), while Schleicher looked to such diverse doctrines emanating from biological research as scientific materialism and Darwinian evolution (Sections 4.2 and 4.3).

Nineteenth-century scholars who wished to link linguistic form with cultural and psychological factors generally preferred humanistic models, although their humanism was frequently one informed by the latest discoveries and advances in the natural sciences. Grimm's sound laws were part of historicist discourse (Section 2.4). Humboldt and Steinthal's research into language was merely one aspect of their broader projects, which extended across what would today be considered such fields as history, literary studies, anthropology and psychology (Chapter 3). Whitney's convictions were rooted in the 'Common Sense' philosophy he had imbibed as a schoolboy, combined with uniformitarianism stemming from geology (Sections 5.3 and 5.4).

In the twentieth century, linguistics remained embedded in a network of interdisciplinary exchange. Although Saussure hived off *la langue* as the private possession of linguists, in his choice of terminology he allied this notion with the sociology of Émile Durkheim (Section 8.3). In elaborating structuralism, the Prague School linguists described linguistic structure in the idiom of Gestalt psychology (Sections 10.1 and 10.2), and Jakobson later sought to assimilate his work to the master science of cybernetics (Section 13.3). In Britain in this era, the linguistic research of Firth and Malinowski was aligned with anthropology (Chapter 12), as was the American structuralism of Boas, Sapir and Whorf (Chapters 14 and 15). Malinowski, Sapir and Whorf were also enamoured of early analytic philosophy (Sections 12.3 and 15.3). Bloomfield shared their anthropological interest in 'exotic' languages and penchant for early analytic philosophy, but he learnt his most abiding scientific lessons from behaviourist psychology (Chapter 16).

The character of linguistic scholarship was also influenced, at each point in our story, by the social and political environment outside the academy. Grimm's historicism was in no small part a political project: his linguistic research was intended to aid in the cultivation of the German national consciousness (Section 2.4). Schleicher's scientific materialism was similarly bound up with his liberal political commitments (Section 4.2), just as Steinthal's *Völkerpsychologie* was intimately connected with the issue of Jewish minority identity in the German nation (Section 3.4). Firth (Section 12.1), Malinowski (Section 12.2), and Boas and Sapir's (Section 14.2) work was facilitated by states that supported linguistic and anthropological research as an instrument of colonial control. Sapir (Sections 15.1 and 15.3), Bloomfield (Sections 16.2 and 16.3) and Jakobson (Section 13.3) all strove to present their research in a manner congenial to the utilitarian disposition of American philanthropies and the US government.

Even the Neogrammarians' retreat into esoteric technical topics could be understood as conservative quietism in Bismarck's Germany (Section 7.3).

We ended our story just after World War II, when political and economic power, and along with it international academic and cultural influence, shifted from Central and Western Europe to North America. This was a watershed moment in world history, which was not without its significance for those who studied language. Linguistic scholarship continued without break after the war but – as we presaged in Chapters 13 and 16 – the tone of the field was now set in America, by scholars raised and trained on that continent as well as those who had fled fascism and war in Europe.

Bibliography

Aarsleff, Hans (1982), *From Locke to Saussure: Essays on the Study of Language and Intellectual History*, Minneapolis: University of Minnesota Press.

Adelung, Johann Christoph, and Johann Severin Vater (1806–17), *Mithridates, oder allgemeine Sprachenkunde*, Berlin: Vossische Buchhandlung.

Alter, Stephen G. (1999), *Darwinism and the Linguistic Image: Language, Race, and Natural Theology in the Nineteenth Century*, Baltimore: Johns Hopkins University Press.

Alter, Stephen G. (2005), *William Dwight Whitney and the Science of Language*, Baltimore: Johns Hopkins University Press.

Amsterdamska, Olga (1987), *Schools of Thought: The Development of Linguistics from Bopp to Saussure*, Dordrecht: Reidel.

Anderson, Stephen R. (2021 [1985]), *Phonology in the Twentieth Century: Second Edition, Revised and Expanded*, Berlin: Language Science Press.

Angell, James Rowland (1907), 'The province of functional psychology', *The Psychological Review* 14:2, 61–91.

Arnauld, Antoine, and Claude Lancelot (1660), *Grammaire générale et raisonnée contenant les fondemens de l'art de parler, expliqués d'une manière claire et naturelle*, Paris: Pierre le Petit. (English translation: Arnauld and Lancelot 1975 [1660].)

Archaimbault, Sylvie (2010), 'Peter Simon Pallas (1741–1811), un naturaliste parmi les mots', *Histoire Épistémologie Langage* 32:1, 69–91.

Arnauld, Antoine, and Claude Lancelot (1975 [1660]), *General and Rational Grammar: The Port-Royal Grammar*, trans. Jacques Rieux and Bernard E. Rollin, The Hague: Mouton. (French original: Arnauld and Lancelot 1660.)

Ash, Mitchell G. (1995), *Gestalt Psychology in German Culture, 1890–1967: Holism and the Quest for Objectivity*, Cambridge: Cambridge University Press.

Ashby, Michael, and Marija Tabain (2020), 'Fifty years of JIPA', *Journal of the International Phonetic Association* 50:3, 445–8.

Auroux, Sylvain, E. F. Konrad Koerner, Hans-Josef Niederehe and Kees Versteegh (eds) (2000–6), *History of the Language Sciences – Geschichte der Sprachwissenschaften – Histoire des sciences du langage: An International Handbook on the Evolution of the Study of Language from the Beginnings to the Present*, 3 vols, Berlin: Walter de Gruyter.

Baudouin de Courtenay, Jan (1895), *Versuch einer Theorie phonetischer Alternationen*, Strassburg: Trübner. (English translation: Baudouin de Courtenay 1972 [1895].)

Baudouin de Courtenay, Jan (1972 [1877]), 'Detailed program of lectures (1876–77)', in Baudouin de Courtenay (1972), pp. 92–113. (Russian original: 'Podrobnaja programma lekcij . . . v 1876–1877 uč. Godu'.)

Baudouin de Courtenay, Jan (1972 [1895]), 'An attempt at a theory of phonetic alternations: A chapter from psychophonetics', in Baudouin de Courtenay (1972), pp. 144–212. (German original: Baudouin de Courtenay 1895.)

Baudouin de Courtenay (1972), *A Baudouin de Courtenay Reader: The Beginnings of Structural Linguistics*, ed. and trans. Edward Stankiewicz, Bloomington: Indiana University Press.
Beiser, Frederick C. (2011), *The German Historicist Tradition*, Oxford: Oxford University Press.
Beiser, Frederick C. (2014), *After Hegel: German philosophy 1840–1900*, Princeton: Princeton University Press.
Belke, Ingrid (ed.) (1971), *Moritz Lazarus und Heymann Steinthal: die Begründer der Völkerpsychologie in ihren Briefen*, Tübingen: Mohr.
Bell, Alexander Melville (1867), *Visible Speech: The Science of Universal Alphabetics*, London: Simkin, Marshall.
Benedict, Ruth (1946), *The Chrysanthemum and the Sword: Patterns of Japanese Culture*, Boston: Houghton Mifflin.
Benetka, Gerhard (1995), *Psychologie in Wien: Sozial- und Theoriegeschichte des Wiener Psychologischen Instituts 1922–1938*, Vienna: WUV-Universtätsverlag.
Benfey, Theodor (1869), *Geschichte der Sprachwissenschaft und orientalischen Philologie in Deutschland, seit dem Anfange des 19. Jahrhunderts mit einem Rückblick auf die früheren Zeiten*, Munich: Cotta'sche Buchhandlung.
Bleek, Wilhelm (1862–9), *A Comparative Grammar of South African Languages*, 2 vols, London: Trübner.
Bloch, Bernard (1948), 'A set of postulates for phonemic analysis', *Language* 24:1, 3–46.
Bloch, Bernard (1949), Obituary for Leonard Bloomfield, *Language* 25:2, 87–98.
Bloch, Bernard, and George Trager (1942), *Outline of Linguistic Analysis*, Baltimore: Linguistic Society of America.
Bloomfield, Leonard (1909–10), 'A semasiological differentiation in Germanic secondary ablaut', *Modern Philology* 7, 245–88, 345–82. (Introduction reprinted in Hockett 1970, pp. 1–6.)
Bloomfield, Leonard (1914), *An Introduction to the Study of Language*, New York: Henry Holt.
Bloomfield, Leonard (1922), Review of Sapir (1921), *The Classical Weekly* 15, 142–3. (Reprinted in Hockett 1970, pp. 95–100.)
Bloomfield, Leonard (1924), Review of Saussure (1922 [1916]), *Modern Language Journal* 8, 317–19. (Reprinted in Hockett 1970, pp. 106–8.)
Bloomfield, Leonard (1925), 'Why a linguistic society?', *Language* 1, 1–5. (Reprinted in Hockett 1970, pp. 109–12.)
Bloomfield, Leonard (1926), 'A set of postulates for a science of language', *Language* 2, 153–64. (Reprinted in Hockett 1970, pp. 128–38.)
Bloomfield, Leonard (1930 [1929]), 'Linguistics as a science', *Studies in Philology*, 553–7. (Reprinted in Hockett 1970, pp. 227–30.)
Bloomfield, Leonard (1933), *Language*, New York: Henry Holt.
Bloomfield, Leonard (1936 [1935]), 'Language or ideas?', *Language* 12, 89–95. (Reprinted in Hockett 1970, pp. 322–8.)
Bloomfield, Leonard (1938), *Linguistic Aspects of Science* (= International Encyclopedia of Unified Science, vol. 1, no. 4), Chicago: University of Chicago Press.
Bloomfield, Leonard (1942), *Outline Guide for the Practical Study of Foreign Languages*, Baltimore: Linguistic Society of America.
Boas, Franz (1887a), 'The occurrence of similar inventions in areas widely apart', *Science* 9:224, 485–6.
Boas, Franz (1887b), Response to Powell (1887), *Science* 9:229, 614.
Boas, Franz (1889), 'On alternating sounds', *American Anthropologist* 2:1, 47–54.
Boas, Franz (ed.) (1911), *Handbook of American Indian Languages*, Part I, Washington DC: Government Printing Office.

Boas, Franz, and Ella Cara Deloria (1941), *Dakota Grammar*, Washington DC: Government Printing Office.
Bod, Rens (2010), *De vergeten wetenschappen. Een geschiedenis van de humaniora*, Amsterdam: Bakker. (English translation: Bod 2013 [2010].)
Bod, Rens (2013 [2010]), *A New History of the Humanities: The Search for Principles and Patterns from Antiquity to the Present*, Oxford: Oxford University Press. (Dutch original: Bod 2010.)
Bopp, Franz (1816), *Über das Conjugationssystem der Sanskritsprache in Vergleichung mit jenem der griechischen, lateinischen, persischen und germanischen Sprache*, Frankfurt am Main: Andräische Buchhandlung.
Bopp, Franz (1820), 'Analytical comparison of the Sanskrit, Greek, Latin, and Teutonic languages, shewing the original identity of their grammatical structure', *Annals of Oriental Literature* 1, 1–64.
Bopp, Franz (1833–52), *Vergleichende Grammatik des Sanskrit, Zend, Griechischen, Lateinischen, Litthauischen, Gothischen und Deutschen*, 6 vols, Berlin: Dümmler. (English translation: Bopp 1845–53.)
Bopp, Franz (1841), *Über die Verwandtschaft der malayisch-polynesischen Sprachen mit den indisch-europäischen*, Berlin: Dümmler.
Bopp, Franz (1845–53), *A Comparative Grammar of the Sanskrit, Zend, Greek, Latin, Lithuanian, Gothic, German, and Sclavonic Languages*, trans. Edward B. Eastwick, 3 vols, London: Madden and Malcolm. (German original: Bopp 1833–52.)
Borsche, Tilman (1989), 'Die innere Form der Sprache. Betrachtungen zu einem Mythos der Humboldt-Herme(neu)tik', in *Wilhelm von Humboldts Sprachdenken. Symposion zum 150. Todestag*, ed. Hans-Werner Scharf, Essen: Reimer Hobbing, pp. 47–65.
Bourdeau, Michel (2018), 'Auguste Comte', *Stanford Encyclopedia of Philosophy* (Summer 2018 Edition), ed. Edward N. Zalta. https://plato.stanford.edu/archives/sum2018/entries/comte/
Bréal, Michel (1866), 'De la forme et de la fonction des mots', *Revue des Cours littéraires de la France et de l'étranger* 5 (29 December), 65–71. (English translation: Bréal 1991 [1866].)
Bréal, Michel (1868), *Les Idées latentes du langage*, Paris: Hachette. (English translation: Bréal 1991 [1868].)
Bréal, Michel (1897), *Essai de sémantique (science des significations)*, Paris: Hachette. (English translation: Bréal 1900 [1897].)
Bréal, Michel (1900 [1897]), *Semantics: Studies in the Science of Meaning*, trans. Nina Cust, London: Heinemann. (French original: Bréal 1897.)
Bréal, Michel (1991 [1866]), 'On the form and function of words', in Bréal (1991), pp. 50–62. (French original: Bréal 1866.)
Bréal, Michel (1991 [1868]), 'The latent concepts of language', in Bréal (1991), pp. 79–92. (French original: Bréal 1868.)
Bréal, Michel (1991), *The Beginnings of Semantics: Essays, Lectures and Reviews*, ed. and trans. George Wolf, London: Duckworth.
Brinton, Daniel Garrison (1890 [1888]), 'The earliest form of human speech, as revealed by American tongues', in *Essays of an Americanist*, ed. Daniel Garrison Brinton, Philadelphia: Porter & Coates, pp. 390–409.
Brugman, Karl (1876a), 'Nasalis sonans in der indogermanischen Grundsprache', *Studien zur griechischen und lateinischen Grammatik* 9, 285–338.
Brugman, Karl (1876b), 'Zur Geschichte der Stammabstufenden Declinationen. Erste Abhandlung: die Nomina auf *-ar-* und *-tar-*', *Studien zur griechischen und lateinischen Grammatik* 9, 361–406.
Brugman, Karl (1884), 'Zur Frage nach den Verwandtschaftsverhältnissen der indogermanischen Sprachen', *Internationale Zeitschrift für Allgemeine Sprachwissenschaft* 1, 226–56.

Brugman, Karl (1897 [1894]), 'Zum Gedächtniss W. D. Whitney's', in *The Whitney Memorial Meeting*, ed. Charles R. Lanman, Boston: Ginn, pp. 74–81.
Bühler, Karl (1927), *Die Krise der Psychologie*, Jena: Fischer.
Bühler, Karl (1931), 'Phonetik und Phonologie', *Travaux du Cercle Linguistique de Prague* 4, 22–53.
Bühler, Karl (1934), *Sprachtheorie: Die Darstellungsfunktion der Sprache*, Jena: Fischer. (English translation: Bühler 2011 [1934].)
Bühler, Karl (1960), *Das Gestaltprinzip im Leben des Menschen und der Tiere*, Bern: Huber.
Bühler, Karl (2011 [1934]), *Theory of Language: The Representational Function of Language*, trans. Donald Fraser Goodwin and Achim Eschbach, Amsterdam: John Benjamins. (German original: Bühler 1934.)
Bunsen, Christian Karl Josias (1854), *Christianity and Mankind: Their Beginnings and Prospects*, London: Longman, Brown, Green, and Longmans.
Bunzl, Matti (1996), 'Franz Boas and the Humboldtian tradition: From *Volksgeist* and *Nationalcharakter* to an anthropological concept of culture', in Volksgeist *as Method and Ethic: Essays on Boasian Ethnography and the German Anthropological Tradition*, ed. George W. Stocking Jr., Madison: University of Wisconsin Press, pp. 17–78.
Caldwell, Robert (1856), *A Comparative Grammar of the Dravidian or South-Indian Family of Languages*, London: Harrison.
Campbell, Lyle (2020 [1998]), *Historical Linguistics: An Introduction*, 4th edition, Edinburgh: Edinburgh University Press.
Carnap, Rudolf (1931a), 'Überwindung der Metaphysik durch logische Analyse der Sprache', *Erkenntnis* 2, 219–41. (English translation: Carnap 1959 [1931].)
Carnap, Rudolf (1931b), 'Die physikalische Sprache als Universalsprache der Wissenschaft', *Erkenntnis* 2, 432–65. (English translation: Carnap 1934 [1931].)
Carnap, Rudolf (1934 [1931]), *The Unity of Science*, trans. Max Black, London: Kegan Paul. (German original: Carnap 1931b.)
Carnap, Rudolf (1959 [1931]), 'The elimination of metaphysics through logical analysis of language', trans. Arthur Pap, in *Logical Positivism*, ed. Alfred Jules Ayer, Glencoe, IL: The Free Press, pp. 60–81 (German original: Carnap 1931a).
Carroll, John B. (ed.) (1956), *Language, Thought, and Reality: Selected Writings of Benjamin Lee Whorf*, Cambridge, MA: MIT Press.
Cassirer, Ernst (1945), 'Structuralism in modern linguistics', *Word* 1, 99–120.
Chase, Stuart (1938), *The Tyranny of Words*, New York: Harcourt, Brace.
Christy, Craig T. (1983), *Uniformitarianism in Linguistics*, Amsterdam: John Benjamins.
Condillac, Etienne Bonnot de (1746), *Essai sur l'origine des connoissances humaines*, 2 vols, Amsterdam: Mortier. (English translation: Condillac 2001 [1746].)
Condillac, Etienne Bonnot de (2001 [1746]), *Essay on the Origin of Human Knowledge*, ed. and trans. Hans Aarsleff, Cambridge: Cambridge University Press. (French original: Condillac 1746.)
Coseriu, Eugenio (1967), 'Georg von der Gabelentz et la linguistique synchronique', *Word* 23, 74–110.
Curtius, Georg (1876), 'Nachwort', *Studien zur griechischen und lateinischen Grammatik* 9, 468.
Darnell, Regna (1990), *Edward Sapir: Linguist, Anthropologist, Humanist*, Berkeley: University of California Press.
Darnell, Regna (1998), *And Along Came Boas: Continuity and Revolution in Americanist Anthropology*, Amsterdam: John Benjamins.
Darwin, Charles (1859), *On the Origin of Species by Means of Natural Selection, or the Preservation of Favoured Races in the Struggle for Life*, London: Murray.

Darwin, Charles (1861 [1859]), *On the Origin of Species*, London: Murray. (3rd edition of Darwin 1859.)
Darwin, Charles (1871), *The Descent of Man, and Selection in Relation to Sex*, London: Murray.
Daston, Lorraine, and Peter Galison (2007), *Objectivity*, New York: Zone Books.
Delbrück, Berthold (1901), *Grundfragen der Sprachforschung, mit Rücksicht auf W. Wundts Völkerpsychologie*, Strassburg: Trübner.
Delbrück, Berthold (1919 [1880]), *Einleitung in das Studium der indogermanischen Sprachen. Ein Beitrag zur Geschichte und Methodik der vergleichenden Sprachforschung*, Leipzig: Breitkopf und Härtel.
Deloria, Ella Cara (1932), *Dakota Texts*, New York: Stechert.
Deutscher, Guy (2010), *Through the Language Glass: Why the World Looks Different in Other Languages*, New York: Random House.
Diez, Friedrich Christian (1836–44), *Grammatik der romanischen Sprachen*, 3 vols, Bonn: Weber.
Dosse, François (1991), *Histoire du structuralisme, I. Le champ du signe, 1945–1966*, Paris: La Découverte. (English translation: Dosse 1997 [1991].)
Dosse, François (1992), *Histoire du structuralisme, II. Le chant du cygne, de 1967 à nos jours*, Paris: La Découverte. (English translation: Dosse 1997 [1992].)
Dosse, François (1997 [1991]), *History of Structuralism, Volume 1: The Rising Sign, 1945–1966*, trans. Deborah Glassman, Minneapolis: University of Minnesota Press. (French original: Dosse 1991.)
Dosse, François (1997 [1992]), *History of Structuralism, Volume 2: The Sign Sets, 1967–Present*, trans. Deborah Glassman, Minneapolis: University of Minnesota Press. (French original: Dosse 1992.)
Durnovo, Nikolaj, Bohuslav Havránek, Roman Jakobson, Vilém Mathesius, Jan Mukařovský, Nikolai Trubetzkoy and Bohumil Trnka (1929), 'Thèses présentées au Premier Congrès des philologues slaves', in *Mélanges linguistiques dédiés au Premier Congrès des Philologues Slaves*, Prague: Jednota Československých Matematiků a Fysiků, pp. 5–29. (English translation: Durnovo et al. 1978 [1929].)
Durnovo, Nikolaj, Bohuslav Havránek, Roman Jakobson, Vilém Mathesius, Jan Mukařovský, Nikolai Trubetzkoy and Bohumil Trnka (1978 [1929]), 'Manifesto', in *Recycling the Prague Linguistic Circle*, ed. and trans. Marta K. Johnson, Ann Arbor: Karoma, pp. 1–31. (French original: Durnovo et al. 1929.)
Edwards, Paul N. (1997), *The Closed World: Computers and the Politics of Discourse in Cold War America*, Cambridge, MA: MIT Press.
Ehrenfels, Christian von (1890), 'Über Gestaltqualitäten', *Vierteljahrsschrift für wissenschaftliche Philosophie* 14, 249–92.
Elffers-van Ketel, Els (1991), *The Historiography of Grammatical Concepts: 19th and 20th-Century Changes in the Subject-Predicate Conception and the Problem of Their Historical Reconstruction*, Amsterdam: Rodopi.
Errington, J. Joseph (2008), *Linguistics in a Colonial World: A Story of Language, Meaning, and Power*, Oxford: Blackwell.
Eschbach, Achim (ed.) (1984), *Bühler-Studien*, 2 vols, Frankfurt am Main: Suhrkamp.
Firth, John Rupert (1957), *Papers in Linguistics, 1934–1951*, London: Oxford University Press.
Firth, John Rupert (1964 [1930 and 1937]), *The Tongues of Men* (1937) and *Speech* (1930), Oxford: Oxford University Press.
Firth, John Rupert (1968), *Selected Papers of J. R. Firth, 1952–59*, ed. Frank R. Palmer, Bloomington: Indiana University Press.
Formigari, Lia (2001), *Il Linguaggio. Storia della teorie*, Rome: Laterza. (English translation: Formigari 2004 [2001].)

Formigari, Lia (2004 [2001]), *A History of Language Philosophies*, trans. Gabriel Poole, Amsterdam: John Benjamins. (Italian original: Formigari 2001.)

Formigari, Lia (2018), 'Wilhelm Wundt and the *Lautgesetze* controversy', *History and Philosophy of the Language Sciences* (17 January). https://hiphilangsci.net/2018/01/17/wundt-lautgesetze/

Fortis, Jean-Michel (2019), 'On Sapir's notion of form/pattern and its aesthetic background', in McElvenny (2019a), pp. 59–88.

Fought, John G. (2001), 'The "Bloomfieldian School" and descriptive linguistics', in Auroux et al. (2000–6), vol. 2, pp. 1950–66.

Friedrich, Janette (ed.) (2018), *Karl Bühlers* Krise der Psychologie*: Positionen, Bezüge und Kontroversen im Wien der 1920er/30er Jahre*, Cham: Springer.

Gabelentz, Georg von der (1893), 'Baskisch und Berberisch', *Sitzungsberichte der königlich-preußischen Akademie der Wissenschaften zu Berlin*, Philologische-historische Classe (22 June), 593–613.

Gabelentz, Georg von der (1894), *Die Verwandtschaft des Baskischen mit den Berbersprachen Nord-Africas, nachgewiesen von Georg von der Gabelentz*, ed. Albrecht Graf von der Schulenburg, Braunschweig: Sattler.

Gabelentz, Georg von der (2016 [1891]), *Die Sprachwissenschaft, ihre Aufgaben, Methoden, und bisherigen Ergebnisse*, critical edition, ed. Manfred Ringmacher and James McElvenny, Berlin: Language Science Press.

Gabelentz, Hans Conon von der (1861–73), 'Die melanesischen Sprachen nach ihrem grammatischen Bau und ihrer Verwandtschaft unter sich und mit den malaiisch-polynesischen Sprachen untersucht', *Abhandlungen der Königlich-Sächsischen Akademie der Wissenschaften zu Leipzig*, Philologische-historische Classe 3, 1–266; 7, 1–186.

Gardiner, Alan Henderson (1932), *Theory of Speech and Language*, Oxford: Oxford University Press.

Geoghegan, Bernard Dionysius (2011), 'From information theory to French theory: Jakobson, Lévi-Strauss, and the cybernetic apparatus', *Critical Inquiry* 38:1, 96–126.

Geoghegan, Bernard Dionysius (2023), *Code: From Information Theory to French Theory*, Durham, NC: Duke University Press.

Gessner, Conrad (2009 [1555]), *Mithridate/Mithridates*, ed. and trans. Bernard Colombat and Manfred Peters, Geneva: Librairie Droz.

Ginsborg, Hannah (2019), 'Kant's aesthetics and teleology', *Stanford Encyclopedia of Philosophy* (Winter 2019 Edition), ed. E. N. Zalta, Stanford: Metaphysics Research Lab, Stanford University. https://plato.stanford.edu/archives/win2019/entries/kant-aesthetics/

Ginschel, Gunhild (1989 [1967]), *Der Junge Jacob Grimm: 1805–1819*, Berlin and Stuttgart: Hirzel.

Gleick, James (2011), *The Information*, London: Fourth Estate.

Goethe, Johann Wolfgang von (1877 [1817–24]), 'Zur Morphologie', *Goethe's Werke*, vol. 33, ed. Salomon Kalischer, Berlin: Dümmler.

Goldsmith, John A., and Bernard Laks (2019), *Battle in the Mind Fields*, Chicago: University of Chicago Press.

Gregory, Frederick (1977), *Scientific Materialism in Nineteenth-Century Germany*, Dordrecht: Reidel.

Grimm, Jacob (1822–37 [1819]), *Deutsche Grammatik*, 4 vols, Göttingen: Dieterich'sche Buchhandlung.

Grimm, Jacob (1840 [1819]), *Deutsche Grammatik*, 3rd edition, Göttingen: Dieterich'sche Buchhandlung.

Grimm, Jacob, and Wilhelm Grimm (1812–15), *Kinder- und Hausmärchen*, 2 vols, Berlin: Realschulbuchhandlung.
Grimm, Jacob, Wilhelm Grimm, et al. (eds) (1854–1960), *Deutsches Wörterbuch*, 16 vols, Leipzig: Hirzel.
Haeckel, Ernst (1866), *Generelle Morphologie der Organismen*, 2 vols, Berlin: Georg Reimer.
Haeckel, Ernst (1899), *Die Welträthsel, gemeinverständliche Studien über monistische Philosophie*, Stuttgart: Kröner.
Hall, Robert A. (1990), *A Life for Language: A Biographical Memoir of Leonard Bloomfield*, Amsterdam: John Benjamins.
Halliday, Michael A. K. (1985), *An Introduction to Functional Grammar*, London: Arnold.
Harrington, Anne (1996), *Reenchanted Science: Holism in German Culture from Wilhelm II to Hitler*, Princeton: Princeton University Press.
Harris, Roy, and Talbot J. Taylor (1997 [1989]), *Landmarks in Linguistic Thought I: The Western Tradition from Socrates to Saussure*, London: Routledge.
Harris, Zellig S. (1942), 'Morpheme alternants in linguistic analysis', *Language* 18:2, 169–80.
Harris, Zellig S. (1951), *Methods in Structural Linguistics*, Chicago: University of Chicago Press.
Heims, Steve J. (1991), *The Cybernetics Group*, Cambridge, MA: MIT Press.
Herder, Johann Gottfried von (1772), *Abhandlung über den Ursprung der Sprache*, Berlin: Voß. (English translation: Herder 2002 [1772].)
Herder, Johann Gottfried von (2002 [1772]), 'Treatise on the origin of language', in *Herder: Philosophical Writings*, ed. and trans. Michael N. Forster, Cambridge: Cambridge University Press, pp. 65–164. (German original: Herder 1772.)
Hirschkop, Ken (2019), *Linguistic Turns, 1890–1950: Writing on Language as Social Theory*, Oxford: Oxford University Press.
Hiż, Henry, and Pierre Swiggers (1990), 'Leonard Bloomfield, the logical positivist', *Semiotica* 79:3/4, 257–70.
Hockett, Charles F. (1958), *A Course in Modern Linguistics*, New York: Macmillan.
Hockett, Charles F. (ed.) (1970), *A Leonard Bloomfield Anthology*, Bloomington: Indiana University Press.
Hockett, Charles F. (1980), 'Preserving the heritage', in *First Person Singular*, ed. Boyd H. Davis and Raymond K. O'Cain, Amsterdam: John Benjamins, pp. 97–107.
Hockett, Charles F. (1987), 'Letters from Bloomfield to Michelson and Sapir', in *Leonard Bloomfield: Essays on His Life and Work*, ed. Robert A. Hall, Jr., Amsterdam: John Benjamins, pp. 39–60.
Hoijer, Harry (ed.) (1954a), *Language in Culture: Proceedings of a Conference on the Interrelations of Language and Other Aspects of Culture*, Chicago: University of Chicago Press.
Hoijer, Harry (1954b), 'The Sapir–Whorf hypothesis', in Hoijer (1954a), pp. 92–105.
Honeybone, Patrick (2005), 'J. R. Firth', in *Key Thinkers in Linguistics and the Philosophy of Language*, ed. Siobhan Chapman and Christopher Routledge, Edinburgh: Edinburgh University Press, pp. 80–6.
Humboldt, Wilhelm von (1836), *Über die Verschiedenheit des menschlichen Sprachbaues und ihren Einfluß auf die geistige Entwicklung des Menschengeschlechts*, ed. Alexander von Humboldt, Berlin: Dümmler. (English translation: Humboldt 1988 [1836].)
Humboldt, Wilhelm von (1905 [1820]), 'Über das vergleichende Sprachstudium in Beziehung auf die verschiedenen Epochen der Sprachentwicklung', in Humboldt (1905), pp. 1–34. (English translation: Humboldt 1997 [1820].)
Humboldt, Wilhelm von (1905 [1822]), 'Über das Entstehen der grammatischen Formen

und ihren Einfluss auf die Ideenentwicklung', in Humboldt (1905), pp. 285–313. (English translation: Humboldt 1997 [1822]).

Humboldt, Wilhelm von (1905), *Wilhelm von Humboldts gesammelte Schriften*, ed. Albert Leitzmann, vol. 4, Berlin: Behr.

Humboldt, Wilhelm von (1988 [1836]), *On Language: The Diversity of Human Language Structure and its Influence on the Mental Development of Mankind*, trans. Peter Heath, Cambridge: Cambridge University Press. (German original: Humboldt 1836.)

Humboldt, Wilhelm von (1997 [1820]), 'On the comparative study of language and its relation to the different periods of language development', in Humboldt (1997), pp. 1–22. (German original: Humboldt 1905 [1820].)

Humboldt, Wilhelm von (1997 [1822]), 'On the origin of grammatical forms and their influence on the development of ideas', in Humboldt (1997), pp. 23–51. (German original: Humboldt 1905 [1822].)

Humboldt, Wilhelm von (1997), *Wilhelm von Humboldt: Essays on Language*, ed. Theo Harden and Daniel J. Farrelly, trans. John Wieczorek and Ian Roe, Frankfurt am Main: Peter Lang.

Hurch, Bernhard, and Kathrin Purgay (2019), 'The Basque–Berber connection of Georg von der Gabelentz', in McElvenny (2019c), pp. 57–97.

Hurston, Zora Neale (1990 [1935]), *Mules and Men*, New York: HarperCollins.

Hymes, Dell, and John Fought (1981 [1975]), *American Structuralism*, The Hague: Mouton.

Innis, Robert (1982), *Karl Bühler: Semiotic Foundations of Language Theory*, New York: Plenum Press.

Jakobson, Roman (1971 [1929]), 'Retrospect', in Jakobson (1971), pp. 711–12. (Original Czech source of opening quotation: Jakobson 2012 [1929]).

Jakobson, Roman (1971 [1939]), 'Les lois phoniques du langage enfantin et leur place dans la phonologie générale', in Jakobson (1971), pp. 317–27.

Jakobson, Roman (1971 [1960]), 'The Kazan' School of Polish linguistics and its place in the international development of phonology', in Jakobson (1971), pp. 394–428.

Jakobson, Roman (1971), *Selected Writings, Volume II: Word and Language*, ed. Roman Jakobson, The Hague: Mouton.

Jakobson, Roman (1981 [1960]), 'Linguistics and poetics', in *Selected Writings, Volume III: Poetry of Grammar and Grammar of Poetry*, The Hague: Mouton, pp. 18–51. (An abridged version with the title 'The speech event and the functions of language' is reproduced in Jakobson 1990, pp. 69–79.)

Jakobson, Roman (1990), *On Language*, ed. Linda R. Waugh and Monique Monville-Burston, Cambridge, MA: Harvard University Press.

Jakobson, Roman (2012 [1929]), 'Romantické všeslovanství – nová slavistika', in *Selected Writings, Volume IX,1 Completion, Volume 2/Part 1*, ed. Jindřich Toman, Berlin: De Gruyter, pp. 231–3.

Jakobson, Roman, counter-signed by N. S. Trubetzkoy and Serge Karcevski (1971 [1928]), 'Proposition au Premier Congrès International de Linguistes: Quelles sont les méthodes les mieux appropriées à un exposé complet et pratique de la phonologie d'une langue quelconque?', in Jakobson (1971), pp. 3–6.

Jankowsky, Kurt (2001), 'The crisis of historical-comparative linguistics in the 1860s', in Auroux et al. (2000–6), vol. 2, pp. 1326–38.

Jendreieck, Helmut (1975), *Hegel und Jacob Grimm: Ein Beitrag zur Geschichte der Wissenschaftstheorie*, Berlin: Erich Schmidt.

Jespersen, Otto (1922), *Language: Its Nature, Development and Origin*, London: Allen & Unwin.

Jones, William (1807 [1786]), 'The Third Anniversary Discourse, on the Hindus', in Jones (1807), pp. 24–46.

Jones, William (1807 [1792]), 'The Ninth Anniversary Discourse, on the Origin and Families of Nations', in Jones (1807), pp. 185–204.
Jones, William (1807), *The Works of Sir William Jones*, vol. 3, ed. Lord Teignmouth, London: Stockdale and Walker.
Joseph, John E. (1996), 'The immediate sources of the "Sapir–Whorf hypothesis"', *Historiographia Linguistica* 23:3, 365–404. (Revised and expanded version in chapter 4 of Joseph 2002.)
Joseph, John E. (2001), 'The exportation of structuralist ideas from linguistics to other fields: An overview', in Auroux et al. (2000–6), vol. 2, pp. 1880–908.
Joseph, John E. (2002), *From Whitney to Chomsky: Essays on the History of American Linguistics*, Amsterdam: John Benjamins.
Joseph, John E. (2012), *Saussure*, Oxford: Oxford University Press.
Joseph, John E. (2017), 'Ferdinand de Saussure', *Oxford Research Encyclopedia of Linguistics*. DOI: 10.1093/acrefore/9780199384655.013.385
Joseph, John E., Nigel Love and Talbot J. Taylor (2001), *Landmarks in Linguistic Thought II: The Western Tradition in the Twentieth Century*, London: Routledge.
Kant, Immanuel (1787 [1781]), *Critik der reinen Vernunft*, Riga: Hartknoch. (English translation: Kant 1998 [1781].)
Kant, Immanuel (1998 [1781]), *Critique of Pure Reason*, ed. and trans. Paul Guyer and Allen W. Wood, Cambridge: Cambridge University Press. (German original: Kant 1787 [1781].)
Kaplan, Judith (2019), 'Visual formalisms in comparative-historical linguistics', in McElvenny (2019a), pp. 1–33.
Klautke, Egbert (2013), *The Mind of the Nation:* Völkerpsychologie *in Germany, 1851–1955*, New York: Berghahn.
Knobloch, Clemens (1991), 'Introduction', in Wegener (1991 [1885]), pp. xi–li.
Koerner, E. F. Konrad (1978 [1974]), 'Animadversions on some recent claims regarding the relationship between Georg von der Gabelentz and Ferdinand de Saussure', in *Toward a Historiography of Linguistics: Selected Essays*, ed. E. F. Konrad Koerner, Amsterdam: John Benjamins, pp. 137–52.
Koerner, E. F. Konrad (2002), 'On the sources of the Sapir-Whorf hypothesis', in *Toward a History of American Linguistics*, ed. E. F. Konrad Koerner, London: Routledge, pp. 39–62.
Koerner, E. F. Konrad (2008), 'Hermann Paul and general linguistic theory', *Language Sciences* 30, 102–32.
Kohrt, Manfred, and Kerstin Kucharczik (2001), 'Die Wurzeln des Strukturalismus in der Sprachwissenschaft des 19. Jahrhunderts', in Auroux et al. (2000–6), vol. 2, pp. 1719–35.
Kortlandt, Frederick (2010), *Studies in Germanic, Indo-European and Indo-Uralic*, Amsterdam: Rodopi.
Korzybski, Alfred (1933), *Science and Sanity: An Introduction to Non-Aristotelian Systems and General Semantics*, Lancaster, PA: International Non-Aristotelian Library.
Kruszewski, Mikołaj (1881), 'K voprosu o gune: Isledovanie v oblasti staroslavjanskago vokalizma', *Russkuj Filologičeskij Vestnik* 5:1, 1–109. (Published in Kruszewski's own German translation also in 1881: *Ueber die Lautabwechslung*, Kazan: Universitätsbuchdrückerei; English translation: Kruszewski 1995 [1881].)
Kruszewski, Mikołaj (1995 [1881]), 'On sound alternation', in *Mikołaj Kruszewski: Writings in General Linguistics*, trans. Robert Austerlitz, ed. E. F. Konrad Koerner, Amsterdam: John Benjamins, pp. 3–35. (Russian and German originals: Kruszewski 1881.)
Kuhn, Thomas (1962), *The Structure of Scientific Revolutions*, Chicago: University of Chicago Press.

Kuryłowicz, Jerzy (1927), 'ə indo-européen et h hittite', in *Symbolae grammaticae in honorem Ioannis Rozwadowski*, vol. 1, Krakow: Gebethner & Wolff, pp. 95–104.
Law, Vivien (2003), *The History of Linguistics in Europe: From Plato to 1600*, Cambridge: Cambridge University Press.
Lazarus, Moritz (1884 [1856–67]), *Geist und Sprache: Eine psychologische Monographie*, Berlin: Dümmler.
Leahy, Thomas Hardy (2018 [1987]), *A History of Psychology: From Antiquity to Modernity*, New York: Routledge.
Lee, Penny (1996), *The Whorf Theory Complex: A Critical Reconstruction*, Amsterdam: John Benjamins.
Lefmann, Salomon (1870), *August Schleicher: Skizze*, Leipzig: Teubner.
Lefmann, Salomon (1891–7), *Franz Bopp, sein Leben und seine Wissenschaft*, 2 vols and *Nachtrag*, Berlin: Reimer.
Lehmann, Christian (2015 [1982]), *Thoughts on Grammaticalization*, Berlin: Language Science Press.
Lehmann, Winfried (1967), *A Reader in Nineteenth-Century Historical Indo-European Linguistics*, Bloomington: Indiana University Press.
Lepschy, Giulio (ed.) (1994–8), *History of Linguistics*, 4 vols, London: Addison Wesley Longman.
Lepsius, Richard (1861), 'Über die Umschrift und Lautverhältnisse einiger hinterasiatischer Sprachen, namentlich der Chinesischen und der Tibetischen', *Abhandlungen der Königlichen Akademie der Wissenschaften zu Berlinaus dem Jahre 1860*, 449–96.
Lepsius, Richard (1863), *Standard Alphabet for Reducing Unwritten Languages and Foreign Graphic Systems to Uniform Orthography in European Letters*, London: Williams & Norgate.
Leskien, August (1876), *Die Declination im Slavisch-Lithauischen und Germanischen*, Leipzig: Hirzel.
Lévi-Strauss, Claude (1949), *Les structures élémentaires de la parenté*, Paris: Presses universitaires de France. (English translation: Lévi-Strauss 1969 [1949].)
Lévi-Strauss, Claude (1963 [1958]), *Structural Anthropology*, trans. Claire Jacobson and Brooke Grundfest Schoepf, New York: Basic Books. (An English translation, with additional content, of the French original: Lévi-Strauss 1974 [1958].)
Lévi-Strauss, Claude (1969 [1949]), *The Elementary Structures of Kinship*, trans. James H. Bell, John R. von Sturmer and Rodney Needham, Boston: Beacon Press. (French original: Lévi-Strauss 1949.)
Lévi-Strauss, Claude (1974 [1958]), *Anthropologie structurale*, Paris: Plon. (English translation: Lévi-Strauss 1963 [1958].)
Locke, John (1975 [1690]), *An Essay Concerning Human Understanding*, ed. Peter H. Nidditch, Oxford: Oxford University Press.
Lotze, Hermann (1851), *Allgemeine Physiologie des koerperlichen Lebens*, Leipzig: Wiedmann.
Lyell, Charles (1830–3), *Principles of Geology: Being an Attempt to Explain the Former Changes of the Earth's Surface, by Reference to Causes now in Operation*, 3 vols, London: John Murray.
Lyell, Charles (1863), *The Geological Evidences of the Antiquity of Man*, London: John Murray.
Maaß, Holger (2003), 'Karl Vosslers Sprachphilosophie und die romanische Philologie des 19. Jahrhunderts. Eine wissenssoziologische Betrachtung', in *Traditionen der Entgrenzung. Beiträge zur romanistischen Wissenschaftsgeschichte*, ed. F. Estelmann, P. Krügel and O. Müller, Frankfurt: Peter Lang, pp. 43–55.
McElvenny, James (2014), 'Ogden and Richards' *The Meaning of Meaning* and early analytic philosophy', *Language Sciences* 41, 212–21.

McElvenny, James (2015), 'The application of C.K. Ogden's semiotics in Basic English', *Language Problems and Language Planning* 39:2, 187–204.

McElvenny, James (2016a), 'The secret history of grammaticalization', *History and Philosophy of the Language Sciences*. https://hiphilangsci.net/2016/04/28/the-secret-history-of-grammaticalization/ (Expanded French translation: McElvenny 2020.)

McElvenny, James (2016b), 'The fate of form in the Humboldtian tradition: The *Formungstrieb* of Georg von der Gabelentz', *Language and Communication* 47, 30–42.

McElvenny, James (2017), 'Georg von der Gabelentz', *Oxford Research Encyclopedia of Linguistics*. DOI: 10.1093/acrefore/9780199384655.013.379

McElvenny, James (2018a), *Language and Meaning in the Age of Modernism: C. K. Ogden and His Contemporaries*, Edinburgh: Edinburgh University Press.

McElvenny, James (2018b), 'August Schleicher and materialism in 19th-century linguistics', *Historiographia Linguistica* 45:1/2, 133–52.

McElvenny, James (ed.) (2019a), *Form and Formalism in Linguistics*, Berlin: Language Science Press.

McElvenny, James (2019b), 'Alternating sounds and the formal franchise in phonology', in McElvenny (2019a), pp. 35–58.

McElvenny, James (ed.) (2019c), *Gabelentz and the Science of Language*, Amsterdam: Amsterdam University Press.

McElvenny, James (2020), 'La grammaticalisation et la circulation internationale des idées linguistiques', in *Les linguistes allemandes du XIXème siècle et leurs interlocuteurs étrangers*, ed. Jacques François, Paris: Éditions de la Société de Linguistique de Paris, pp. 201–12. (English original: McElvenny 2016a.)

McElvenny, James (2021), 'Language complexity in historical perspective: The enduring tropes of natural growth and abnormal contact', *Frontiers in Communication*. DOI: 10.3389/fcomm.2021.621712

McElvenny, James (ed.) (2022), *Interviews in the History of Linguistics: Volume I*, Berlin: Language Science Press.

McElvenny, James (ed.) (2023a), *The Limits of Structuralism: Forgotten Texts in the History of Modern Linguistics*, Oxford: Oxford University Press.

McElvenny, James (2023b), 'Scouting the limits of structuralism', in McElvenny (2023a), pp. 1–10.

McElvenny, James (2023c), 'Gabelentz' typology: Humboldtian linguistics on the threshold of structuralism', in McElvenny (2023a), pp. 81–101.

McElvenny, James, and Clemens Knobloch (2023), 'From *Sprachtheorie* to semantics and cybernetics: Karl Bühler's "Pocketbook on practical semantics"', *Semiotica* 251, 39–54.

McGetchin, Douglas T. (2009), *Indology, Indomania and Orientalism: Ancient India's Rebirth in Modern Germany*, Madison, NJ: Fairleigh Dickinson University Press.

Mackert, Michael (1993), 'The roots of Franz Boas' view of linguistic categories as a window to the human mind', *Historiographia Linguistica* 20:2/3, 331–51.

Mackert, Michael (1994), 'Franz Boas' theory of phonetics', *Historiographia Linguistica* 21:3, 351–86.

MacMahon, Michael K. C. (1986), 'The International Phonetic Association: The first 100 years', *Journal of the International Phonetic Association* 16:1, 30–8.

Madvig, Johan Nicolai (1875), *Kleine philologische Schriften*, Leipzig: Teubner.

Malinowski, Bronislaw (1935), *Coral Gardens and Their Magic*, 2 vols, London: Allen & Unwin.

Malinowski, Bronislaw (1956 [1923]), 'The problem of meaning in primitive languages', in Ogden and Richards (1956 [1923]), pp. 296–336.

Mandelbaum, David G. (ed.) (1949), *Selected Writings of Edward Sapir in Language, Culture and Personality*, Berkeley: University of California Press.

Martinet, André (1980 [1960]), *Éléments de linguistique générale*, Paris: Armin Colin.

Mason, Otis T. (1887), 'The occurrence of similar inventions in areas widely apart', *Science* 9:226, 534–5.

Mathesius, Vilém (1975 [1961]), *A Functional Analysis of Present-Day English on a General Linguistic Basis*, trans. Libuše Diškova, ed. Josef Vachek, The Hague: Mouton.

Matthews, Peter H. (1993), *Grammatical Theory in the United States from Bloomfield to Chomsky*, Cambridge: Cambridge University Press.

Mead, Margaret (1928), *Coming of Age in Samoa: A Psychological Study of Primitive Youth for Western Civilisation*, New York: Morrow.

Messling, Markus (2016), *Gebeugter Geist. Rassismus und Erkenntnis in der modernen europäischen Philologie*, Göttingen: Wallstein.

Miklosich, Franz von (1852–75), *Vergleichende Grammatik der slavischen Sprachen*, 4 vols, Vienna: Braumüller.

Möller, Hermann (1880), Review of F. Kluge, *Beiträge zur Geschichte der germanischen Conjugation*, Strassburg: K. J. Trübner (1879), *Englische Studien* 3, 148–64.

Morgan, Lewis Henry (1877), *Ancient Society, or Researches in the Lines of Human Progress, from Savagery through Barbarism to Civilization*, New York: Holt.

Morpurgo Davies, Anna (1975), 'Language classification in the nineteenth century', in Sebeok (1975), pp. 607–716.

Morpurgo Davies, Anna (1998), *History of Linguistics, Volume IV: Nineteenth-Century Linguistics*, London: Longman. (Volume 4 of the series Lepschy 1994–8.)

Mueller-Vollmer, Kurt, and Markus Messling (2021), 'Wilhelm von Humboldt', *Stanford Encyclopedia of Philosophy* (Winter 2021 Edition), ed. Edward N. Zalta. https://plato.stanford.edu/archives/win2021/entries/wilhelm-humboldt/

Mugdan, Joachim (1985), 'The origin of the phoneme: Farewell to a myth', *Lingua Posnaniensis* 28, 137–50.

Mugdan, Joachim (2011), 'On the origins of the term *phoneme*', *Historiographia Linguistica* 38:1/2, 85–110.

Mugdan, Joachim (2014), 'More on the origins of the phoneme', *Historiographia Linguistica* 41:1, 185–7.

Mugdan, Joachim (2021), 'Jan Baudouin de Courtenay', *Oxford Bibliographies in Linguistics*. DOI: 10.1093/obo/9780199772810-0276

Müller, Friedrich Max (1861), *Lectures on the Science of Language*, first series, London: Longman.

Müller, Friedrich Max (1864), *Lectures on the Science of Language*, second series, London: Longman.

Müller, Friedrich Max (1870), 'The science of language', *Nature* 1, 256–9.

Nerlich, Brigitte (1990), *Change in Language: Whitney, Bréal, and Wegener*, London: Routledge.

Nerlich, Brigitte, and David D. Clarke (1996), *Language, Action, and Context: The Early History of Pragmatics in Europe and America, 1780–1930*, Amsterdam: Benjamins.

Newmeyer, Frederick J. (2022), *American Linguistics in Transition: From Post-Bloomfieldian Structuralism to Generative Grammar*, Oxford: Oxford University Press.

Ogden, Charles Kay (1933 [1930]), *Basic English: A General Introduction with Rules and Grammar*, London: Kegan Paul.

Ogden, Charles Kay, and Ivor Armstrong Richards (1956 [1923]), *The Meaning of Meaning*, London: Kegan Paul.

Osthoff, Hermann, and Karl Brugman (1878), 'Vorwort', *Morphologische Untersuchungen* 1, i–xx.

Passy, Paul (1887), *Les sons du français, leur formation, leur combinaison, leur représentation*, Paris: Firmin-Didot.
Paul, Hermann (1880), *Principien der Sprachgeschichte*, Halle (Saale): Niemeyer.
Paul, Hermann (1885), Review of Wegener (1885), *Literarisches Centralblatt für Deutschland* 36 (29 August), col. 1230.
Paul, Hermann (1920 [1880]), *Prinzipien der Sprachgeschichte*, Halle (Saale): Niemeyer.
Pitman, Isaac (1840 [1837]), *Phonography, or Writing by Sound, Being also a New and Natural System of Shorthand*, London: Bagster.
Plato (1891 [1871]), 'Cratylus', in *The Dialogues of Plato*, ed. and trans. Benjamin Jowett, Oxford: Oxford University Press, pp. 251–390.
Porter, Theodore (1986), *The Rise of Statistical Thinking, 1820–1900*, Princeton: Princeton University Press.
Pott, August Friedrich (1833–6), *Etymologische Forschungen auf dem Gebiete der indogermanischen Sprachen*, 2 vols, Lemgo: Meyer.
Powell, John Wesley (ed.) (1880 [1877]), *Introduction to the Study of Indian Languages*, Washington DC: Smithsonian Institution.
Powell, John Wesley (1887), 'Museums of ethnology and their classification', *Science* 9:229, 612–14.
Putschke, Wolfgang (2001), 'Die Dialektologie, ihr Beitrag zur historischen Sprachwissenschaft im 19. Jahrhundert und ihre Kritik am junggrammatischen Programm', in Auroux et al. (2000–6), vol. 2, pp. 1498–512.
Rébori, Victoria (2002), 'The legacy of J. R. Firth: A report on recent research', *Historiographia Linguistica* 29:1/2, 165–90. (See also the follow-up discussion between Rébori and Leendert Plug in *Historiographia Linguistica* 31:2/3 [2004], 469–77.)
Richards, Robert J. (2002a), *The Romantic Conception of Life: Science and Philosophy in the Age of Goethe*, Chicago: University of Chicago Press.
Richards, Robert J. (2002b), 'The linguistic creation of man: Charles Darwin, August Schleicher, Ernst Haeckel, and the missing link in nineteenth-century evolutionary theory', in *Experimenting in Tongues: Studies in Science and Language*, ed. Matthies Dörries, Stanford: Stanford University Press, pp. 21–48.
Richards, Robert J. (2008), *The Tragic Sense of Life: Ernst Haeckel and the Struggle over Evolutionary Thought*, Chicago: University of Chicago Press.
Ringer, Fritz K. (1969), *The Decline of the German Mandarins: The German Academic Community, 1890–1933*, Cambridge, MA: Harvard University Press.
Ringmacher, Manfred (1996), *Organismus der Sprachidee: H. Steinthals Weg von Humboldt zu Humboldt*, Paderborn: Schöningh.
Ringmacher, Manfred (2001a), 'Die Klassifizierung der Sprachen in der Mitte des 19. Jahrhunderts', in Auroux et al. (2000–6), vol. 2, pp. 1427–35.
Ringmacher, Manfred (2001b), 'Sprachtypologie und Ethnologie in Europa am Ende des 19. Jahrhunderts', in Auroux et al. (2000–6), vol. 2, pp. 1435–42.
Rischel, Jørgen (2001), 'The Cercle linguistique de Copenhague and glossematics', in Auroux et al. (2000–6), vol. 2, pp. 1790–806.
Robins, Robert H. (1997 [1967]), *A Short History of Linguistics*, London: Routledge.
Rudwick, Martin J. S. (2005), *Bursting the Limits of Time: The Reconstruction of Geohistory in the Age of Revolution*, Chicago: University of Chicago Press.
Rüegg, Walter (2004), 'Themes', in *A History of the University in Europe, Volume 3: Universities in the Nineteenth and Early Twentieth Centuries (1800–1945)*, ed. Walter Rüegg, Cambridge: Cambridge University Press, pp. 3–31.
Russell, Bertrand (1918–19), 'The philosophy of logical atomism', *The Monist* 28, 495–527; 29, 32–63, 190–222, 345–80.

Said, Edward (2003 [1978]), *Orientalism*, London: Penguin Books.
Sapir, Edward (1907), 'Herder's *Ursprung der Sprache*', *Modern Philology* 5:1, 109–42.
Sapir, Edward (1921), *Language*, New York: Harcourt, Brace.
Sapir, Edward (1923), 'An approach to symbolism', review of Ogden and Richards (1923), *The Freeman* 7:22, 572–3. (Reprinted in Mandelbaum 1949, pp. 150–9.)
Sapir, Edward (1929 [1928]), 'The status of linguistics as a science', *Language* 5, 207–14. (Reprinted in Mandelbaum 1949, pp. 160–6.)
Sapir, Edward (1929), 'Foundations of language', *International Auxiliary Language Association in the United States, Inc.: Annual Meeting, May 19, 1930*, New York: IALA, pp. 16–18.
Sapir, Edward (1949 [1924]), 'The grammarian and his language', in Mandelbaum (1949), pp. 150–9. (Original published in *American Mercury* 1 [1924], 149–55.)
Saussure, Ferdinand de (1879), *Mémoire sur le système primitif des voyelles dans les langues indo-européennes*, Leipzig: B. G. Teubner.
Saussure, Ferdinand de (1922 [1916]), *Cours de linguistique générale*, ed. Charles Bally and Albert Sechehaye, Paris: Payot. (English translation: Saussure 1959 [1916].)
Saussure, Ferdinand de (1959 [1916]), *Course in General Linguistics*, trans. Wade Baskin, New York: Philosophical Library. (French original: Saussure 1922 [1916].)
Schlegel, August Wilhelm (1818), *Observations sur la langue et la littérature provençales*, Paris: Librairie grecque-latine-allemande.
Schlegel, August Wilhelm (1832), 'Grammatischer Unterschied', 'Literarische Scherze', in *Museumsalmanach für das Jahr 1832*, ed. Amadeus Wendt, Leipzig: Weidmann, p. 321.
Schlegel, August Wilhelm (1847 [1815]), Review of *Altdeutsche Wälder*, in *August Wilhelm von Schlegel's sämmtliche Werke*, vol. 12, ed. Eduard Böcking, Leipzig: Weidmann, pp. 383–426.
Schlegel, Friedrich (1808), *Ueber die Sprache und Weisheit der Indier*, Heidelberg: Mohr und Zimmer. (English translation: Schlegel 1900 [1808].)
Schlegel, Friedrich (1900 [1808]), 'On the Indian language, literature and philosophy', in *The Æsthetic and Miscellaneous Works of Friedrich von Schlegel*, ed. and trans. E. J. Millington, London: George Bell and Sons, pp. 425–536. (German original: Schlegel 1808.)
Schleicher, August (1850), *Die Sprachen Europas in systematischer Uebersicht*, Bonn: König.
Schleicher, August (1859), 'Zur Morphologie der Sprache', *Mémoires de l'Académie Impériale des Sciences de St.-Petersbourg* 1:7, 1–38.
Schleicher, August (1860), *Die Deutsche Sprache*, Stuttgart: Cotta.
Schleicher, August (1861–2), *Compendium der vergleichenden Grammatik der indogermanischen Sprachen*, 2 vols, Weimar: Böhlau. (English translation: Schleicher 1874–7 [1861–2].)
Schleicher, August (1863), *Die Darwinsche Theorie und die Sprachwissenschaft*, Weimar: Böhlau. (English translation: Schleicher 1869 [1863].)
Schleicher, August (1865a), *Über die Bedeutung der Sprache für die Naturgeschichte des Menschen*, Weimar: Böhlau.
Schleicher, August (1865b), *Die Unterscheidung von Nomen und Verbum in der lautlichen Form*, Leipzig: Hirzel.
Schleicher, August (1868), 'Eine fabel in indogermanischer ursprache', *Beiträge zur vergleichenden Sprachforschung* 5, 206–8.
Schleicher, August (1869 [1863]), *Darwinism Tested by the Science of Language*, trans. Alex V. W. Bikkers, London: John Camden Hotton. (German original: Schleicher 1863.)
Schleicher, August (1871 [1861–2]), *Compendium der vergleichenden Grammatik der indogermanischen Sprachen*, 2 vols, ed. August Leskien and Johannes Schmidt, Weimar: Böhlau. (3rd edition of Schleicher 1861–2.)
Schleicher, August (1874–7 [1861–2]), *A Compendium of the Comparative Grammar of the*

Indo-European, Sanskrit, Greek and Latin Languages, trans. Herbert Bendall, London: Trübner. (German original: Schleicher 1861–2.)

Schmidt, Johannes (1872), *Die Verwandtschaftsverhältnisse der indogermanischen Sprachen*, Weimar: Böhlau.

Schmidt, Johannes (1871–5), *Zur Geschichte des indogermanischen Vocalismus*, 2 vols, Weimar: Böhlau.

Schmidt, Johannes (1887), 'Schleichers Auffassung der Lautgesetze', *Zeitschrift für vergleichende Sprachforschung* 28, 303–12.

Schuchardt, Hugo (1893), Review of Gabelenz (1893), *Literaturblatt für germanische und romanische Philologie* 14, 334–8.

Schuchardt, Hugo (1928 [1870]), 'Über die Klassifikation der romanischen Mundarten', in Schuchardt (1928), pp. 166–88.

Schuchardt, Hugo (1928 [1885]), 'Über die Lautgesetze. Gegen die Junggrammatiker', in Schuchardt (1928), pp. 51–87. (English translation: Schuchardt 1972 [1885].)

Schuchardt, Hugo (1928), *Hugo Schuchardt-Brevier: Ein Vademecum der allgemeinen Sprachwissenschaft*, ed. Leo Spitzer, Halle (Saale): Niemeyer.

Schuchardt, Hugo (1972 [1885]), 'On sound laws: Against the Neogrammarians', in *Schuchardt, the Neogrammarians, and the Transformational Theory of Phonological Change*, ed. Theo Vennemann and Terence H. Wilbur, Königstein um Taunus: Athenäum, pp. 39–72. (German original: Schuchardt 1928 [1885].)

Sebeok, Thomas A. (ed.) (1975) *Historiography of Linguistics*, 2 vols, vol. 13 of *Current Trends in Linguistics*, The Hague: Mouton.

Sedley, David (2020), 'Plato's *Cratylus*', *Stanford Encyclopedia of Philosophy* (Winter 2020 Edition), Edward N. Zalta (ed.), URL = <https://plato.stanford.edu/archives/win2020/entries/plato-cratylus/>.

Senft, Gunter (2009), 'Bronislaw Kasper Malinowski', in *Culture and Language Use*, ed. Gunter Senft, Jan-Ola Östman and Jef Verschueren, Amsterdam: John Benjamins, pp. 210–25.

Sériot, Patrick (2012 [1999]), *Structure et totalité. Les origines intellectuelles du structuralisme en Europe centrale et orientale*, Limoges: Lambert-Lucas. (English translation: Sériot 2014.)

Sériot, Patrick (2014), *Structure and the Whole: East, West and Non-Darwinian Biology in the Origins of Structural Linguistics*, trans. Amy Jacob-Colas, Berlin: Mouton de Gruyter. (French original: Sériot 2012 [1999].)

Sériot, Patrick (2023), 'Roman Jakobson, language unions and structuralism in Russia: Encounter or misunderstanding?', in McElvenny (2023a), pp. 139–58.

Shannon, Claude (1948), 'A mathematical theory of communication', *The Bell System Technical Journal* 27, 379–423, 623–56.

Shannon, Claude, and Warren Weaver (1949), *The Mathematical Theory of Communication*, Urbana: University of Illinois Press.

Shcherba, Lev (1912), *Russkie glasnye v kačestvennom i količestvennom otnošenii* [Russian vowels in their qualitative and quantitative relationships], St Petersburg: Erlich.

Solleveld, Floris (2023), '"Primitive" structures, polysynthesis, and Peter Stephen Du Ponceau', in McElvenny (2023a), pp. 11–28.

Stadler, Friedrich (2011), *Studien zum Wiener Kreis. Ursprung, Entwicklung und Wirkung des Logischen Empirismus im Kontext*, Frankfurt am Main: Suhrkamp. (English translation: Stadler 2015 [2011].)

Stadler, Friedrich (2015 [2011]), *The Vienna Circle: Studies in the Origins, Development, and Influence of Logical Empiricism*, Vienna: Springer. (German original: Stadler 2011.)

Stang, Nicholas F. (2018 [2016]), 'Kant's transcendental idealism', *Stanford Encyclopedia of Philosophy* (Winter 2018 Edition), ed. Edward N. Zalta. https://plato.stanford.edu/archives/win2018/entries/kant-transcendental-idealism/
Steinthal, H. (1855), *Grammatik, Logik und Psychologie, ihre Prinzipien und Verhältniß zueinander*, Berlin: Dümmler.
Steinthal, H. (1860a), *Charakteristik der hauptsächlichsten Typen des Sprachbaues*, Berlin: Dümmler.
Steinthal, H. (1860b), 'Mathematische Sprachwissenschaft', *Zeitschrift für Völkerpsychologie und Sprachwissenschaft* 1, 432–5.
Steinthal, H. (1865), Review of Schleicher (1865b), *Zeitschrift für Völkerpsychologie und Sprachwissenschaft* 3, 497–506.
Steinthal, H. (1871), *Abriss der Sprachwissenschaft, 1. Teil: Die Sprache im Allgemeinen. Einleitung in die Psychologie und Sprachwissenschaft*, Berlin: Dümmler.
Steinthal, H. (1875), 'Antikritik. Gegen Whitney', *Zeitschrift für Völkerpsychologie und Sprachwissenschaft* 8, 216–50.
Sütterlin, Ludwig (1902), *Das Wesen der sprachlichen Gebilde: Kritische Bemerkungen zu Wilhelm Wundts Sprachpsychologie*, Heidelberg: Winter.
Swadesh, Morris (1934), 'The phonemic principle', *Language* 10:2, 117–29.
Sweet, Henry (1877), *Handbook of Phonetics*, Oxford: Oxford University Press.
Thomas, Margaret (2011), *Fifty Key Thinkers on Language and Linguistics*, London: Routledge.
Thomas, Margaret (2023), 'Boas' "purely analytical approach" to language classification in the backdrop to American structuralism', in McElvenny (2023a), pp. 51–69.
Titchener, Edward B. (1898), 'The postulates of structural psychology', *Philosophical Review* 7:5, 449–65.
Titchener, Edward B. (1909), *Lectures on the Experimental Psychology of the Thought-Processes*, New York: Macmillan.
Toman, Jindřich (1995), *The Magic of a Common Language: Jakobson, Mathesius, Trubetzkoy, and the Prague Linguistic Circle*, Cambridge, MA: MIT Press.
Trabant, Jürgen (1986), *Apeliotes oder der Sinn der Sprache, Wilhelm von Humboldts Sprachbild*, Munich: Wilhelm Fink. (French translation: Trabant 1992.)
Trabant, Jürgen (1992), *Humboldt ou le sens du langage*, Liège: Mardaga. (German original: Trabant 1986.)
Trabant, Jürgen (2012), *Weltansichten: Wilhelm von Humboldts Sprachprojekt*, Munich: Beck.
Trautmann, Thomas (1997), *Aryans and British India*, Berkeley: University of California Press.
Trautmann-Waller, Céline (2006), *Aux origines d'une science allemande de la culture: linguistique et psychologie des peuples chez Heymann Steinthal*, Paris: CNRS.
Trubetzkoy, Nikolai (1939), *Grundzüge der Phonologie*, Prague: Cercle Linguistique. (English translation: Trubetzkoy 1969 [1939].)
Trubetzkoy, Nikolai (1969 [1939]), *Principles of Phonology*, Berkeley: University of California Press. (German original: Trubetzkoy 1939.)
Trubetzkoy, Nikolai (1991 [1925]), 'The Legacy of Genghiz Khan', in *The Legacy of Genghiz Khan and Other Essays on Russia's Identity*, ed. and trans. Anatoly Liberman, Ann Arbor: Michigan Slavic Publications, pp. 161–232.
Turner, James (2014), *Philology: The Forgotten Origins of the Modern Humanities*, Princeton: Princeton University Press.
Tynianov, Juri, and Roman Jakobson (1928), 'Problemy izucheniya yazyka i literatury', *Novyi LEF, New Left Front of the Arts* 12, 36–7. (English translation: Tynianov and Jakobson 1972 [1928].)
Tynianov, Juri, and Roman Jakobson (1972 [1928]), 'Problems in the study of language and

literature', in *The Structuralists: From Marx to Lévi-Strauss*, ed. Richard De George and Fernande De George, trans. Richard De George, New York: Anchor Books, pp. 80–3. (Russian original: Tynianov and Jakobson 1928.)

Underhill, James W. (2009), *Humboldt, Worldview and Language*, Edinburgh: Edinburgh University Press.

Ungeheuer, Gerold (2004 [1967]), 'Die kybernetische Grundlage der Sprachtheorie von Karl Bühler', in *Sprache und Kommunikation*, ed. Karin Kolb and H. Walter Schmitz, Münster: Nodus, pp. 128–46.

Van de Walle, Jürgen (2008), 'Roman Jakobson, cybernetics and information theory: A critical assessment', *Folia Linguistica Historica* 29, 87–128.

Verein Ernst Mach (2006 [1929]), 'Wissenschaftliche Weltauffassung: der Wiener Kreis', in *Wiener Kreis*, ed. Michael Stöltzner and Thomas E. Uebel, Hamburg: Felix Meiner, pp. 1–29.

Vermeulen, Han F. (2018), *Before Boas: The Genesis of Ethnography and Ethnology in the German Enlightenment*, Lincoln: University of Nebraska Press.

Verner, Karl (1877), 'Eine Ausnahme der ersten Lautverschiebung', *Zeitschrift für vergleichende Sprachforschung* 23, 97–130.

Viëtor, Wilhelm (1882), *Der Sprachunterricht muss umkehren!*, Heilbronn: Henninger.

Voegelin, Charles F. ['Carl'], and Florence M. Voegelin (1963), 'On the history of structuralizing in 20th century America', *Anthropological Linguistics* 5, 12–37.

Vogel, Annemete von, and James McElvenny (2019), 'The Gabelentz family in their own words', in McElvenny (2019c), pp. 13–26.

Vogt, Carl (1846), *Physiologische Briefe für Gebildete aller Stände*, vol. 2, Giessen: Ricker'sche Buchhandlung.

Vossler, Karl (1904), *Positivismus und Idealismus in der Sprachwissenschaft*, Heidelberg: Winter.

Vossler, Karl (1905), *Sprache als Schöpfung und Entwicklung*, Heidelberg: Winter.

Watson, John B. (1913), 'Psychology as the behaviorist views it', *Psychological Review* 20, 158–77.

Watson, John B. (1926), 'What is behaviorism?', *Harper's Magazine* 152, 723–9.

Watson, John B., and Rosalie Rayner (1920), 'Conditioned emotional reactions', *Journal of Experimental Psychology* 10, 421–8.

Waugh, Linda, and Monique Monville-Burston (2002), 'Introduction', in *Roman Jakobson Selected Writings: Phonological Studies*, Berlin: De Gruyter, pp. v–xcviii.

Wegener, Philipp (1885), *Untersuchungen über die Grundfragen des Sprachlebens*, Halle: Niemeyer. (English translation: Wegener 1971 [1885].)

Wegener, Philipp (1971 [1885]), *Speech and Reasons: Language Disorder in Mental Disease. A Translation of 'The Life of Speech' by Philipp Wegener*, trans. Wilfred D. Abse, Charlottesville: University of Virginia Press. (German original: Wegener 1885.)

Wegener, Philipp (1991 [1885]), *Untersuchungen über die Grundfragen des Sprachlebens*, reprint of Wegener (1885) with introduction by Clemens Knobloch, Amsterdam: John Benjamins.

Weil, Henri (1844), *De l'ordre des mots dans les langues anciennes comparées aux langues modernes*, Paris: Joubert. (English translation: Weil 1978 [1844].)

Weil, Henri (1978 [1844]), *The Order of Words in the Ancient Languages Compared with that of the Modern Languages*, trans. Charles W. Super, Amsterdam: John Benjamins. (French original: Weil 1844.)

Weiss, Albert Paul (1925), 'One set of postulates for a behavioristic psychology', *Psychological Review* 32:1, 83–7.

Wenker, Georg (1877), *Das rheinische Platt*, Düsseldorf: Self-published.

Whitney, William Dwight (1867), *Language and the Study of Language: Twelve Lectures on the Principles of Linguistic Science*, London: Trübner.
Whitney, William Dwight (1873 [1871]), 'Schleicher and the physical theory of language', in Whitney (1873), pp. 298–331.
Whitney, William Dwight (1873 [1872]), 'Steinthal and the psychological theory of language', in Whitney (1873), pp. 332–75.
Whitney, William Dwight (1873), *Oriental and Linguistic Studies*, vol. 1, New York: Scribner, Armstrong.
Whitney, William Dwight (1874), 'The elements of English pronunciation', in *Oriental and Linguistic Studies*, vol. 2, ed. William Dwight Whitney, New York: Scribner, Armstrong, pp. 202–76.
Whitney, William Dwight (1875), *The Life and Growth of Language*, London: King. (German translation: Whitney 1876 [1875].)
Whitney, William Dwight (1876 [1875]), *Leben und Wachstum der Sprache*, trans. August Leskien, Leipzig: Brockhaus. (English original: Whitney 1875.)
Whorf, Benjamin Lee (1956 [1936]), 'The punctual and segmentive aspects of verbs in Hopi', in Carroll (1956), pp. 51–6.
Whorf, Benjamin Lee (1956 [1940]), 'Science and linguistics', in Carroll (1956), pp. 207–19.
Whorf, Benjamin Lee (1956 [1941]a), 'The relation of habitual thought and behavior to language', in Carroll (1956), pp. 134–59.
Whorf, Benjamin Lee (1956 [1941]b), 'Languages and logic', in Carroll (1956), pp. 233–45.
Whorf, Benjamin Lee (1956 [1942]), 'Language, mind, and reality', in Carroll (1956), pp. 246–70.
Whorf, Benjamin Lee (1956 [1950]), 'An American Indian model of the universe', in Carroll (1956), pp. 57–64.
Wiener, Norbert (1948), *Cybernetics: Or Control and Communication in the Animal and the Machine*, Cambridge, MA: MIT Press.
Wundt, Wilhelm (1886), 'Ueber den Begriff des Gesetzes, mit Rücksicht auf die Frage der Ausnahmslosigkeit der Lautgesetze', *Philosophische Studien* 3, 195–215.
Wundt, Wilhelm (1900), *Völkerpsychologie, eine Untersuchung der Entwicklungsgesetze von Sprache, Mythus und Sitte*, vol. 1, *Die Sprache*, Leipzig: Engelmann.
Wundt, Wilhelm (1908 [1883]), *Logik. Eine Untersuchung der Prinzipien der Erkenntniss und der Methoden wissenschafticher Forschung*, vol. 3, *Logik der Geisteswissenschaften*. Stuttgart: Enke.
Young, Michael W. (2004), *Malinowski: Odyssey of an Anthropologist, 1884–1920*, New Haven, CT: Yale University Press.
Zeuß, Johann Kaspar (1853), *Grammatica Celtica*, 2 vols, Leipzig: Weidmann.
Ziemer, Frank (1886), Review of Wegener (1885), *Berliner philologische Wochenschrift* 6, 181–5.

Index

Adelung, Johann Christoph, 11
aesthetics, 167
agglutinative languages, 21–2, 27, 30–1, 42–3
agglutination theory, 12–13, 43, 51–3
allophone, 71, 91, 174
Alphabetical Conferences, 95–6
analogy, 62–3, 71
'analytic' languages *see* 'synthetic' and 'analytic' languages
analytic philosophy, 101, 157–62, 171
arbitrariness, 10–12, 23–4, 53–4, 86–8, 164
Aristotle, 23
Arnauld, Antoine, 12

Bally, Charles, 83
Basic English, 160–1
Bastian, Adolf, 145, 146
Baudouin de Courtenay, Jan, 92–4, 98, 101–2, 106, 165
behaviourism, 131–2, 168–71, 172–3, 175
Bell, Alexander Melville, 96
Benedict, Ruth, 143–4
Benfey, Theodor, 6
Bismarck, Otto von, 78
Blair, Hugh, 53
Bleek, Wilhelm, 34
Bloch, Bernard, 173, 174, 175
Bloomfield, Leonard, 89, 107, 142, 163–75
Bloomfield, Maurice, 166
Blumenbach, Johannes Friedrich, 9–10, 41, 42
Boas, Franz, 107, 142–50, 151, 155–7, 163, 165–6
Bolsheviks, 102
Bonaparte, Napoleon, 15
Bopp, Franz, 11–14, 34–5, 43
Bréal, Michel, 87–8, 112–13

Brinton, Daniel Garrison, 143, 148, 149–50, 156
Brugman, Karl, 59–60, 65, 68, 75, 80–1, 82, 88
Bühler, Karl, 130–6
Bunsen, Christian Karl Josias, 95

Caldwell, Robert, 34
Campbell, George, 53
Carnap, Rudolf, 171–3
Carroll, John B., 153
Cassirer, Ernst, 105
catastrophism, 55–6
character of languages, 25–7, 29–30
Chase, Stuart, 160
Chomsky, Noam, 108, 175
codification controversy, 15
cognitive revolution, 175
comparative anatomy, 9–10
complementary distribution, 174
Comte, Auguste, 76–7, 170
Condillac, Étienne Bonnot de, 23–4, 88
conditioning, 168–9
context, 111–12, 120–8
Copenhagen Linguistic Circle, 107
Croce, Bendetto, 77, 167
cubism, 106
Curtius, Georg, 36, 59, 72, 80–1
Cuvier, Georges, 9–10, 41, 56
cybernetics, 138–40

Darwinism, 37–41, 41–2, 49, 53, 56–7
Delbrück, Berthold, 65
Deloria, Ella Cara, 144
diachrony *see* synchrony and diachrony
Diez, Friedrich Christian, 34
Dilthey, Wilhelm, 114–15
distinctive features, 102–3, 104–5

distributional analysis, 121, 173–5
double articulation, 133–4, 135, 165
Droysen, Johann Gustav, 114–15
duality of patterning *see* double articulation
Dufriche-Desgenettes, Antoni, 92
Durkheim, Émile, 89

eclipsing stance, 6
economy in language change, 51–3
Ehrenfels, Christian von, 106
Einstein, Albert, 154–5
emotive language, 127–8
energeia see *ergon* and *energeia*
Enlightenment, 9
ergon and *energeia*, 26, 134
Esperanto, 160
etymology, 10, 16–17, 30
Eurasianism, 102
evolution of language, 10–11, 23–4, 26, 41–3, 45, 49, 125–8, 148, 156–7

Firth, John Rupert, 118–22, 132
'formal' vs 'formless' languages, 30–2, 45
French Revolution, 15

Gabelentz, Georg von der, 67–8, 70–1, 88–9, 115, 148
Gabelentz, Hans Conon von der, 34
Gardiner, Alan Henderson, 132–3
general grammar, 12–13
General Semantics, 160
Gessner, Conrad, 11
Gestalt psychology, 103, 105–6, 131
glossomatics, 107
Goethe, Johann Wolfgang von, 41–2, 45
grammaire générale see general grammar
'grammatical' subject and predicate *see* 'logical' and 'grammatical' subject and predicate
grammaticalisation, 43
Grimm, Jacob, 14–17, 35, 39
Grimm, Wilhelm, 14, 39
Grimm's Law, 16–17, 61–2, 69, 73

Haeckel, Ernst, 40–1, 42
Halle, Morris, 108
Halliday, Michael, 117
Harris, Zellig, 174, 175
Hegel, Georg Wilhelm Friedrich, 59, 77

Heidegger, Martin, 172
Herbart, Johann Friedrich, 110
Herder, Johann Gottfried von, 24, 49, 156
hermeneutics, 114–15, 132
historical materialism *see* materialism
historicism, 14–16, 35, 45, 114
Hjelmslev, Louis, 107
Hockett, Charles, 133–4, 175
Hoijer, Harry, 152
holism, 105
Humboldt, Alexander von, 145–6
Humboldt, Wilhelm von, 13, 22–7, 29–30, 42–3, 45, 47–8, 77, 110, 134, 145–6, 149–50, 155–7, 167
Hurston, Zora Neale, 144

idealism, 75–8
incorporation, 27, 31–2
inflection, 20–1, 27, 30–2, 42–3
information structure, 115–17
information theory, 138–40
inner form of languages, 9, 29–32, 43–5, 48, 149, 155–6, 164
international language movement, 160–1
introspection, 130, 168
International Phonetic Alphabet, 97
International Phonetic Association, 97
isolating languages, 21–2, 27, 30–1, 42–3

Jakobson, Roman, 100–8, 136–40
Jespersen, Otto, 17
Jones, Sir William, 7–8, 152

Kant, Immanuel, 20–1, 25, 26, 42, 77
Karcevsky, Serge, 104
Korzybski, Alfred, 160
Kruszewski, Mikołaj, 92–4
Kuryłowicz, Jerzy, 82

Lancelot, Claude, 12
langue vs. *parole*, 83–4, 94, 120, 134, 139, 167
Lazarus, Moritz, 28, 114, 145
Leibniz, Gottfried Wilhelm, 10–11, 23
Lepsius, Karl Richard, 34, 95
Leskien, August, 37, 62, 65, 68, 75
Lévi-Strauss, Claude, 107, 139
linguistic relativity *see* Sapir-Whorf hypothesis
'Little Albert' experiment, 168–9

Locke, John, 10, 23–4, 53–4
'logical' and 'grammatical' subject and predicate, 115–16
logical positivism, 101, 171–3
Lotze, Hermann, 45
Lyell, Charles, 55, 56

Madvig, Johan Nicolai, 113
Malinowski, Bronislaw, 118, 123–8, 132, 158
markedness, 104–5
Martinet, André, 133–4
Mason, Otis T., 146
materialism, 38–41, 44, 49, 77, 170
Mathesius, Vilém, 100, 117
Mead, Margaret, 143–4
'mechanical' languages *see* 'organic' vs 'mechanical' languages
Miklosich, Franz von, 34
Mithridates, 11
Möller, Hermann, 82
monism, 38, 40, 44, 170
Morgan, Lewis Henry, 144–5
morpheme, 94, 165, 174
morphology, 41–3, 149, 156
Mosaic ethnology, 8
Moscow Linguistic Circle, 104
Müller, Friedrich Max, 48–50, 53, 56–7, 96

Napoleonic Wars, 15
Naturphilosophie, 38–9, 42
Neogrammarians, 58–66, 80–3, 88–9, 93, 105, 109, 110–11, 113, 115–17, 118, 165–6, 169
Neurath, Otto, 171–3
Noah, 8, 55
nomenclature, 23, 84

October Revolution, 102
Ogden, Charles Kay, 123, 127–8, 158–9, 160–1
onomatopoeia, 86, 106
'organic' vs 'mechanical' languages, 20–1, 43
'organism' of languages, 21, 25–7, 37, 48, 88, 89, 157
Organon model, 131–2
origins of language *see* evolution of language
Osthoff, Hermann, 59–60, 65, 68, 81

Pallas, Peter Simon, 11
Pāṇini, 13, 88, 166
participant observation, 118
Passy, Paul, 97–8
Paul, Hermann, 63–6, 68, 89, 110–11, 115–17
phatic communion, 125, 137
philologer passage, 7
phoneme, 91–9, 101–3, 121, 133, 149, 164–5, 173–4
phonetics, 96–8
physicalism, 171–2
Pitman, Isaac, 97
Plato, 131
polysynthesis *see* incorporation
Port-Royal grammar, 12
positivism, 75–8, 114, 170
postcolonial studies, 7
Pott, August Friedrich, 34
Powell, John Wesley, 143, 146–7, 148
Prague Circle, 100–3, 133, 135–6, 137–8, 173
progressivism, 169, 170
prosodic phonology, 121
psychic unity of mankind, 145
Putnam, Frederic W., 147

Rask, Rasmus, 17, 113
Rayner, Rosalie, 168–9
Reform Movement, 97
Reid, Thomas, 53
Revolution of 1848, 39–40
Rhenish Fan, 72–3
Richards, Ivor Armstrong, 123, 127–8, 158–9
Romanticism, 9, 21, 38–9, 43
Romic, 97–8
Rousseau, Jean-Jacques, 43
Russell, Bertrand, 158–9, 160, 171
Russian Futurism, 106

Said, Edward, 7
Sapir, Edward, 107, 142, 143, 144, 151–3, 156–7, 157–9, 160–1, 163–7, 173
Sapir-Whorf hypothesis, 151–62
Saussure, Ferdinand de, 80–9, 92, 94–5, 103–5, 120, 134, 166–7
Savigny, Friedrich Carl von, 14–16
Schlegel, August Wilhelm, 11, 13–14, 16, 21–2, 26–7

Schlegel, Friedrich, 8–11, 16, 19–21, 43
Schleicher, August, 35–45, 48, 49, 56–7, 64, 68, 88, 135, 149, 156, 170
Schleicher's fable, 36–7
Schleiden, Matthias, 40
Schmidt, Johannes, 37, 68, 74–5
Schuchardt, Hugo, 69
scientific materialism *see* materialism
scientific realism, 36
Sechehaye, Albert, 83
semantics, 87–8, 112–13
sensationism, 24, 112
sensualism *see* sensationism
Shannon, Claude, 138, 139
Shcherba, Lev, 98, 102
shorthand, 97
signifier and signified, 84, 102, 104
sound law, 16–17, 36, 60–3, 69–72
Sprachbund, 102
Standard Average European, 153–4, 163
statistics, 51–3, 70–1
Steinthal, Heymann, 27–32, 43–5, 47–8, 54, 63–4, 110, 145, 149
Stewart, Dugald, 53
structuralism, 80, 82, 100–8, 142, 166–7
Sütterlin, Ludwig, 65
Swadesh, Morris, 173–4
Sweet, Henry, 97–8
synchrony and diachrony, 86–7, 88–9
syntax, 115–17
'synthetic' and 'analytic' languages, 22, 32, 43

teleology, 20–1, 42, 69–70
theosophy, 161
Titchener, Edward B., 100
Trager, George, 175
Trubetzkoy, Nikolai, 100–6, 135–6
Tynianov, Juri, 104
typology, 19, 41

Uldall, Hans Jørgen, 107
uniformitarianism, 54–7, 62–3
unity of science, 171–3
'usual' and 'occasional' meaning, 115

value, 84–5
variationist approaches to language, 51–3, 136
Vater, Johann Severin, 11
Verner, Karl, 61–2
Vienna Circle, 101, 171
Viëtor, Wilhelm, 97
Visible Speech, 96
Voegelin, C. F. 'Carl' and Florence, 6, 167
Vogt, Carl, 40–1
Völkerpsychologie, 27–9, 64–5, 110, 114, 145
Volksgeist, 14–17, 28, 64
Vossler, Karl, 75–8, 165, 167

Wackernagel, Jacob, 166
Watson, John B., 168–9
wave theory, 72–5
Weaver, Warren, 138, 139
Wegener, Philipp, 109–15, 124–5, 132
Weil, Henri, 115
Weiss, Albert Paul, 169, 172
Wenker, Georg, 72–3
Whitney, Josiah Dwight, 55
Whitney, William Dwight, 47–57, 65, 68, 72, 87, 96, 109–10, 142, 166
Whorf, Benjamin Lee, 142, 151–2, 153–5, 159–62
Wiener, Norbert, 138–9
Wittgenstein, 158–9, 160, 171
Wundt, Wilhelm, 28, 64–5, 70, 100, 106, 110, 130, 169

Zarncke, Friedrich, 59
zaum, 106
Zeuß, Johann Kaspar, 34
Ziemer, Frank, 113

EU representative:
Easy Access System Europe
Mustamäe tee 50, 10621 Tallinn, Estonia
Gpsr.requests@easproject.com

www.ingramcontent.com/pod-product-compliance
Lightning Source LLC
Chambersburg PA
CBHW070816250426
43671CB00037B/2507